Elliot

Cooking from the ♥

# OFFAL GOOD

Takes Guts!!!

CLARKSON POTTER/PUBLISHERS
NEW YORK

# OFFAL GOOD

Chris Cosentino with Michael Harlan Turkell

**COOKING FROM THE HEART, WITH GUTS**

PHOTOGRAPHS BY MICHAEL HARLAN TURKELL

Published in the United States by Clarkson Potter/Publishers,
an imprint of the Crown Publishing Group, a division of
Penguin Random House LLC, New York.
crownpublishing.com
clarksonpotter.com



Library of Congress Cataloging-in-Publication Data
Names: Cosentino, Chris, author. | Turkell, Michael Harlan,
photographer (expression)
Title: Offal Good / Chris Cosentino with Michael Harlan Turkell ;
photographs by Michael Harlan Turkell.
Description: First edition. | New York : Clarkson Potter, 2017.
Identifiers: LCCN 2016039390 (print) | LCCN 2016041470
(ebook) | ISBN 9780770435127 (hardback) | ISBN
9780770435134 (Ebook)
Subjects: LCSH: Cooking (Variety meats) | BISAC: COOKING /
Specific Ingredients / Meat. | COOKING / Specific Ingredients /
Game. | COOKING /
Reference. | LCGFT: Cookbooks.
Classification: LCC TX749.5.V37 C67 2017 (print) | LCC
TX749.5.V37 (ebook) |
DDC 641.3/6—dc23
LC record available at https://lccn.loc.gov/2016039390

ISBN 978-0-7704-3512-7
eISBN 978-0-7704-3513-4

Printed in China

Book design by Debbie Glasserman
Jacket design by Debbie Glasserman
Jacket photography: (Front) Evan Sung, (Back) Michael Harlan Turkell

10 9 8 7 6 5 4 3 2 1

First Edition

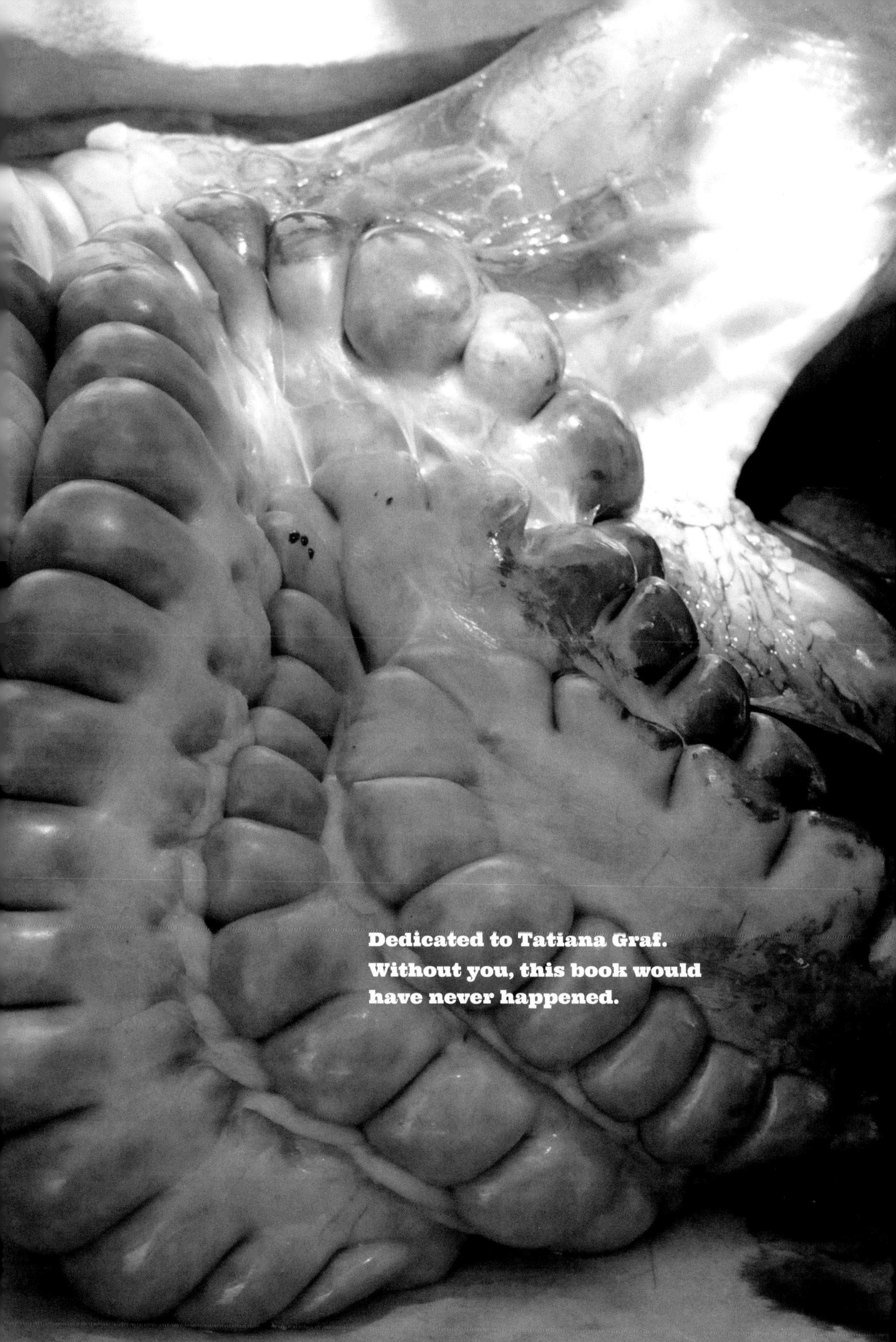

**Dedicated to Tatiana Graf.
Without you, this book would
have never happened.**

# CONTENTS

# FOREWORD

**BY ANDREW ZIMMERN**

Creativity is courageous. Pass it on.

Albert Einstein said that decades ago. And it's what I think about every time I see Chris Cosentino. Courageous and creative, and passing it on is how he lives. You can see it in much of this book, a peek into the creative process of a brilliant and talented chef, dedicated to a simple set of principles. In his hands, the fifth quarter of an animal becomes something more than just parts. First, cooking offal requires real *cooking*. It's a transformative process, typically in multiple stages that takes an ingredient of mixed reputation and lifts it up to the shelf that holds life's great treasures. Second, it's soundly civic in the best sense of the word. Using every part of animal (or plant for that matter) is a moral obligation in a world where so many go without food, yet where so many others waste 40 percent of what foods they buy, and because our planet's mathematical equation for supplying all of us with all we need to eat and drink is an unsustainable proposition. Cosentino isn't just a clever culinarian, he is a philosopher poet, demonstrating lessons on ethics and the nature of taste, and changing our ideas about pleasure simply by turning out a plate of his delicious pigskin spaghetti and clams. But I'm getting ahead of myself.

People are more important than food. Trust me on this. And I'm not saying you have to be a good person to be a great cook, but I am telling you that as much as I love Chris' food, he is one of finest people I know and one of my dearest friends. I knew of Chris by reputation before I met him in 2008. I was shooting an episode of *Bizarre Foods* and I'd wanted to see what this young chef was all about. He was brash, and had an intensity and determination that assaulted your senses. He spoke fast, he thought fast, he started four sentences before completing any of them but they all made sense to me. He loved art and street culture, skateboards and bikes. He was also the most curious person I had met in a long time. He pressed me for information on foods I'd eaten, chefs I knew. He stared me down through his thick black glasses and spent the better part of a half an hour discussing pig blood homogenization and various heating techniques that he spent months working out. The goal was a mousse that had the essential natural flavor of cooked blood, but with bright red color and soft smooth texture. Stalking his neighbor and friend, Harold McGee, for advice was part of the story but I lost track very quickly as I ate the blood mousse dish that evoked all the aromas and textures of ramen. I had seconds.

Chris took me to a local Szechuan restaurant called Spices (terrible name, great food) for some mid-afternoon snacks and we laughed, ate, and I saw that HUGE Cosentino smile for the first time. I was convinced that this young chef was destined for as much greatness as he could handle. But I was unprepared for what happened next. We got into my car and I got the last of several texts from home that had thrown me off-kilter all day. A kid with the flu, plus a delay in my travel back home, had gotten me into a lengthy conversation with my wife about parental responsibility, and my lack of it. My show was in its second season and demands on my time had quadrupled. I had no clue how to handle any of it. I was turning into a shitty parent and an ignorant husband. I hadn't done anything spontaneous with a friend in a year. Worst of all, I knew in my heart the situation was going to get worse before it got better. So I'm looking at my phone in the back of the car and Chris looked at me with what I now call his soft-eyes look. It's the look of someone who's had his balls put through more than one set of pasta rollers in his life. It's the look of someone needing to empathically connect with another person because he's sick and tired of phony bull-shitters pretending everything is always "great!" He asks me, "What's up, dude?" And I told him, and I told him some more of my story, and I told him some more.

We spent the next half hour realizing we had more in common than we ever imagined. I learned that his wife, Tatiana, and son, Easton, mean more to him than anything in the world and he struggled with some of the same time and presence issues that I did. He was as petrified of fatherhood as I was—our kids were both 3 at the time—and we bonded over the circumstance of our childhoods and the impending doom we were sure to wreak on our children. Thankfully we were wrong, but because of that day we became fast friends. We've done Disney with our families. I've had the privilege of visiting Easton at school and surprising Tatiana at work. Getting the call from him telling me he was going public with his personal take on the horrific vagaries of food television at the MAD conference or using a where-to-eat guide called *Chef's Feed*, to start a national conversation about mental illness (his own) are the types of things I adore this man for. He's a leader. Fearless when push comes to shove.

The day he called and told me he was going to compete on *Top Chef Masters*, I felt sorry for the rest of my friends doing the show. He's that good. Need more proof? You've got his brilliant book in your hands. I've eaten half the dishes in this stunner and you will cook out of it again and again. You'll come to understand the humor of Big Brain Little Brain, and then eat it, and you'll find nothing funny at all about how simply delicious that dish is. If you were expecting a lengthy forward with a nifty recap of the book so you could decide whether to buy it or not while you're standing in the bookstore, I'm sorry. You should be buying it because of the man who wrote it and the subject matter speaks for itself. This is a book by a chef who knows food like few do, who has a point of view about what we eat that makes him a unique voice.

No art ever came out of not risking your neck. Eudora Welty said that. I wish I did. She wasn't talking about Chris, but she could have been.

# FARMYARD BLUES

## (OR THE BALLAD OF COSENTINO)

BY FERGUS HENDERSON

Dum—dum—dum—dum! Variety meats, yeah yeah!
Offal's the name, offal's the game.

Ladies and gentlemen, I give you . . . CHRIS COSENTINO! The expletive master, but always charming. The human Tigger of the kitchen as he bounces around, effing and blinding but—all ways charming. It's guts a-go-go with this boy, go! Gooooo!

Praises to the pig-oh oooh, nose to tail, yeah, YEAH, YEAH! Porky romance: two lovers, two cheeks, two ears, and double up for four trotters. Stick your lips together baby, the sticky sticky shake. Pucker up baby!

Man, oh man, where do you find udders like those? Thank you for the mammaries moo moo ooh ooooh. Changing paddock, now this is beef, what a relief . . . The farmyard dance is about to start!

Strut like a chicken, cock-a-doodle-doo, bing bing bing the farmer plays along badly, he's been at the moonshine already. The goats don't mind, they've been at that moonshine too.

Those sheep show independent thought, baah baah baah baah, what a surprise! Setting up a percussion section with two buckets and a paint pot.

LAMB BAMB this party has to stop, my lovelies! The reason you're here is you're grown for the pot! Simmer simmer simmer, we crave your brains cooked with black butter and capers! I'm sorry my dearests we desire your tripe, braised slowly to steady us, oh oh oh-hooo! Ox tongue how long do you need in a brine each day? Becoming more flavorsome and what can I say . . . except kidneys, the shining jewels in the offally crown.

The sheep start to drum a slow retreat . . . brump-brup-brump, saying return to your stables and paddocks! Wait and see, if you appear on Chris' menu tomorrow be chirpy chirpy all of you. You are not ending your life as a burger patty, this is no end for a happy animal. You've been nurtured by Chris, cooked with love by Chris, and this sounds good to us.

Yea haah!!!!

# INTRODUCTION

## THE OLD AND THE NEW

I've spent two decades learning about, cooking, and getting creative with offal. It's become my signature as a chef. But the irony is, when I was a kid, I used to run from tripe. Literally. Whenever my great-grandmother Rosalie would make *trippa napoletana,* I'd run out of the house, hoping to escape the smell.

Her prep kitchen was in the basement, and right when you walked in, a wall of wretchedness would smack you in the face. It reeked of digestion, that sulfuric hard-boiled-egg stink. I loved spending time downstairs with her, jarring the garden's bulk of tomatoes, but I wouldn't help if the air hadn't cleared. Upstairs, in the "regular" kitchen, hand-cranked pasta dried on racks. But even there, for every ribbon of fettuccine, there was a scary offal-based dish like sofrit (liver, kidney, heart, and lung with onion and tomato), which Rosalie served over polenta. I remember thinking, "A grandmother should spoil you—not serve you food that you think is spoiled!"

There were other elements of my Italian heritage, though, that I more eagerly participated in. Watching my great-grandmother stirring marinara or going around the neighborhood to collect fallen chestnuts for *crema di castagne.* Rosalie would pick dandelion flowers for dandelion wine. She'd press crunchy, sweet, buttery pizzelle cookies. At the time, I was unaware how these Old World flavors were forming my palate. I was unwittingly eating *la cucina povera,* literally "the poor kitchen," the same sort of food my family had been cooking for generations. We were honoring our past traditions, while living in contemporary New England.

When I was with the other side of my family—my mother's—I'd dig for quahogs in the same Rhode Island town that her English ancestors, the Eastons, founded in 1639. In Newport, at the southernmost point of Aquidneck Island, you'll find a place still called Easton's Beach. In this commercial fishing community, most of our meals were fish. My maternal grandparents, Helen and Thurston Easton, made roasts for special occasions, but most of the time, dinner was cod, scrod, flounder, bluefish, and tautog. Their clam chowder was broth based, instead of the more expensive cream version. Food for them was convivial, and dinnertime was for family bonding. Every year, on the Sunday before Christmas, they invited up to two hundred people over for tea sandwiches filled with lobster salad, egg salad, tuna salad, ham salad, and roast beef. But there weren't many prime cuts of meat in our diet.

When we did eat meat, it was ground—and in a casing. My family was best known for Easton's Sausage Company, established by William H. Easton in 1860. The factory closed in 1942, during World War II, because it became impossible to get the foreign spices needed, but also there was a shift away from offal that we still see today. My grandfather didn't make a single link after that.

But the Easton family recipe, lightly seasoned with citrus and sage, lives on at Boccalone, my salumi company. (And the Easton name continues in my family—it's my son's name.)

As a chef, I've been riding on the coattails of thousands of grandmas cooking before me, taking those tried-and-true relics and making them anew. Those meals of Grandma Rosalie's cucina povera, the nearly forgotten taste of the Easton sausage: what I do today traces directly back to those moments with my family, when they were cooking and feeding me the tastes of our heritage. And it's funny to think how much I hated Rosalie's tripe back then.

**INTO THE OFFCUTS**

The tagline for Boccalone is "Tasty Salted Pig Parts," which might seem amusing now, but in my grandparents' time, making the most of every scrap of meat they had, every cut from the animal, was fundamental. This was true for most people, for most of history. Morton Salt published a book in 1930 with instructions on how to raise and butcher your own hog at home. This meant that people were eating, enjoying, and nourishing themselves beyond the chops or shoulders. Offal is all the other parts: the variety meats, the odd bits, the fifth quarter, the guts, the innards, the umbles, humble pie, bits and bobs. And, even though they're not technically internal organs, I also include the skin, head, tails, and feet—other parts that have fallen out of favor.

Eating offal was—and is—definitely not awful. Different cuts of steak may be delicious, but they are mostly delicious in the same basic way. Offal, though, gives you an amazing variety of textures and flavors. Pig skin can be luxurious and velvety when braised; turned into a wild, rich "spaghetti"; or puffed into crisp, airy chicharrones. Livers can be pureed smooth and silky, humming with mineral earthiness, or knocking you over with their meaty aroma when seared hard. I grew to love all these cuts and became passionate about learning more and more about them—their traditional uses, their biological structure, the nutrition they provide (many are far more nutritious than muscle meats), and, of course, how to highlight their best features.

Recognizing ingredients, tasting their distinct qualities, and working to bring out their best is the ideology I've always believed in as a chef. It's what, in essence, this book is about: accepting offal for offal, and understanding its character, its breadth, its versatility and deliciousness.

But, like I said, I wasn't always this way. There was that feared trippa. I remember having to be tricked by a crispy bacon wrap to eat liver hors d'oeuvres at my parents' parties. Usually I'd be glued to the TV, watching as *Mutual of Omaha's Wild Kingdom* host Marlin Perkins narrated the sight of bears catching salmon as they swam upstream. What I didn't realize then was that the bears ate the belly first, pitching the carcass for their cubs. Within the rules of hierarchy, offal is for the strong. That flipped somewhere along the line in America. It's time to flip it back.

That said, I'm not *really* doing anything different here. Most every culture in the world eats and appreciates offal. Using these organs is the right thing to do. It makes meat eating more sustainable, as it literally means we get many more meals out of each slaughtered animal. I was inspired by the movement of buying whole animals and wanted to have the know-how to cook all the cuts of meat that are available when sold that way. But, like I said, for most of human history, that's how it *had* to be done. I don't think of my way of cooking as a revelation or trendsetting.

Offal was part of the American pantry. It continues to be a little more so in the South, with its pickled pig's feet, hog maws, and chitterlings (chitlins)—and also in many Asian and Latin American immigrant communities—but in the rest of the country it's fallen off. An issue with offal has always been its perishability; in some cases and climates, more than a few hours old and it could get pretty scary. But when canning became more prolific during the Great Depression, these cuts made their way to supermarket shelves (and bomb shelters).

After World War II and the postwar economic boom, though, offal was suddenly seen as a thing of the past by people tired of eating potted meat. Skeletal meat, like rib eyes and porterhouses, gained popularity as it became more accessible to a population that had been eating "lesser" offal. This new generation wanted steaks on the table, and decades later, that still holds true.

Today, butchering and sausage making is in vogue, as many chefs and home cooks look back to culinary traditions for inspiration and instruction. But there's still a disparity of knowledge when it comes to offal. I read Upton Sinclair's *The Jungle* in high school and remember it highlighting the poor conditions and disgusting habits of the meatpacking industry during the early 1900s. As a salumi maker, I often hear the misconception that sausage is only made from the lesser, unwanted parts of an animal; maybe this is thanks to the modern-day hot dog with its emulsified pink goo. In the mid-twentieth century, meat began to be mass-produced through factory farming. Offal was going to waste because there was no demand for it. It was being ground into pet food and sometimes used as feed for the same type of animal, a practice brought to light during the late twentieth century's mad cow disease epidemic. Only now are we starting to realize how important sustainable farming is, and to use the whole animal. Eating offal is an extension of honoring an animal that was harvested for our consumption. As a chef, my greatest goal is to close this circle.

### MY LIFE, FROM HEAD TO TAIL

I grew up with ADHD; I was a Ritalin kid. I couldn't read a book because I couldn't sit still long enough to concentrate on one. When I was fourteen, I got a dishwashing job at IHOP. I'd watch the two guys working the line, pounding out four hundred plates during a shift, keeping track of hundreds of egg orders, and I was mesmerized by their speed, their precision, and their craft. Still, I rebelled and acted out until my junior year of high school, when I realized that if I didn't change my ways, I wouldn't graduate on time. My most likely options would be jail, the military, or cooking.

I got my act together enough to graduate and decided to pursue a culinary degree at Johnson & Wales. Because of my lousy record, I was accepted to the school conditionally, and I had to check in weekly with the dean, Bill Day, who happened to be from my hometown. He watched out for me through all four years. From carving ice sculptures to manning the omelet station, I developed a strong sense of responsibility that I'd never felt before. Eventually, I received a fellowship and began teaching my peers. I knew then that this is what I wanted to do: cook, learn, and teach.

After graduating from culinary school, I leapt at an opportunity to move to Washington, D.C., and work for renowned chef Mark Miller at Red Sage. There I had my first experience working with whole animals, refined my sausage making, and most importantly, met my future wife, Tatiana, who worked for the restaurant in marketing and PR. I then worked for Bob Kinkead's An American Brasserie, where he taught me how to pair flavors of the familiar with the unfamiliar, how to introduce something new to the guest by luring them in with something they already knew. (My Oxtail & Skate recipe, page 125, is based on his oxtail ragù with salsify and skate.)

Tatiana and I moved to San Francisco in 1996, encouraged by the promise of desirable weather, bountiful produce, and fresh perspectives on food. I took a job at Rubicon with chef Traci Des Jardins and began buying stacks of used cookbooks at Green Apple Books. It became an obsession. I worked in my off-hours at a sandwich shop to make ends meet, but still I'd spend all my money collecting cookbooks, old and new. One day, I picked up a book that struck a chord deep in me: a Time-Life book on offal called *Variety Meats* from The Good Cook/Techniques & Recipes series. I first read it on the walk back to my house along Clement Street, stopping for a bowl of congee with a poached egg soaked in soy sauce, a big pile of fried shallots, herbs, peanuts, and plenty of pig organs. Including coffee, the meal cost only four dollars. It was so eye-opening to find that something so simple, delicious, and filling could cost so little. I'd hit up dim sum houses with glistening red pork and whole roasted ducks hanging in the windows. I wandered around New May Wah Supermarket and stared at tendons, tripe, and cubes of coagulated pig's blood. There you even could buy the whole pig with its uterus intact. These things captivated me. Meanwhile, San Francisco revealed itself to be part of a region full of so much food potential, but outside of French restaurants or "ethnic" cuisines, offal was rarely found. This fact made an abstract impression on me, one that I'd fully understand only later.

After a few jobs and a stint returning to an old passion, competitive cycling, Tatiana and I traveled and worked through Europe for inspiration, being exposed to great French traditions of meat and offal cooking. Coming back to the United States, I saw foie gras, sweetbreads, and chicken liver in French restaurants, and turkey giblets on the Thanksgiving table, but little other offal in between.

I became enamored with a lot of Asian cuisines, with their bright flavors and, more importantly, appreciation for many textures—the spectrum of soft textures, as well as the chewy, sticky, gelatinous, and gristly bits that are so delicious if you open your mind to them.

Then, I had the honor of working at Chez Panisse, the legendary restaurant in Berkeley owned by Alice Waters. There I met a rancher named Don Watson. In the spring, his lambs were pasture-raised, milk-fed, and harvested just after weaning, beautifully flavored from the fields they grazed. Working with him and his well-raised whole animals marked the beginning of my access to offal in the Bay Area.

In 2002, I became chef at Incanto restaurant in San Francisco. Mark Pastore, the owner, created the restaurant to serve regional Italian cuisine. I was excited by the opportunity to return to and explore my Italian heritage, and my interest in offal had become a guiding principle. There I focused on using cuts that others didn't, or wouldn't, to show the deliciousness—and the value—of these ingredients. I brought the spirit of cucina povera into my kitchen every day, while insisting on using inspiring ingredients from the farmers I most admired, like Don Watson and Andy Griffin from Mariquita Farm. The first offal-based dishes I put on the menu were pâté (liver, kidney, spleen), chicken liver mousse, foie gras, and sweetbreads. These were commonly known to guests, thanks to haute French cuisine, but they were often served only in the fanciest restaurants, and I wanted to present them in our comfortable, dressed-down environment. Gradually, I started to introduce beef heart (grilled with beets and horseradish), beef tongue (with potatoes and poached eggs), pork tongue, and pigs' heads, feet or trotters (which became my favorite). We started bringing in whole pigs and lamb, and going deeper and deeper into the bowels of anatomy—cockscomb and duck testicles, poultry tongues, gizzards, hearts.

In winter of 2014, after two decades in San Francisco, I finally opened my own restaurant. I called it Cockscomb, after the prominent but underused part of the rooster. Cockscomb blends my adopted city's diverse culinary influences, while paying homage to my background as a chef. I finally have an oyster bar resonant of my Newport days and a wood-fired oven that subtly smokes and fire-kisses our food. It's a place where, among other things, I showcase offal as worthy of craftsmanship and creativity, as an American cook taking cues from my Italian and English heritage, all the while looking toward the future of cooking. Today I continue to experience the passion I felt as both a student and teacher in cooking school. I've taken all the lessons I've learned along the way, from my great-grandmother's once-feared tripe, to Mark Miller's incorporation of flavors from around the world, to Bob Kinkead's strategy of combining the familiar with the unfamiliar, to the global travels that have inspired me, and I try to cook guts with both my brains and my balls.

That's what this book is about. It's tradition and innovation, it's honoring the animals we eat, it's exploring the unique qualities of our ingredients, no matter how humble the bits.

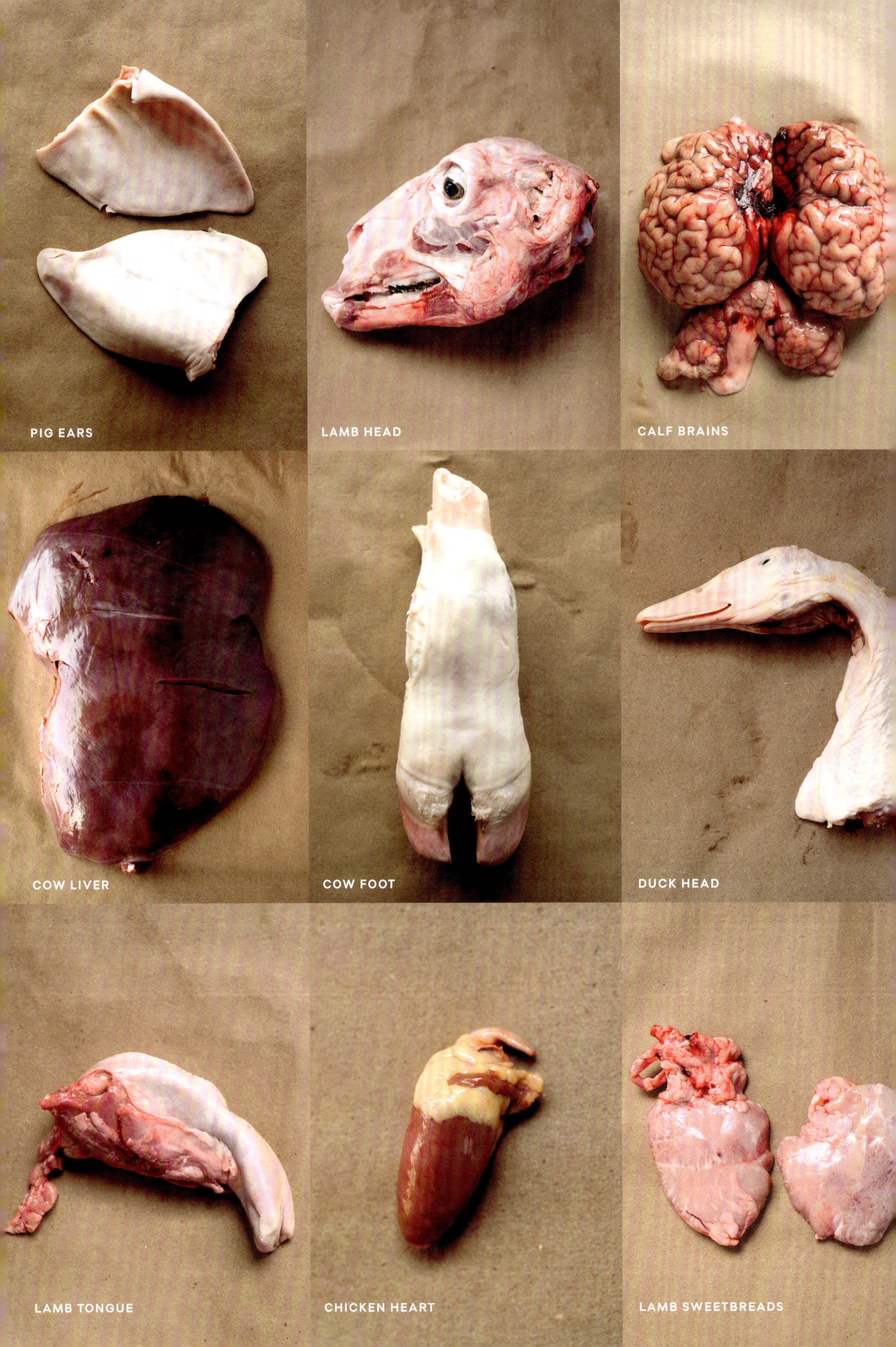
PIG EARS
LAMB HEAD
CALF BRAINS
COW LIVER
COW FOOT
DUCK HEAD
LAMB TONGUE
CHICKEN HEART
LAMB SWEETBREADS

# THE ORGANS

**"ONLY A GENERATION AGO, EVEN IN OUR CITIES, THE WHOLE BEEF OR PORK OR LAMB CARCASS WAS DISSECTED BEFORE THE EYES OF THE HOUSEWIFE BY HER LOCAL BUTCHER, AND OUR MANY FARM FAMILIES DID THE JOB THEMSELVES. . . . FEW AMERICANS ANY LONGER RECOGNIZE, THEREFORE—MUCH LESS EAT—THE FULL RANGE OF EDIBLE PRODUCTS EVEN OUR MOST COMMON FOOD ANIMALS CAN SUPPLY, AND GASTRONOMIC POSSIBILITIES NECESSARILY BECOME MORE LIMITED FOR THE AVERAGE AMERICAN FAMILY."**

—CALVIN W. SCHWABE, *UNMENTIONABLE CUISINE,* 1979

In this section, we'll look at all the organs, from head (well, skin) to toe (or claw) from the most commonly eaten land animals. While some of the cuts in this book, like tongue and feet, aren't technically "internal organs" such as tripe or liver, I include them because they're delicious and often under-appreciated as well. Think of this as a tour through the anatomy, but from a cook's view. I'll share some of my favorite preparations or uses of these cuts, and tips on how to initially prep them for further cooking.

But before you can cook them, you have to get your hands on them. I could wax poetic about how buying a whole animal is the best way to get great offal, but for those of us who can't, perhaps economically, or who don't have the time (or space) to be able to process all the meat, I urge you to develop a relationship with a good butcher. They'll help you define what to look for: how to determine the freshness of a cut, what questions to ask, and how to recognize a properly raised animal. There's a sourcing list in the back of this book that names some of my most trusted purveyors, whom I now call my friends. But my first words of advice are always to befriend your local butcher.

# SKIN

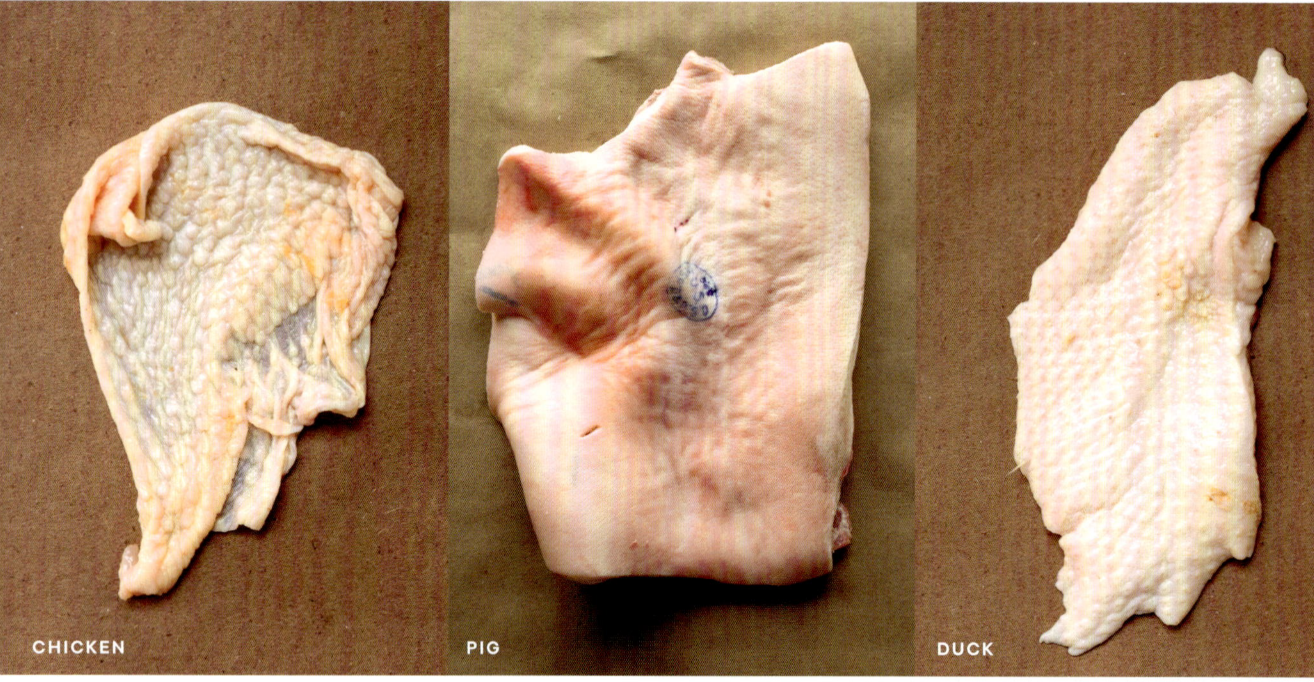


When we think of an animal's organs from head to tail, it's easy to forget the fact that skin is the first organ we face. Skin is like the wrapping on a present: You're happy to see it, because it means there's something special inside. But once opened, it's overlooked in lieu of the interior contents.

The largest organ of an animal, skin is what protects an animal from harm and disease. But skin also allows moisture to penetrate, making it the true gateway offal in more ways than one.

Pork skins provide the world with some of the greatest fatty snacks we know, like crackling chicharrones (see pages 141–143), the crisp-fried snack found in many Latin American cuisines. These vary in how much meat, if any, is still attached, and, with different techniques, crisped skin may shatter like glass or puff up like Rice Krispies. For another take, there's Ciccioli (page 139), an Emilia-Romagna dish comprised of scratchings (rinds) and sinew, braised and pressed into a puck-shaped patty. And of course, everyone loves a crisp piece of chicken or duck skin.

Tattoo artists have been known to practice their skills on pigskin, and, speaking of ink, the USDA inspection stamp you often see stamped onto pigs' skin is edible, made from natural coloring agents such as annatto, carotene, chlorophyll, saffron, and turmeric.

But let's get back to the meat of it. . . .

**COW** In the United States, it's really unusual to use cowhide for culinary purposes—it's much more profitable as leather—so you will likely not have access to it. But that doesn't mean it's inedible. In Nigeria, for instance, it's called *ponmo,* and it's beloved when stewed until tender. The Nigerian government did try to ban it, not because it's dangerous to consume, but because they wanted people to tan it and sell it as leather for revenue. Ponmo lovers are fighting back.

**PIG** When whole pigs are sold, they've usually been already dehaired via a scalding, shaving, and scrubbing process. Sometimes, though, I'll still end up with bristly pig and will have to give it a close shave with a Bic and then blowtorch the follicles as a precaution. No one wants hair in their food. When working with skin, first give it a look to see if there are any stray hairs and get rid of them.

Many muscle cuts, such as ham or butt, are sold skin on. The best example of this is pork belly, which is most commonly used as bacon. Sear or roast these cuts skin-side up, so that it gets crispy and all that lovely subcutaneous fat can render down through the meat.

In recipes where only the skin is used, like Cracklins Cacio e Pepe (page 143), it's important to physically remove the subcutaneous fat before cooking it. If you don't, you'll be unnecessarily rendering out fat in the cooking process, which takes time and, depending on your cooking method, may end up giving you too much fat in the pan. So try to cut off any easily accessed layers of fat. Then bring a pot of water to a boil, add the skin with a couple tablespoons of salt and vinegar, and drop the temperature to a simmer. This tenderizes the skin and gets rid of some of the funk. The timing depends on what the final product will be and can take two hours or more—consult some of the recipes in this book or elsewhere to get a sense of the proper doneness for different applications.

Once cooked, lay the skins out on sheet trays and flatten them with another weighted tray, then chill the skins in the fridge. Once chilled, you can use a bench scraper or knife to remove any extra white or clear fat left over. Butchers use skinning knives to remove the fat before processing the skin for a terrine or puffing pork rinds. From this prep point, you can crisp them for chicharrones or cracklins, make jellied skins (which are found in many Asian cultures), or even pickle them. For something even crazier, I like to make spaghetti purely out of skin (see page 134).

**SHEEP** I've never seen lambskin used in a restaurant, but that doesn't mean it can't be. Sheep are shorn for their wool, exposing the skin, which, like cow, is primarily used in fashion. (And contrary to popular belief, lambskin condoms are not actually made from lamb's skin, but lamb's intestines, a practice established during the Roman Empire.) If you do get some lambskin, follow the same procedure described above for pig skin.

**FOWL** When cooking with chicken, duck, turkey, or goose skin, use this process: First, look to make sure there aren't any quills left in there. If there are, use pin-bone tweezers (usually for deboning fish) to pull them out. There are many ways to skin a chicken—just make a cut somewhere, and start lifting the skin away from the body while trimming it away from any attaching muscle; usually you can do this with just your hands. Once you have the skin in hand, bring a pot of water to a boil with a touch of salt and quickly blanch the skin for a few seconds, which helps remove some of the impurities and makes it easier to work with, then shock it in salted and slightly vinegary ice water to stop it from cooking further. Let the skin chill in the fridge and scrape off the fat, which will be slightly more translucent, using a bench scraper or a dull knife.

In my restaurant kitchen, I've found that the cleanest way to render the fat from poultry skin is to do it sous vide. I season the skin with salt and black pepper and then vacuum-pack it with aromatics like bay leaves. I circulate it in water at 185°F (85°C) for 45 minutes, then chill it in an ice-water bath or in the refrigerator to set the skin.

From there, I like to fry them up like chicharrones. Make sure to use a neutral but high–smoke point oil heated to 375°F. Once they're fried to a golden color, drain them on paper towels, and season with salt. For a perfectly flat and crispy chip, instead of frying the skins, I like to bake them laid flat on a sheet tray and sandwiched by two Silpats (see Crisp Skins, page 234).

Gribenes (Yiddish for "scraps") are a by-product of rendering schmaltz. They're a lot like cracklings and are great in sandwiches.

# HEAD

CHICKEN PIG COW

For some reason, it's illegal to sell whole cow heads in California. New York, too. Ask your local government and the USDA to change these laws, so we can all enjoy the delicacy that many Texans and Mexicans know as barbacoa (which can be lamb's head as well), usually slow-cooked over a fire or buried in the ground to bake.

There's no better centerpiece to a meal than serving a whole head, which, because of availability, usually means pig's head. The beauty of the head is the variety of muscles, flavors, and textures—mellow tongue, meaty cheek, fatty jowl, and the silky little bits of meat scattered throughout. Try the Whole Fried Pig's Head (page 142) or Smothered Lamb's Head, (page 202). Maybe someday, we'll be able to have cow's head at the table as well. And save that skull. It makes for some of the best broth you've ever had.

**COW** *Tête de veau* is a well-known boiled calf's head recipe found across France, and though the name of this dish references a whole head, it's most often seen as a combination of different cuts—tongue, cheeks, and sometimes brains. A whole head is equally delicious, if not more so, as the sum of its parts. That said, I do love a good headcheese, a terrine made from picked head meat set into jellied aspic. No matter how you're

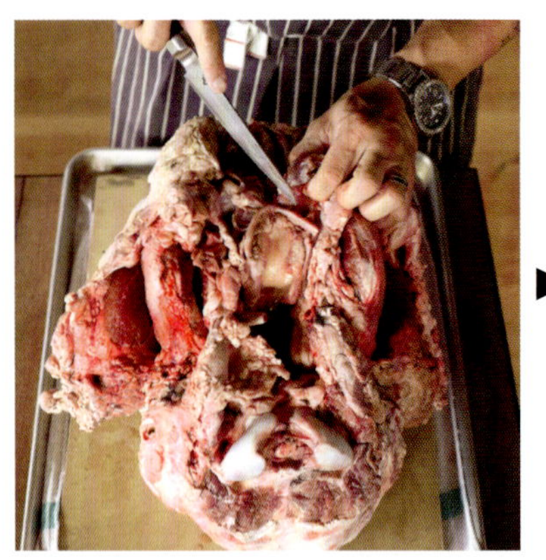

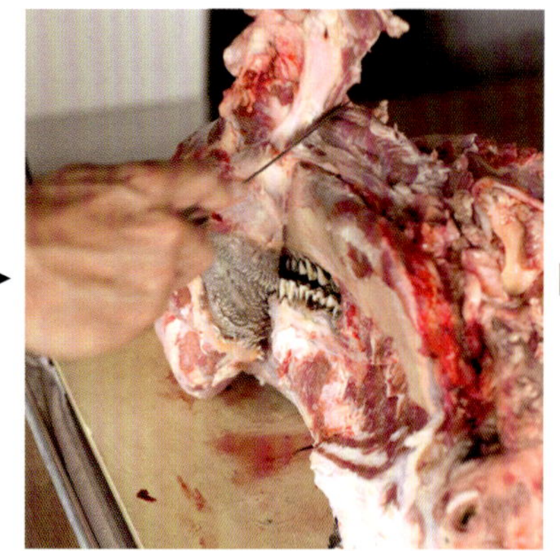

planning to use a cow's head, though, let it soak overnight in a brine (see pages 283–285). Follow the instructions for deboning a pig's head if you're not planning to cook it whole.

**PIG** You can buy pig's heads whole or deboned as "masks." Whole heads are sold in a couple different forms; the best is "square cut," which is cut straight off the carcass, leaving the entire head intact, with jowls on. I often fry or roast this whole. The other way to get it is with the jowls removed, but why would you want to give up the rich jowls?

A mask looks, honestly, like something out of *The Texas Chainsaw Massacre*. It's best used for things like *coppa di testa* or braised, the meat picked and then crisped to make tacos. I personally like to debone a pig's head myself and pick the meat, but a mask can be convenient if you don't have the time to do the butchery yourself.

Be sure to clean inside the ears (see page 31). Then, either braise the head whole or place it in Ham Brine (page 284) overnight, and then confit it.

To debone the head, flip it upside down with the snout facing away from you. Take a sharp boning or butcher's knife, and start at the center of the chin. Using the tip of the knife, continuously run it along the bone, down to the base of the neck. With your hands, peel back and remove all the meat and skin. Go slowly, being sure not to cut holes in the skin, and lay your knife against the bone so you don't hack up the meat. Once the face is removed from the skull, remove the eyelids, as they always have unwanted hair and dark rings. Remove the tongue from the skull, season both sides of the face, as well as the tongue, and place the skull in the brine for 12 hours. From here, the head can be split it in half and either braised or confited.

**SHEEP** When lambs' heads are available, they tend to come without the skin, but that said, they're really hard to get in the United States. Scrapie, a disease that's genetically similar to mad cow disease, may be the cause of this scare about sheep heads, but this disease has been around since the 1700s and there's little to no evidence that it's even transmittable to humans. Still, as with all offal, go to a reliable source and worry less. The prep and cooking procedures are similar to that of a pig's head, but I prefer to roast a lamb's head whole, in a wood oven if you have one, basted in its own fat; its smaller size lends itself well to this kind of preparation. I also cut the skull and take the brain out prior to cooking, poaching it for later use, because it usually overcooks if you prepare it in the head.

**FOWL** Oh, the ortolan bunting. This small bird is a prized, rare poultry of French culinary lore that was fed like ducks are for foie gras, cooked in Armagnac, and served to diners with a napkin, so that they could put it over their head, savor the aromas, and take a personal moment to bite the head open and suck out the brains without other guests having to watch. This practice was deemed illegal in 2007, but if you fancy a similar but legal experience, try it with squab (see Roasted Squab Heads with Squab Liver Aioli, page 235). There isn't any special prep for birds' heads other than giving them a quick check for feathers and a good rinse.

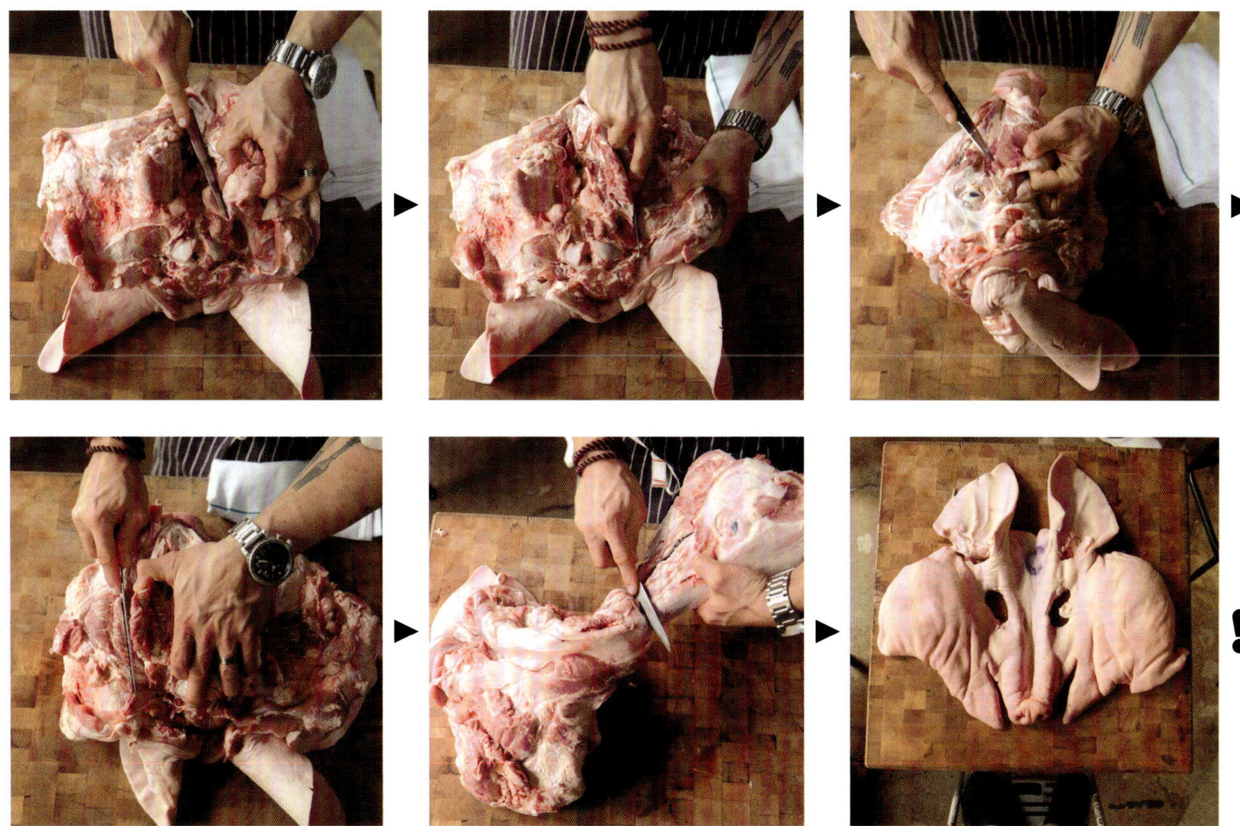

# TONGUE

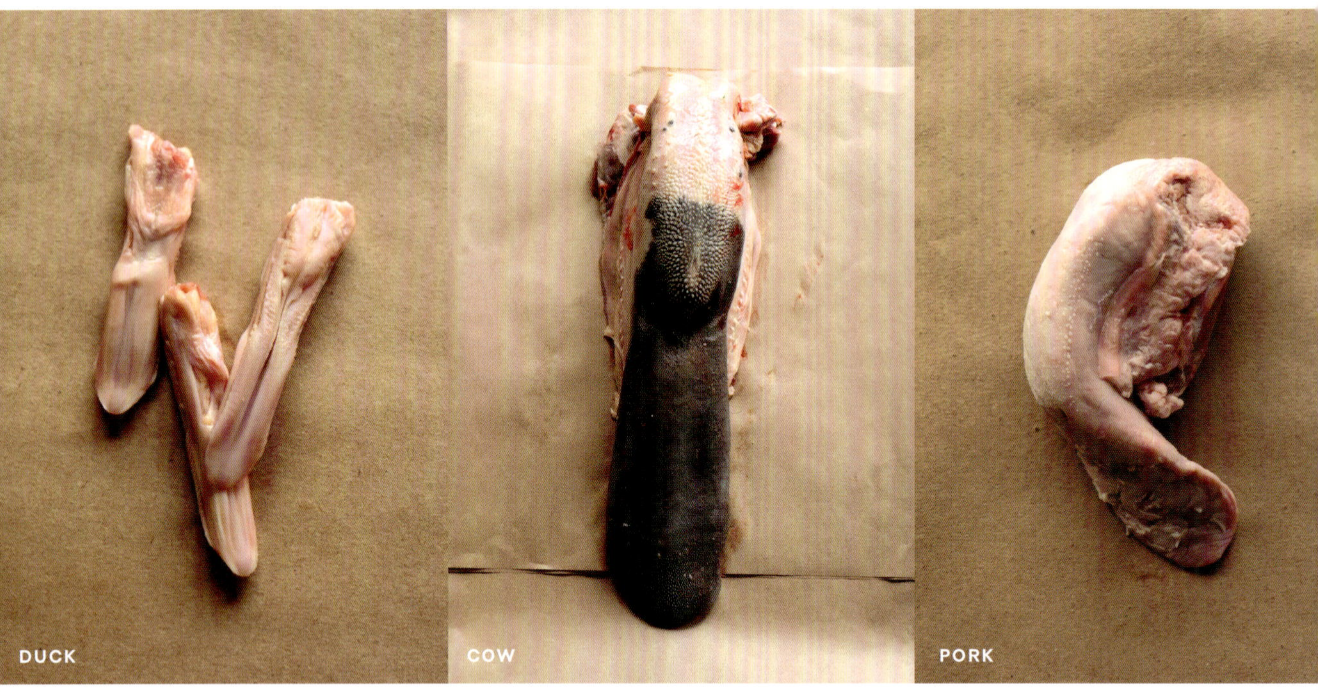


Taste buds are tasty! You know the old adage about how the harder-working the muscle, the more flavor it has? Well, the tongue is one of the hardest-working muscles in the body. And unlike the heart, which is also constantly working, the tongue is very fatty, giving it long, lingering flavor. It's also a great source of iron and vitamin $B_{12}$.

There are several parts to the tongue (tip, middle, and base or end). Tongue is leanest at the tip, becoming increasingly fatty farther back. Though my first stop on almost every trip to New York City is a Jewish deli, like the 2nd Avenue Deli or Katz's, both of which serve center cuts or tips, it was the "tongue experience" at Takashi, a yakiniku restaurant in the West Village, that really enlightened me. Before that, I took tongue for granted as a singular sensation, but tasting three cuts of tongue at Takashi taught me a lot about tongue's versatility. Tongue has the underlying flavor of the animal itself, so it's not the flavor that is the aversion for most people; it's often the texture. When tongue is overcooked, it becomes mealy and mushy. But braised properly, it keeps a bouncy, meaty chew while remaining tender, and it crisps up beautifully after braising. I find grilling tongue, too, to be one of the best expressions of the muscle. To really taste the meat, treat it like a steak and aim for rare to medium rare.

**COW** Beef and veal tongue should be treated the same (and for the most part, pig and lamb, too). For any preparation other than braising or simmering it whole, first lay down a kitchen spoon and place the tongue on it. Put another spoon on top and tightly wrap it all in plastic (and tie it with twine if you want it to be secure). Then, freeze the tongue just until it holds its shape. This keeps the tongue straight and makes it much easier to work with. At this point, you can use a sharp vegetable peeler to remove the tough skin. This is how I prep for tongue tartare—an unusual treatment, but it's perfect raw, well marbled, with so much depth of flavor. Once it's peeled, you can slice and grill it, sear it, or even grind it for sausages.

Beef and veal tongues become very tender when put in Corning Brine (page 283) or marinade for an extended period of time—even upward of a week.

To braise or simmer a whole tongue, don't bother with the peeling referenced above. Put it in a pot with mirepoix and water to cover, bring it to a boil, salt it (unless it's been brined), and simmer until the tongue becomes tender enough so that, when squeezed, the skin separates from the meat; this could be from 1½ to 3 hours, depending on the size and type of tongue. Just keep an eye on it. If the meat shreds when peeled, it's overcooked—it shouldn't come apart in strands. When cooked just right, tongue should peel without much effort; this is easiest to do when it's still warm. Once it's peeled, cool the tongue in its cooking liquid and hold it until you're ready to cook further. This will help keep it moist. Depending on your cut of tongue, there may be a bone toward the base, which looks almost like a wishbone; remove it. From here, you can slice the tongue into thick pieces, cutting it lengthwise across the grain. It's great seared after braising to crisp the edges, transforming it into one of my favorite taco fillings. Order lengua at the next taco truck you see!

**PIG** Pork tongue membranes are much thinner than those on cow tongues, which can make them trickier to peel because sometimes they rip apart rather than coming off in big pieces. Still, they can usually be peeled off easily when fresh. I don't suggest eating them raw, so they should be simmered like cow tongue until firm yet giving. After they're cooked, I use either a spoon or the back of a paring knife to scrape off the membrane. Pig tongues are great in a brine or marinade—and surprisingly good when pickled (see page 151).

**SHEEP** Lamb tongue has an almost identical casing to cow, likely due to the animals' similar grass diet. Follow the same preparation used for beef tongues. I particularly like to use lamb tongue in terrines (see page 206), but they also crisp up nicely with a hard sear, as in my Crispy Lamb's Tongue, Potatoes & Peas (page 205).

**FOWL** You'll almost never find poultry tongues, except for duck, which have this little bone in the middle you have to watch out for when prepping or eating. When the tongues are braised until tender, it's very easy to remove that bone. To do so, place the tongues in salted water with mirepoix, bring to a boil, and then simmer for 30 minutes. Remove the tongues from the stock, squeeze the base of the tongue, and pull out the cartilage; it's the same type of cartilage you would find in a pig's ear. They're a fantastic fried bar snack (see, page 236).

# EARS

Ears are made up of skin and cartilage, and once they're parcooked they become jiggly, with a line of firm cartilage holding their form together. This combination of soft and snappy makes them a perfect candidate for frying. In Spain, *oreja de cerdo* is a typical tapas snack. With all that fat and crunch, pig ears can be transformed into offal's "french fries" (see page 157).

Ears can be used in classic head-based charcuterie, like the Italian coppa di testa, or the French tête de veau, as well as a lining for terrines, providing a toothsome bite while acting as a gelling agent. They're also great for making a super-flavorful and gelatinous stock. Though ears don't have the most pronounced flavor, they do take on other flavors well. Filipinos make *sisig,* a stew of pig jowls and plenty of pig ears, calamansi (a tart hybrid between a mandarin and a kumquat), and hot chiles. It's the most textural chili you've ever had, and it works as an amazing taco filling, too.

**COW** I more readily see cow's ears in pet stores as chew toys than in kitchens. They're less fatty than pig ears. Treat them similarly to the pig procedure that follows, but you may need to braise them for a bit longer.

**PIG** Get *in* there. You'll have to scrub out that layer of stuff from the canal. It's not earwax, but it certainly is something you should remove. A lot of times, the handle of a wooden spoon with a towel wrapped around it works well, like a massive Q-tip.

Pig ears are easy to find sold by the pound. Brine them for 12 hours and braise them, then choose whether you want to either press them into a terrine or deep-fry them. Then place them in a nonreactive pot with mirepoix, aromatics, and unsalted water to cover. Bring this to a boil, skim any scum, then reduce the heat to a simmer and cook for 2 hours, or until tender to the touch. You'll know it's ready when you squeeze the ear between your fingers and your fingertip goes through it easily. You're trying to not only make the exterior tender but the collagen in the interior soft, too.

**SHEEP** These ears can be tough to get, but they should also be treated like pig's ears if you can get your hands on them. Don't confuse these with lamb's ear (*Stachys byzantina*), which is in fact a hardy perennial plant.

**FOWL** Birds *do* have ears, but they're just holes on the sides of their heads. Chickens do have ear lobes though, which can be indicators of what color eggs they lay. The whiter the lobe, the paler the eggshell, and red lobes usually mean brown eggs. If the ear lobes are tinted blue, the eggs usually have a blue hue. But not much to eat here.

Rabbits, of course, have sizable ears. (And yes, rabbits are considered "poultry" by the USDA, which is as weird to me as it is to you.) Rabbit ears are similar in composition to the other ears mentioned above, and I love them braised and then fried as well (see page 237).

# BRAIN

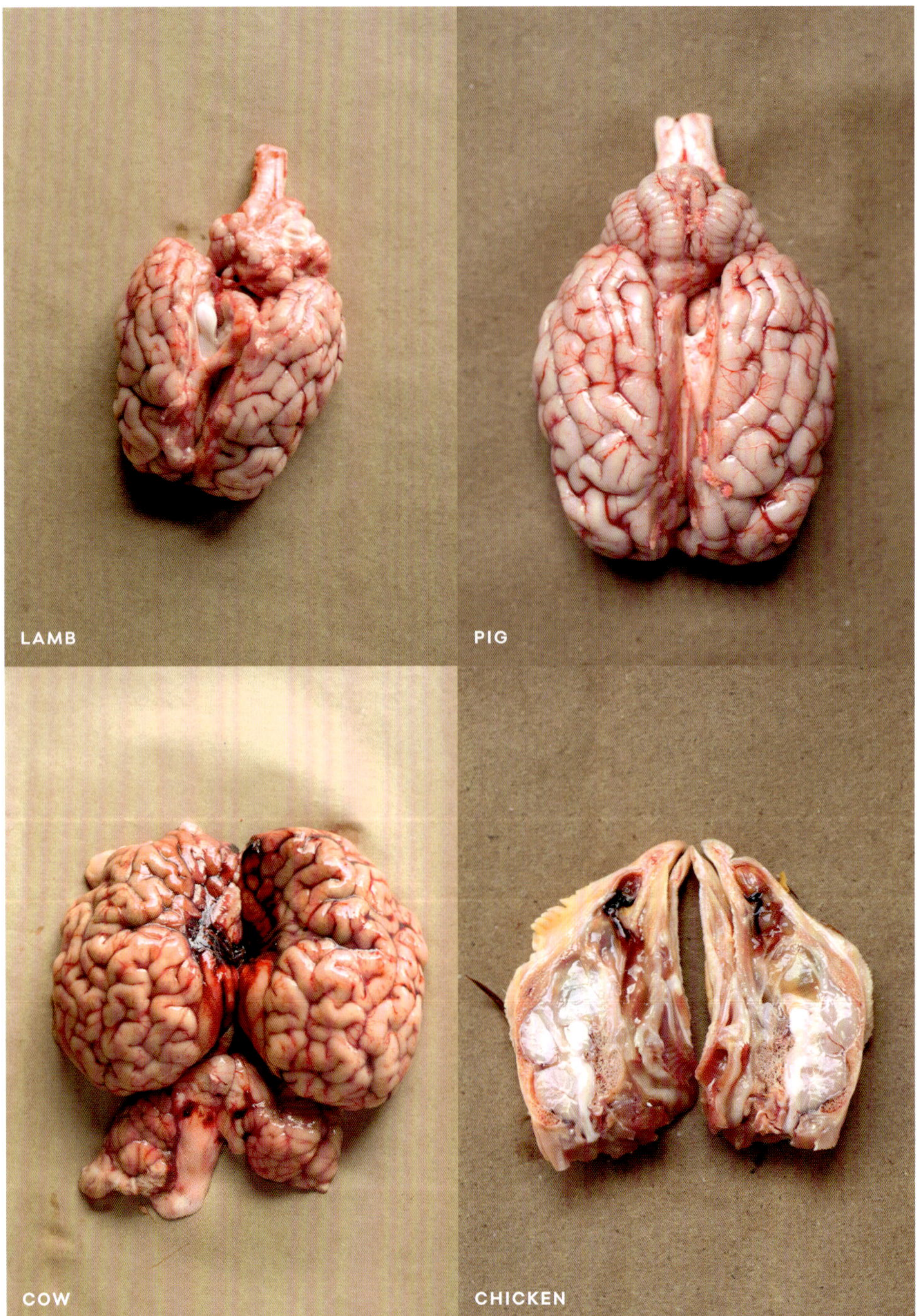

The brain is a giant mass of neurons controlling the nervous system, and it's truly the most complex of all organs. It's more than 50 percent fat, making it the fattiest piece of offal by weight, rich in healthy omega fats as well as cholesterol. Strolling through London's Smithfield Market, I saw a can of Rose's pork brains in milk from the United Kingdom. The amount of cholesterol in this three-ounce can is more than ten times what the average human is supposed to have in a day. It still sits unopened at my home. So, I'm not telling anyone to sit down and eat a brain a day—it's a delicacy, with a creamy, pudding-like texture. Because of its fat content, you can whip it like a mousse and even sear it without oil or butter.

Classical French headcheese, or *fromage de tête,* is often made with pig brains whipped into its cooking liquid. The brains act as a thickening agent for the pâté. And stroll up to most any taco truck in San Francisco, and you'll see Mexican cooks sizzling *tacos de sesos* (beef brain tacos) on the plancha—one of my favorite delicacies!

I know brain eating gets some people pretty squeamish, which is why I'm glad to see zombie movies finally moving away from just focusing on the brains. Modern zombies eat the whole human as a giant flesh ball. Maybe it's their way of thinking sustainably. Horror flicks aside, the greatest fear about eating brain is BSE (bovine spongiform encephalopathy), better known as mad cow disease, which was centralized in the United Kingdom in the 1990s. Humans cannot catch it, but they can contract something similar, called Creutzfeldt-Jakob disease, from eating infected tissue. Now, brains from younger animals are legal in the United States, but in truth, livestock practices have improved. And if you get your brains from a rancher who treats cows humanely, you've essentially nullified the threat of this disease in animals of all ages.

**COW** If you're not getting the head in whole, go to your butcher for the best brains. Ask when they came in—freshest is best, because once they hit the air, they start to degrade in quality; ideally you want the brains to be less than two days old, and check them for any discoloration or any hint of funk in the smell. (This is a case where buying frozen brains is not a bad solution; brains survive freezing pretty well, and it extends their viability for weeks.) For the most part, all brains are prepared using the same process. The first step is to make sure there are no bits of bone by giving the brains a quick rinse. The next step is to soak them to get the blood out. Some people use milk, others use vinegared water, but I prefer to rinse the brains and then poach them in Court Bouillon (page 280); that way they keep their creamy texture. I poach them at a light simmer for just a few minutes, until just done and almost custardy; if they're cooked at too high a heat, everything breaks apart. Once cooked, remove the brains from the liquid and let them cool. Check for membranes on top, which will look like a cloudy veil, and if there are any, peel them off. There are two lobes to a brain, and it's easier to cook them when separated, so use a knife to split them. From here, you can go in many directions—scramble them with eggs, hard-sear them in very hot cast iron, or even bread and fry them, which was prominent as a sandwich in St. Louis during the late 1800s because of the prevalence of beef cattle feedlots in the area. I also love This Is Your Brain on Drugs (page 86), an updated butcher's breakfast, an homage to the early 1900s livestock yards of Chicago, the same ones described in Upton Sinclair's book *The Jungle.*

**PIG** Prepare these like cow brains. Most people only utilize the lobes of pig's brain, but after cooking them for a while, I realized that the cerebellum (the braided "little brain" underneath the back of the lobes) is also good to eat. It's great for a pig's brain iteration of aioli that I make, which was dubbed Brainaise (page 275) by acclaimed San Francisco chef Daniel Patterson.

**SHEEP** Lamb brains can be a little more pungent, due to lamb fat's natural gaminess, but they are so delicious as Lamb Brain on Toast with Creamed Nettles & Morels (page 209). I like to pair them with a more acidic sauce than what I use for cow or pig brains. Also prep them as you do cow brains.

**FOWL** You can't really get bird brains out of the skull, but if you cook the heads, you can suck them out as with the roasted squab heads on page 235.

# SWEETBREADS

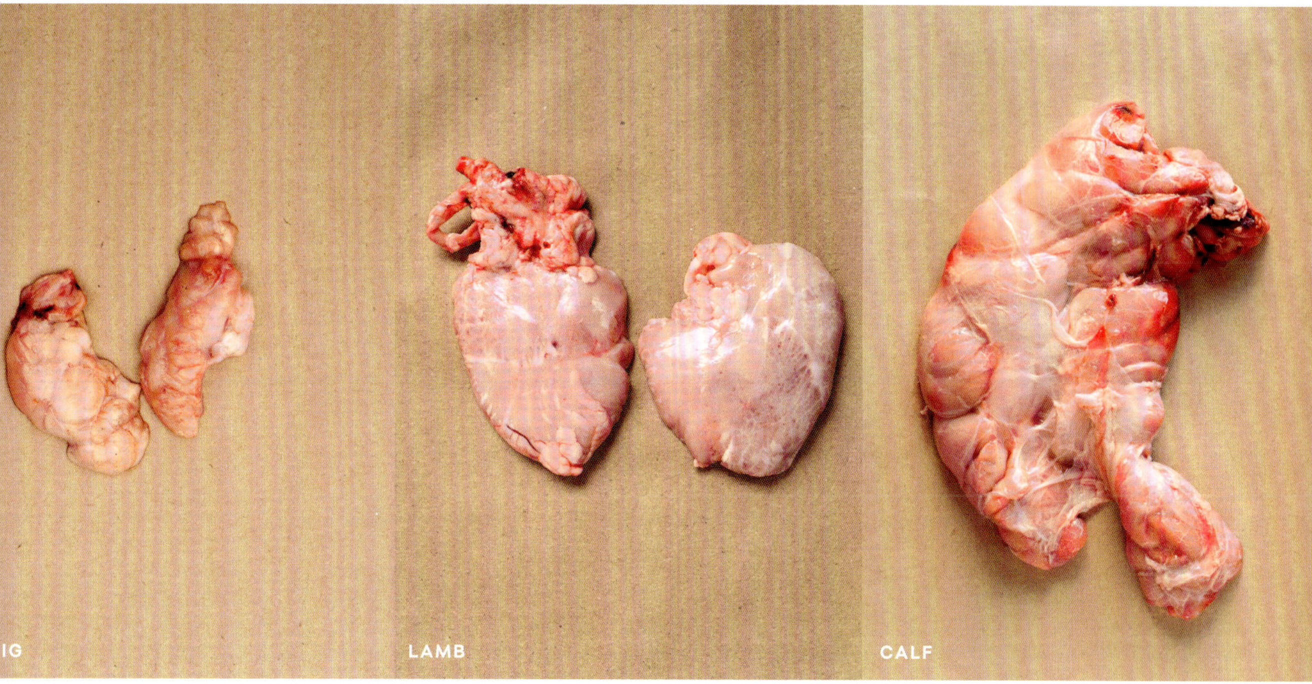


Sweetbreads are neither sweet nor are they bread . . . discuss! And they are not, despite what you may have heard, brains. They're creamy, fatty little nuggets, and the word *sweetbread* refers to the thymus gland (located in the neck) and the pancreas (situated near the stomach). Most commonly harvested from calves or lambs, sweetbreads are highly coveted pieces of offal, known as *ris* in French (calf is *ris de veau*, whereas lamb is *ris d'agneau*).

For some reason, sweetbreads are often the first offal dish that most people are willing to try in a restaurant. They're particularly good fried, but I've also had incredible ones that have been grilled over binchotan charcoal at yakitori counters in Japan. In Argentina, cooks take raw sweetbreads, with the fat left on, and just throw them on the *asado* (grill). Because they're enveloped in fat, they take a while to cook, but the fat renders out and crisps beautifully.

**COW** The vast majority of sweetbreads you'll encounter are from veal calves.

In most cases, you must remove the membrane from sweetbreads before cooking them. Poach them in a Court Bouillon (page 280) until they're just firm. Shock them in salted ice water, press the liquid out (I use two plates weighted by a big can of tomatoes), and then make a shallow incision with a sharp knife and peel away the membrane with your fingertips.

When I was a young cook, working with Traci Des Jardins at Rubicon in San Francisco, the chef Joachim Splichal came in to do a special event. He marched up to me and told me to prep the sweetbreads. I proceeded to peel them all down. I mean *all* the way down. I kept peeling and peeling until I had a pile of nuggets the size of nickels and quarters in front of me. Joachim chewed me out big-time! So how do you know when to stop peeling? Well, you do so basically before the sweetbreads completely fall apart. It's important to leave some fat to keep the sweetbreads intact. I kept tearing away, but once there's no membrane to hold it together, it completely separates. So watch the membrane as you're working, and make sure there's a little still there to keep them together.

Anyway, after the prep, you can poach and then sear them; don't try to sear them raw, as the membrane won't soften without poaching first. Sweetbreads are also often fried. You can deep-fry, but I like to lightly dust them in flour and panfry them, so that I have a bit more control to cook them all evenly. If I am going to deep-fry, I'll dredge them in milk and flour seasoned with salt and pepper.

Finally, if I'm going to grill sweetbreads, I'll start from raw but grill them over medium to medium-high coals, turning them often, so that the fat renders out relatively slowly and keeps the meat nicely moist.

**PIG** Pig sweetbreads are hard to come by on their own, but they should be intact when you buy whole pigs. Prepare them similarly to lamb sweetbreads.

**SHEEP** Lamb sweetbreads are significantly smaller than a calf's, and they are *very* delicate, but they're so damn tasty. They certainly have a stronger flavor, too, and go well with an assertive acidic sauce, as seen in Lamb Sweetbreads, Pine Nuts, Capers & Raisins Agrodolce (page 210). Prep lamb sweetbreads the same way you would cow.

**FOWL** Sweetbreads are not harvested from poultry as a whole, and they aren't found in rabbits.

# LUNGS

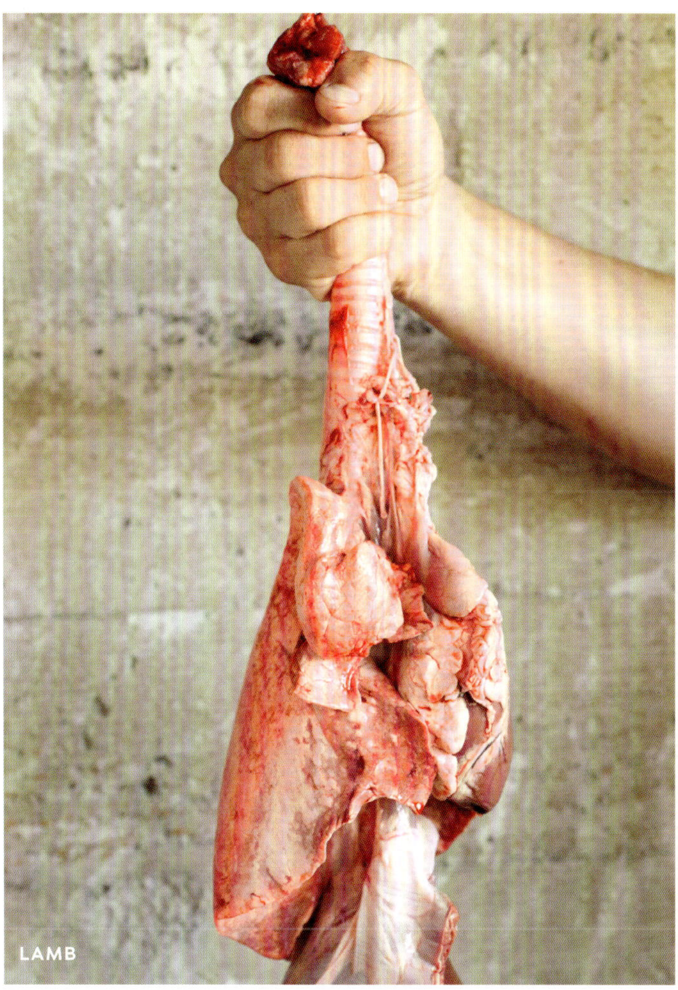

LAMB

The USDA banned livestock lungs for consumption in 1972. They were used as fillers for mixed-meat sausages, but because of a huge pneumonia epidemic in factory-farmed animals, health officials shut down their use in meat fabrication. But lungs are eaten all over the world! Boiled, fried, and ground for pâtés, they're light and less fatty than other organs. They're texturally like angel food cake and are appropriately airy.

*Polmone panino,* whole fried lung sandwich, is served at the offal haven, Mercato Centrale in Florence. In Scotland, haggis incorporates sheep lungs, which means the authentic product can't be imported into the States. I try to utilize lamb pluck, which is the entire esophageal structure, (heart, lungs, liver, and spleen), in dishes like Lamb Pluck Fra Diavolo (page 212), though you can really only get lungs if you work closely with a trusted farmer.

**COW** First, beat the lungs with a wooden spoon to break the capillary blood vessels—kind of like how your grandparents used to tenderize tough steaks. Soak them in salted ice water for 3 hours to get the blood out. I then take a tube or a straw and blow into the lungs to expand them. You'll see that if there's no rib cage, lungs can expand to amazing volumes. I press the lungs to deflate them and expel any extra blood in the cavity as well as any funk.

In a large pot, cover them with cold water and bring them up to a boil, then drain and start anew with fresh, salted water and aromatics and simmer until tender, about 2 hours. Once tender, press them flat, at which point you can slice them easily and consistently. I like to sear them with a little fat.

**PIG** Follow the same path as cow's lungs. Pig lungs will be easier to purchase, especially if you're buying a whole hog. Make sure to check for lesions, though, which are indicators of a bad lung.

**SHEEP** If you can get them (usually only if you buy the whole animal), prep lamb lungs like a cow's.

**FOWL** Turkey Lungs on Toast with Sage Brown Butter (page 238) are a great Thanksgiving appetizer. Prior to cooking, soak them in salted water for 30 minutes to get the blood out. Fowl lungs are commonly found in the carcass of the birds. The larger the bird, the easier they are to find. They are two variegated pieces connected by the trachea, behind the heart.

# HEART

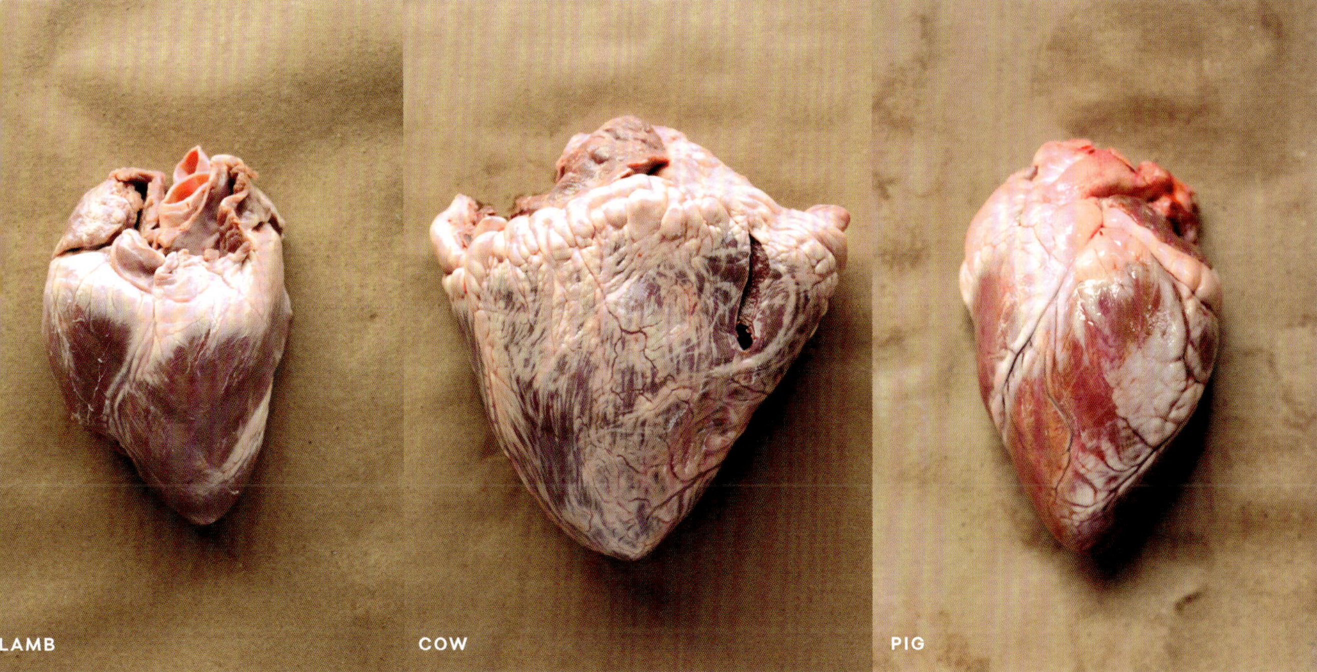


**"I LEFT MY HEART IN SAN FRANCISCO."**

—AS SUNG BY TONY BENNETT

While my heart will always remain in San Francisco, that's not where I found my love of it. My first-ever bite of heart was in London, over a decade ago at Jamie Oliver's Fifteen, where a burly, redheaded beast of a man, Derek Dammann, was chef de cuisine. He's now chef and owner of Maison Publique in Montreal, Quebec, a favorite restaurant of mine and a true destination for deliciousness. But the first time we met, he'd been informed that I was coming into Fifteen for lunch. He'd heard that I served a menu of organ meats back in the States, so Derek took it upon himself to prepare a special tasting. Within minutes of sitting down, out came a grilled beef heart, simply adorned with shaved beets, horseradish, and some fresh herbs, and lightly dressed in vinaigrette—so uncomplicated but with depth and intensity. A pleasant inherent crunchiness from its exterior came with every soft bite, similar to the raw beets the heart was so smartly paired with. Its dense, rich, umami flavor reminded me of something along the lines of a dry-aged steak. The meat was also incredibly lean, antithetical to what I was taught, that "fat is flavor"—a cliché constantly repeated in culinary school and professional kitchens. But heart is flavor-forward on its own, like tasting the purest form of an animal.

*Anticuchos de corazón,* marinated, skewered, and quickly grilled hearts, are a delicious Peruvian street food. Versions ranging from beef to chicken are served from carts lining the streets of Lima. All over Italy, you see chicken hearts cooked on skewers, called spiedini. Japanese yakitori joints fly through chicken hearts. I do a version, Grilled Duck Hearts, Hazelnut Oil & Black Pepper (page 241), that I bet will soon be part of your backyard barbecue repertoire. In France, *coeur de veau farci* is a whole calf's heart packed with forcemeat (ground lean meat emulsified with fat), wrapped in caul fat, braised, and then roasted.

Hearts don't have much fat and are nearly pure muscle fiber—and very well-worked muscle fiber at that. Because of the heart's density, heat has a hard time penetrating the meat. Cooking processes like grilling and sautéing will be slower than expected, and due to this, many people think heart is done before it actually is. Keep it on the fire for a bit longer, another few minutes, and then let it rest properly so all the juices redistribute before cutting into it. To be honest, this also means there is a risk of overcooking, and nobody wants a tough piece of meat. The best way is to cook heart a bit longer, over more gentle heat; you'll also benefit from adding some extra moisture and flavor by brining the meat before cooking.

When shopping for heart, look for ones that are prominently red. (No surprise there, really.) If you want the cow heart intact, ask the butcher to leave it untrimmed. If it's already been cleaned, USDA standards require that it "shall have the 'heart cap' (auricles, arteries, and gristly material), [and] hearts shall be trimmed practically free of fat and shall not have been excessively scored." These procedures don't lessen the quality of the heart meat and will likely be how you see them, as most beef hearts are halved for USDA inspection, to search for blood clots. Pig, lamb, and poultry hearts are sold whole and tend to feel smooth to the touch; if they are soft and spongy, they are not fresh.

**COW** If working with a whole, intact cow's heart, first trim off all of the exterior fat (save it and render it out as tallow, and use it to fry something else later). Slice off the aorta and pulmonary arteries; they'll be sticking out the side. Next, split it open. Trim off the fibrous tissues on the interior, from the top of the heart to the beginning of the chambers. Remove the fascia—the connective tissue collagen—as if you're removing silver skin from a steak or skinning a salmon. Set those trimmings aside and grind them up to make a sugo or ragù later. (See opposite page.)

Cut it into whatever size pieces you desire, leaving the exterior membrane intact. As the meat cooks, the membrane will become very tender.

**PIG** I believe pig hearts should be fully cooked through, no medium rare here—not just my preference, but also the USDA's. I often brine them in Corning or Ham Brine (pages 283 and 284), gently confit them in lard, then shave them thin to serve like charcuterie. They're really nice folded into a crisp green salad. You'll find pig hearts in many types of sausage. I use them in my Blood Sausage (page 164) as the lean meat, reinforcing the porky flavor with the

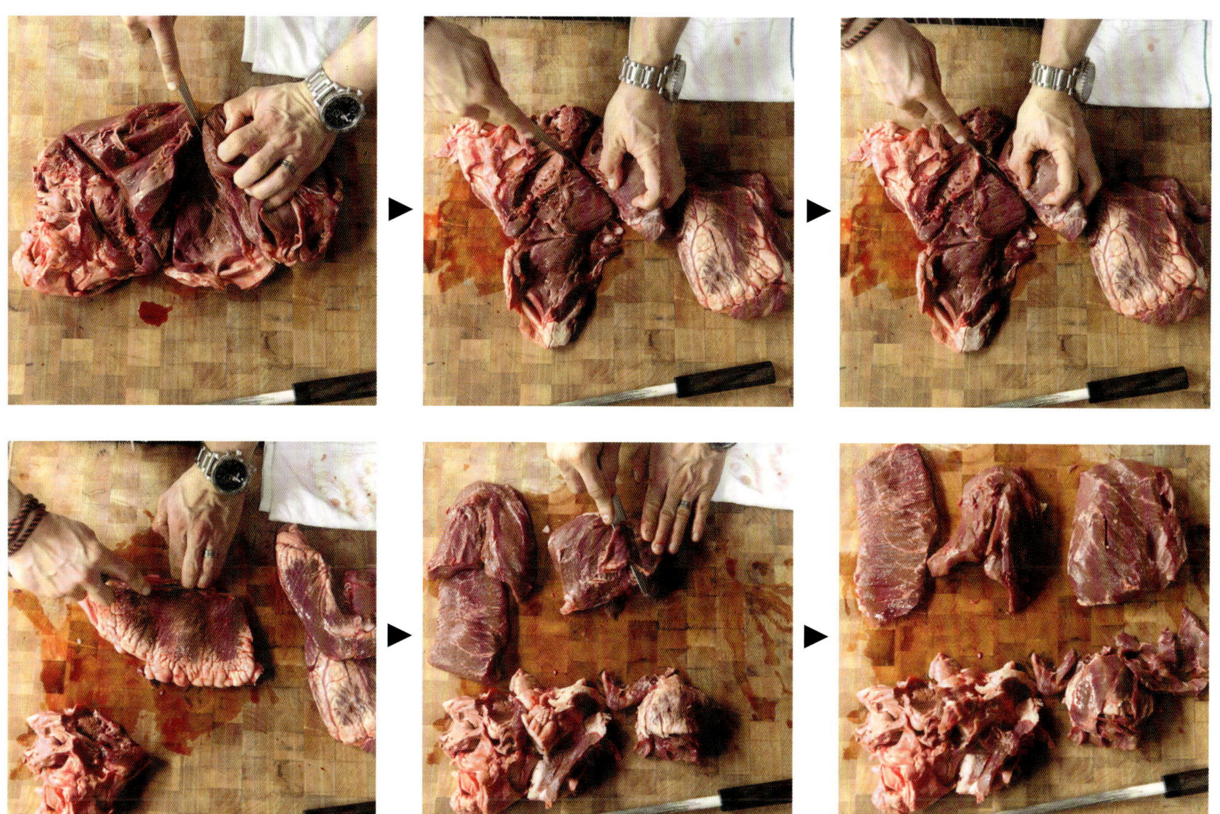

same muscle that pumps the blood. Pig hearts are the ones where you'll notice the biggest taste difference between those properly raised and those that aren't. A heart from a pig with freedom to roam will have a much more intense flavor than that of a factory hog.

**SHEEP** Prep these like cow hearts. Lamb heart can be cooked or served raw, but either way, it always has a bit of a barnyard-y flavor. I like to riff on the Easter tradition of lamb and mint jelly by serving roasted hearts with mint salsa in Lamb Pluck Fra Diavolo (page 212).

**FOWL** Poultry hearts are sold whole and do not need to be split to be cleaned. Just trim the fatty sections and arteries from the top, squeeze the hearts to remove any blood left in the chambers, and they are ready to be cooked.

We all have memories from Thanksgiving of that little giblet sack stuffed inside the cavity of the turkey, pulled out to make gravy and invariably overcooked. The great thing about poultry hearts is their versatility. I've confited them, braised them, grilled them on live fire, roasted them in an oven, and sautéed them in a pan. Even though most heart dishes of smaller fowl aren't usually large enough for stand-alone meals, they're great paired with the breast meat from the animal itself. With bigger birds, like goose and turkey, you can actually stuff the hearts and roast them alongside the rest of the bird. Whether grilling or sautéing, the test for doneness is the same: place your finger slightly into the chamber's opening to see that it's warmed through.

# BLOOD

PIG'S BLOOD, LIQUID

PIG'S BLOOD, COAGULATED

Blood is the life force that brings oxygen from the heart and the lungs to the rest of the body. It carries nutrients through a transportation highway of arteries and veins. But blood gets a bad rap. There's Dracula, communicable diseases, a child's tears when they scrape themselves—all these things have given blood a bad name. But blood is better than that. It's a natural coagulant that makes a scab, which protects you while you heal. In the same vein, in the kitchen, it's an amazing thickener for sauces. And its coagulating powers and rich nutrients are why there are so many blood sausages: Spain and Latin America's *morcilla*, France's *boudin noir*, Italy's *sanguinaccio*, Britain's black pudding, and many more.

Maybe it's because of blood's life-sustaining qualities that various religions have laws about how to deal with blood. Islamic and Jewish law, for instance, closely outlines how blood should be handled during the slaughter of an animal.

Many butchers carry blood in a liquid state; ask for fresh first, then frozen. There are two other forms in which blood can be purchased: in Asian markets you may find it Filipino-style, in which an anticoagulant has been added. It's great used in dishes like Pig's Blood Soup, 'Nduja-Stuffed Dates & Herbs (page 162)—my riff on *dinuguan*, a Filipino stew of meats and offal in blood sauce. Or, in the opposite direction, you can also find coagulated blood cubes in Asian markets, sort of like tofu made of blood. Beef, pork, and duck blood are highly perishable and, when fresh, should be used within one or two days, but they also freeze well. Just be sure to stir it when thawed, as the plasma will separate. Blood is rich in iron and has a metallic minerality, but watch out: it will become gritty if overcooked.

**COW** Beef blood is pretty difficult to get, but if you do, use it in the same way you would pig's blood.

**PIG** There isn't much special prep for blood, except when I make blood mousse, I pasteurize the blood at a low temperature first (see page 173), which is sort of like thermalizing milk when making cheese. This maintains the red color. For Spaghetti, Bloodtarga & Egg Yolk (page 168), I cure blood in the style of the salted, pressed Italian mullet-roe bottarga, using salt and transglutaminase (meat glue), which, once dried and hardened, can be grated as if it's Parmesan cheese. It gives a minerality and depth of flavor to anything you add it to.

**SHEEP** On a Passover Seder plate sits a roasted lamb shank, representing the sacrificial lamb whose blood was used to mark the doorframes of Israelites in Egypt, preventing the death of their firstborns. You, too, can ward off the plagues, or use lamb blood in place of pork in recipes.

**FOWL** Duck blood is probably the most commonly found poultry blood on the market. *Canard à la presse* (pressed duck) is a nineteenth-century French dish for which a duck's neck is quickly broken, rather than slaughtered with a cut and bled out. The duck is then roasted, the meat is taken off the bones and served, and the carcass and the bones are put into a specially designed press that squeezes out the blood and marrow into a satisfyingly fortified sauce.

# LIVER

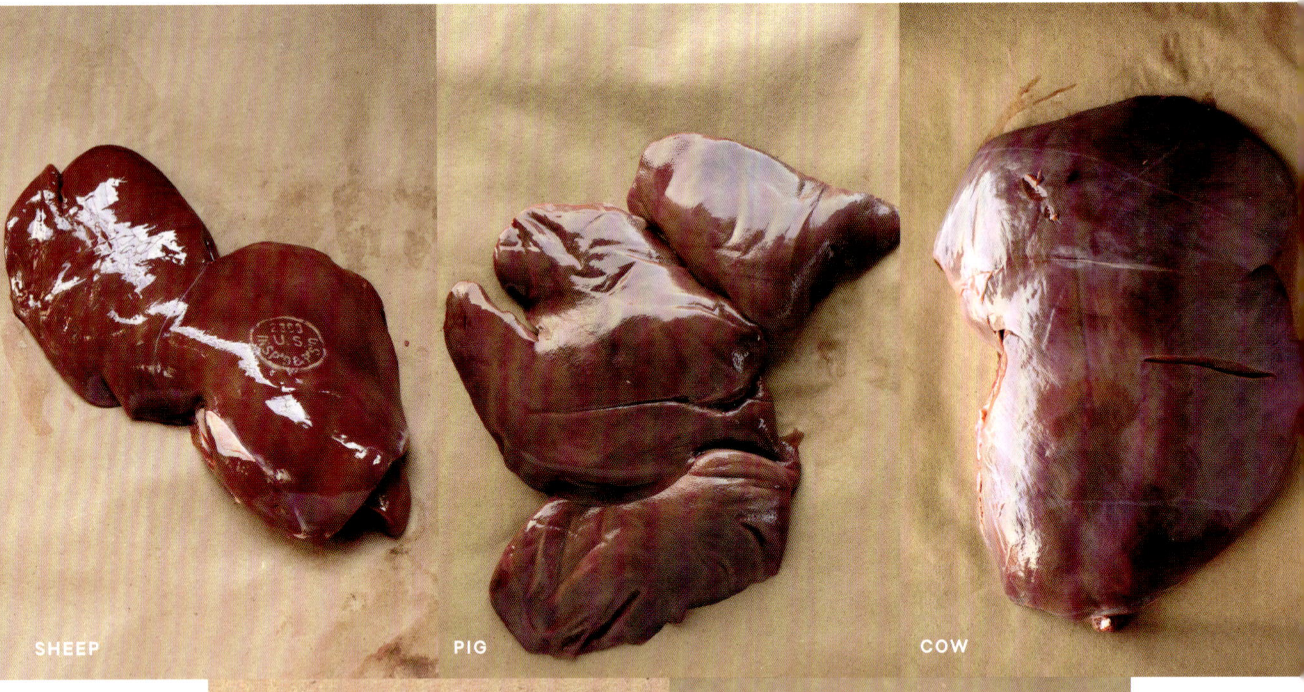

SHEEP PIG COW

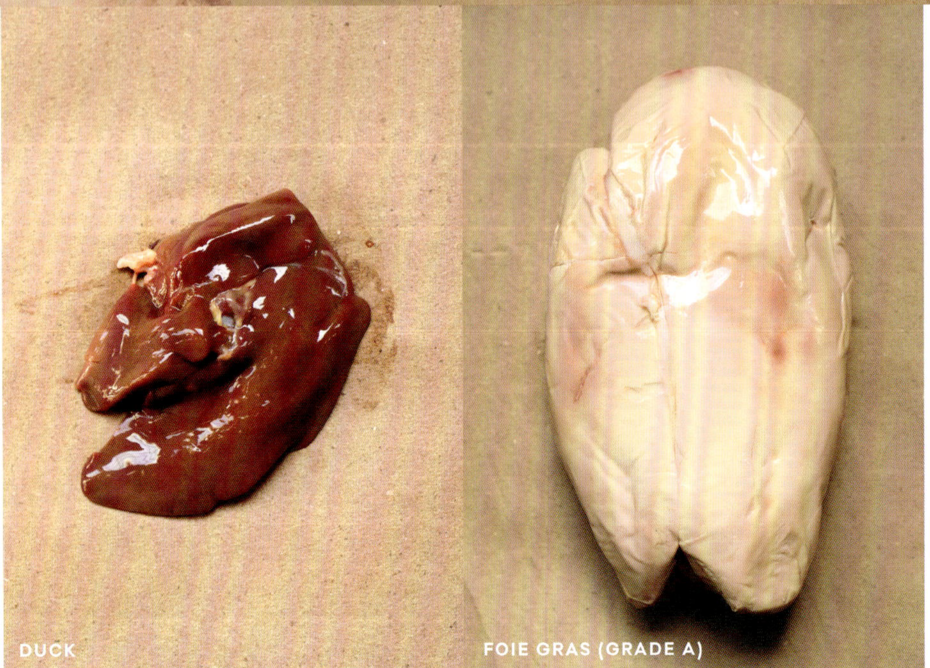

DUCK FOIE GRAS (GRADE A)

Liver is both one of the most commonly enjoyed organs and one that's scared off many an early diner. I, like most people, have had many badly prepared livers, which I blame for liver's sometimes bad rap. When overcooked, it becomes terribly dry and grainy, and its flavor reminds me a little of dirt. But when well cooked, it is creamy and velvety, earthy and minerally with a satisfying meatiness that lingers.

Along with kidney and spleen, liver is one of the filtration organs. There's a common misconception that the filtration organs are full of "bad stuff," when, in fact, liver is highly nutritious, full of vitamins A and $B_{12}$, for starters, which combat colds, diseases, and anemia by fortifying the level of red blood cells in the body. That said, it's also best to buy organic liver. When they start giving animals antibiotics, traces of those chemicals are found in the liver.

Now, I can't talk about liver without bringing up foie gras. It's very rich, like sweet, meaty butter that makes everything it touches taste one hundred times better. It's been banned in California a number of times, and I am a passionate person that has been in the middle of this conversation. It's an engorged duck or goose liver, yes, and is the source of a pretty heated debate, because there is the opinion that it's cruel to produce. But engorged livers also occur naturally in these birds. When these birds fly south for the winter, they survive off their fattened liver, so they don't have to stop during migration. When people produce foie gras, this fattening up of the liver is exaggerated through a process called gavage, which dates as far back as the ancient Egyptians. In gavage, the birds are fed a large amount of warm corn mush through a feeding tube. Yes, they are overfeeding them, but duck anatomy takes it well: the esophagus is less rigid and comparatively larger than the human/mammal esophagus, and designed to hold large amounts of food. The trachea and esophagus are separate, therefore waterfowl do not "gag" when a large amount of food goes down, hence the saying "eating like a duck," which means swallowing something without chewing. And their livers do become enlarged, though not diseased.

**COW** I love using calf's liver, but if you haven't tried beef liver, please do. It has a much more intense natural flavor, so you won't need to add much to it. I love making a spread out of either; try using a recipe like Calf's Liver & Porcini Pâté (page 101), which has flavor for days! With cow, pig, and lamb, check to see if there is a gallbladder attached, which is a little green. If so, you'll want to remove it, as it contains bile and is quite bitter. The skin membrane also needs to be peeled, which can be done by hand. Flip the liver so it's flat-side up, slide a finger underneath the membrane, and start to pull away. Once you're done, search for and remove any veins with a paring knife—they're very fibrous. Calf's liver is smaller and more delicate. Just peel the membrane and remove any large veins.

At this point, the liver is ready to be portioned. Livers have a few distinct lobes that amorphously "hug" other surrounding organs, so each piece won't be totally consistent. You can separate them or keep the liver whole, depending on the preparation. From here, some cooks like to soak it in an ice-water bath or milk to extract some of the intensity. (If the liver is super fresh, I prefer not to soak it.) If you marinate liver, it's very important to dry or blot it off before cooking it in fat to get a good sear. Also, a tip: Once peeled, livers want to adhere to towels. After you blot them dry, oil them a bit so they won't stick.

Cow's and calf's livers have a wide range as an ingredient. They can be seared, pureed to make terrines, added to pâtés, and served rare or even raw, such as in Calf's Liver Crudo, Beets & Balsamic (page 98). When searing liver, though, make sure to bring the liver to temp; that is, take it out of the fridge so it comes to nearly room temp before cooking. Since you don't want to overcook any part of it, doing this allows the interior to come to a nice medium rare by the time you've browned the outside.

**PIG** I love making a "bottarga" out of pig's liver (see page 288), curing and drying it to allow for adding just a dusting of liver to a dish. You simply shave it over the top, like cheese on pasta, and you add a mysterious (or obvious, depending on how much you use) layer of flavor. Pig liver follows the same prep as cow.

**SHEEP** Prep lamb liver as you would cow. I serve raw lamb's liver to highlight its beet-like earthiness (see Lamb Liver Crudo & Bagna Cauda, page 217). Make sure it's super fresh and in beautiful shape—it's an organ that bruises easily. Smoking liver gives it structure, but also adds a depth that befits lamb (see Smoked Lamb Liver, Serrano & Mint Bruschetta, page 220). And you better believe that I also "bottarga" it (see Lamb Liver Bottarga, Mâche, Radish & Sheep's Milk Butter on Toast, page 223).

**FOWL** For chicken livers, the prep is not difficult but requires some detail. Make sure to trim them of veins and remove the membranes and any excess fatty bits before cooking. Also take off the gallbladder, which is green like in other animals, being sure not to pop it; it will make the liver acrid. Foie gras is a bit different and depends on the grade. Grade A is the best for simple presentations, but I use grade B—which is not poorer in quality but a bit veinier and a little less neat in appearance—for torchons. Just remove any interior veins or external clumps of fat. I don't usually soak other poultry livers; I just rinse them in water, though if I'm frying them, I'll let them sit in buttermilk for a bit, as both a bath and flavor boost.

# STOMACH

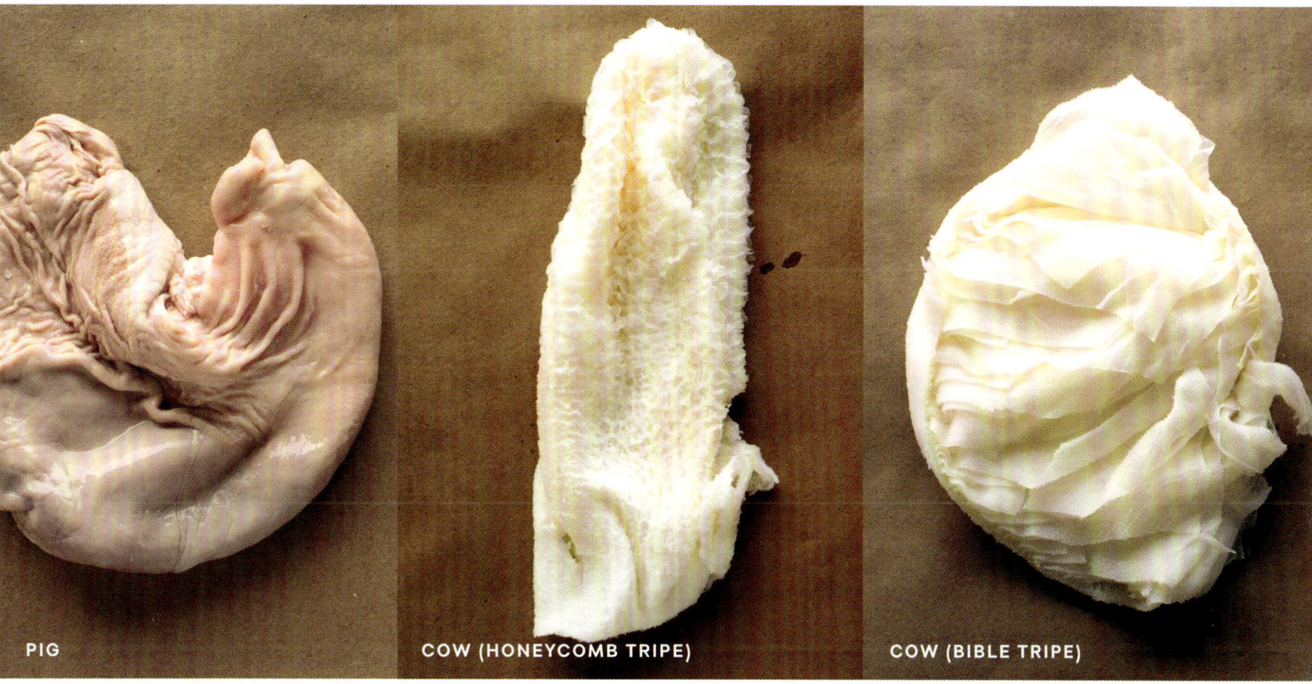

PIG    COW (HONEYCOMB TRIPE)    COW (BIBLE TRIPE)

When it comes to stomachs, animals are separated into two categories: ruminant and nonruminant. Ruminant animals, like cows and lambs, have a plant-based diet and chew their cud. These animals have four-chambered stomachs. Nonruminant animals, like pigs and humans, are omnivores and have single-chambered stomachs. Tripe is a general term for stomach lining—a smooth white muscle and a very tough cut of meat with quite a bit of fat, but one that has ten times the amount of protein as a steak of the same volume.

Nonruminant stomachs are double-lined, and these can be boiled, braised, or used as a great cooking vessel. In Pig Stomach à la Tauntaun (page 180), it's filled with sausage that looks like intestines, a tribute to that scene in *The Empire Strikes Back* when Han Solo stuffed Luke Skywalker into a tauntaun on the snowy plains of Hoth so he wouldn't freeze to death. (Cut it open tableside to serve it. With a lightsaber if you have one.)

I can't believe that the first time I actually *ate* tripe was not at my grandma Rosalie's table but in an old VFW hall, Mike's Kitchen in Warwick, Rhode Island. It was not good, but there was an allure there, maybe because I didn't know what the hell to think of it. Now I love cold tripe salads and dishes like Tripe, Clams, Serrano & Lemon Verbena (page 106), which pairs two of my favorites—tripe and clams—and shows how similar their textures are. And now I eat *menudo*—not the band, but beef tripe in a flavorful broth with chiles, onions, lime, and cilantro; it's also a highly effective Mexican hangover cure. In a similar soupy context, tripe is also notable in Vietnamese pho. Then there's *trippa alla Romana,* braised with tomato and herbs, and tons of Parmesan shaved on top, and *lampredotto,* a Florentine tripe sandwich (see page 112). In the South, I've had hog maws, the muscular lining of a pig's stomach, which is also found in Chinese culture. I've had tripe stuffed as *saumagen* in Germany, and at home as *seimaage* in the Pennsylvania Dutch tradition. It's really a global thing.

**COW** The four chambers of a cow's stomach have their own distinct tastes and textures. They are the blanket (also called mino or, officially, rumen), honeycomb (reticulum), bible or book (omasum), and reed (abomasum). Each chamber has its own method of prep, but all of them have to be cleaned and soaked before being used. First, make sure there's no sand; a quick rinse and scrub will do for that. Then soak the tripe overnight in lightly salted water in the fridge, preferably with ice. This removes some funk and chills the fat, which makes it easier to remove before further cooking.

The blanket is where the cud is held, and while it's often cooked until tender like other tripes, I've found that a relative quick blanch will do, as this tripe is suitable for a near-raw presentation, which highlights its incredible, unique crunch. Tripe Crudo, Hazelnuts & Scallions (page 103) is as uncooked as you will get with tripe in this book.

Honeycomb tripe is probably the most common tripe and is characterized by its telltale honeycomb pattern. It's also sometimes called "nail stomach," because you'll find some of them stuck in there every once in a while. (I've found pieces of barbed wire, bottle caps, and even a LEGO or two in there. Since cows graze off the ground, and they eat most anything in their path, it's safe to say that if you drop something at a cattle ranch, in all likelihood you'll find it in tripe eventually.) For honeycomb, there's green or bleached. Green is colored by grass, but that's easily washed out with a good scrub under water, then a dip in very hot but not-quite boiling vinegar (just under 200°F). This will remove most of the odor, but if you want it odor-free, wash it further with a mixture of flour, water, and salt. (I use a mixture of 1 gallon water, 2 cups flour, and 1 tablespoon salt). Honeycomb also sometimes comes bleached, which is exactly that: cleaned with Clorox. Imagine something that stinks, then add bleach, and when you open up your nostrils wide . . . it's no bueno. In this case, rinse the honeycomb tripe and scrub it under running water, as if you're trying to get a stain out of a shirt. Soak it in ice water with a bit of rock salt as an abrasive and a splash of vinegar, and scrub, scrub, scrub, and scrub again, making sure to get all the sand, grit, and thistle spurs out. If, after all this cleaning, the tripe is still really ripe, do a quick boil in fresh water, rinse it in cold water, and then start over again. Do this until it smells as clean as you want it to, although in many cultures, a little bit of that funk is desired.

Bible tripe is the thinnest of the tripes and is called such because of the number of leaves in the muscle, like the pages in the book. Turn it inside out and spray plenty of cold water inside the leaves. Put it in a big pot with water to cover, bring it up to a boil, and remove it right after it hits a rolling boil. Rinse it in cold water, marinate it with salt and aromatics, and then braise it again to reach the desired texture.

Reed is the fourth and final stomach, and is also called the rennet bag, because it secretes rennet, an enzyme that is used in cheese making. Reed tripe is the most intensely "perfumed" and needs to be cleaned and cooked the most thoroughly. Use the same procedure as for honeycomb tripe.

**PIG** This multilayered stomach has both a lining and outer membrane, which can separate if overcooked. It has to be rinsed thoroughly of its slimy coating, because it usually isn't bleached or processed. Scrub it in water, then bring it up to a boil in fresh water, drain and rinse in cold water, and then braise it with mirepoix and aromatics. It usually comes split open, so if you're going to stuff it, you'll need to sew it closed.

**SHEEP** Lambs are ruminant animals, so their stomachs are treated in the same style as cows'. It's unusual to find all of the stomach in a store or butcher shop, because most lamb tripe is factory cleaned. If you find a proper butcher, you're in for a treat! Lamb tripe takes to braising really well.

**FOWL** Poultry stomachs are usually pitched when butchered, but if you raise your own chickens or have a friend who does, you'll see birds have a two-chambered stomach. The first, the proventriculus, secretes an acid that helps in digestion, while the second, better known as the gizzard (see page 72), is more specialized and grinds up birdseed as if it were a mill. The gizzards are delicious, but the proventriculus is rarely eaten.

## TRIPE COOKING LIQUID

MAKES 2 GALLONS, ENOUGH FOR ABOUT 7 POUNDS OF TRIPE

All tripe, save for the tripe crudo, needs to be cooked. Here's my all-purpose tripe cooking liquid, which has a little savoriness, sweetness, spice, and acidity all in one; I like to cook tripe in this mixture and adjust its cooking time and tenderness based on how the tripe will be served or further cooked in the final dish.

**1 medium carrot**
**1 medium yellow onion**
**2 celery stalks**
**2 garlic heads, split to expose the cloves**
**1 small leek, white and light green parts only**
**1 bulb fennel, tops removed**
**2 bay leaves**
**1 tablespoon sea salt**
**1 tablespoon fennel seeds**
**Peel and juice of 1 lemon**
**1 tablespoon champagne vinegar**
**½ cup white wine**
**2 vanilla bean pods, split lengthwise**

Combine all the ingredients in a large, nonreactive stockpot with 2 gallons of water.

Add the cleaned tripe, bring to a boil over high heat, turn it down to a simmer, and cook for 3 hours, or until the tripe is very tender. (You may adjust this timing for firmer or more tender tripe, depending on the final dish's preparation.)

Let the tripe cool in the cooking liquid overnight. Remove it from the cooking liquid and rinse under water.

Cut the tripe into whatever shape you so desire.

# SPLEEN

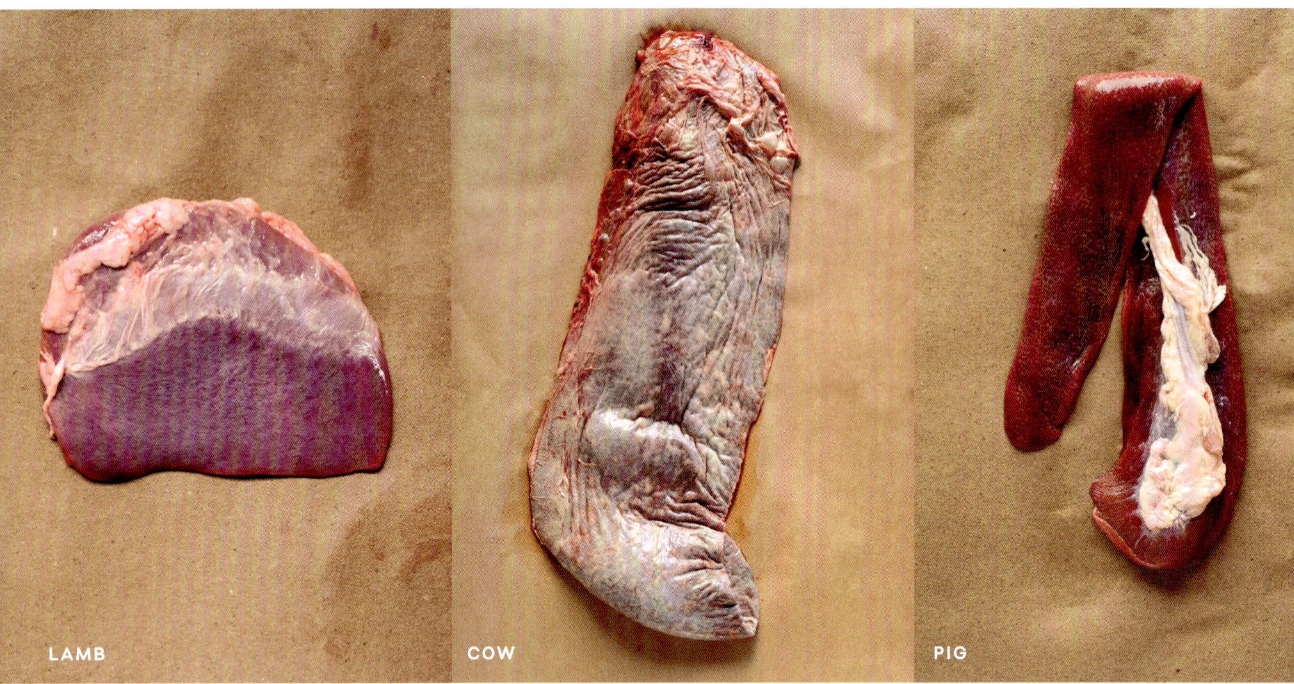


Fergus Henderson's St. John restaurant in London is where I first had pig's spleen; it was rolled with bacon like a pinwheel and braised. With every lush bite, I realized how elevated yet approachable offal can be.

Also called "melts" by butchers, spleen rids the body of old red blood cells and characteristically has a dark color. It takes on a very interesting texture when cooked, a little spongy, but in a good way. Lamb's spleens are very small and pig's are very long. Pork spleens are great in terrines or braised. I love using lamb spleen for *pani ca meusa,* a classic Sicilian street food sandwich topped with salsa picante and caciocavallo cheese.

**COW** To prep cow spleen, use a sharp knife to trim off the outer skin membrane and excess fat, then rinse under cold water to remove any remaining blood. Simmer the spleen in well-salted water with mirepoix for a while, a couple hours even, to cook it through until tender. Once cool to the touch, remove and press it. Pressing removes excess moisture and helps with consistency in cooking. Put the spleen in a perforated pan, put another pan on top, and add weights, like heavy tomato cans. Let the spleen sit for a few hours in the fridge. It's then ready to portion for other applications. Cow spleen is big in the Paleo movement because it is very lean and rich in iron.

**PIG** Long, almost surfboard looking, about a foot by three to four inches wide, pig's spleen attaches to the caul-fat membrane of the stomach, which you should trim off, along with the vein. Portion it into manageable pieces. Soaking is not necessary for pig's spleen; just make sure when you buy it that it's hyper fresh, vibrant red, and not oxidized, but you'll still want to simmer it for 20 to 30 minutes to get the blood out. Then caramelize some mirepoix, deglaze the pot with red wine, and let it reduce by half. Cover this with pork or chicken stock or salted water and fresh aromatics. Add the par-cooked spleen, bring it to a simmer, and cook it gently, partially covered, on the stovetop or in the oven, until tender, about 1 hour. Pig's spleen can be very spongy and needs to be pressed. If it's already rolled, let it cool in the liquid; if not, press the spleen with weighted sheet trays overnight in the fridge. It will firm up and be easy to portion. If it's too tough and chewy from being overcooked, grind it into a burger mix.

**SHEEP** Lamb spleens look like mini livers. I trim off the excess fat and vein and poach them for 10 minutes in Court Bouillon (page 280), skimming the foam. Then I press them as with cow or pig's spleen, and simply sear them in butter. You can soak them in well-salted ice water for 20 to 30 minutes before poaching, if you want to pull out their blood and a little of their bitterness.

**FOWL** These spleens are so wee that they get lost in the giblet mix. You'll have one if you roast a whole bird, but you won't really notice it's there unless you're looking for it. It's right next to the liver.

# KIDNEYS

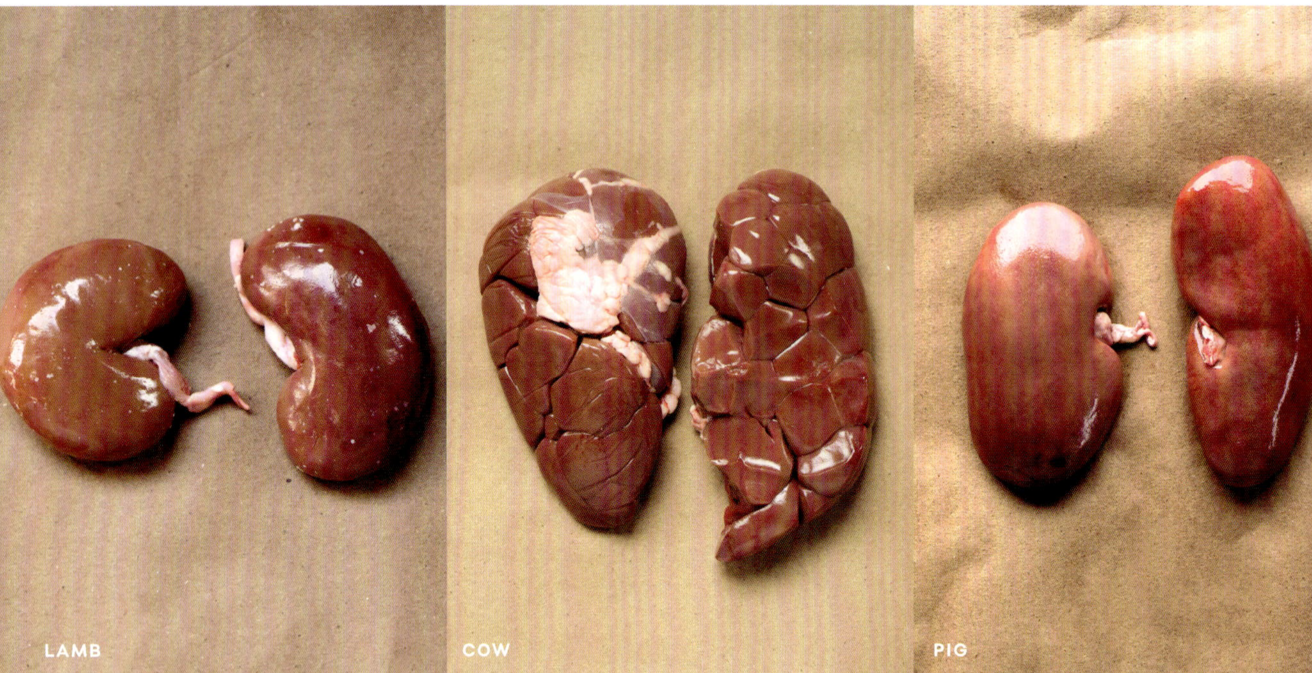


**"MR. LEOPOLD BLOOM ATE WITH RELISH THE INNER ORGANS OF BEASTS AND FOWLS. HE LIKED THICK GIBLET SOUP, NUTTY GIZZARDS, A STUFFED ROAST HEART, LIVER SLICES FRIED WITH CRUST CRUMBS, FRIED HEN CODS' ROES. MOST OF ALL HE LIKED GRILLED MUTTON KIDNEYS WHICH GAVE TO HIS PALATE A FINE TANG OF FAINTLY SCENTED URINE."**

—JAMES JOYCE, *ULYSSES*

Yes, kidneys can smell like a side alley in the heat of the summer. They contain uric acid, a by-product of urine, so you're going to smell pee, but if you treat them properly, they won't taste like pee—they'll be earthy and almost vegetal. I love serving kidneys with asparagus for that reason. Beef and veal kidneys are bigger than pig's. Pork kidneys should come in pairs and should have their fat on them, otherwise they'll dry out. Lamb and pork kidneys look like red kidney beans, whereas calf and beef are a gnarled bunch of granules.

Kidneys wrapped in their own fat, then roasted, are so deeply satisfying. Lamb Kidney, Lentils, Chile & Mint (page 229) and Oyster & Kidney Pie (page 114) are two of my favorite recipes in this book, ones that will make you want to cozy up with a crew of your best mates and just savor the times.

**COW** Cow kidneys are a very different shape than one would expect; they're little nuggets that look almost like an overgrown grape cluster. To prep them, remove the exterior fat but save it either to render down and cook the kidneys in later, or to rewrap the kidneys in once they're fully prepared.

Peel the membrane off. Split the kidneys in half and remove the in/out valves—the fat white clusters that look like little tubes and knobs right in the middle. Remove a good portion of the fat from the internal area with a boning knife. You'll want to keep a little, so the meat stays moist while it cooks, but the more inner fat you take out, the less pee-y it will be. Also, the fresher the kidneys, the less the uric-acid smell. Soaking in milk is a traditional way of leaching out that unwanted flavor, but I find the kidneys don't sear well afterward. If you want to soak them, try salted ice water, which helps remove any impurities without compromising cookability. Make sure to really dry them well before cooking. Oh, and while you're cleaning them, don't cut too deep or spread the kidneys out too thin, because they'll overcook more easily that way.

**PIG** These have that classic kidney-bean, or kidney-pool shape. Pig's kidneys are pretty easy to find. They have an external membrane and an in/out valve that goes down the middle and looks like a skateboard half pipe. Trim out both with a knife, peel back the membrane by hand, and remove any fat inside the kidney. Be sure not to cut too deep or spread

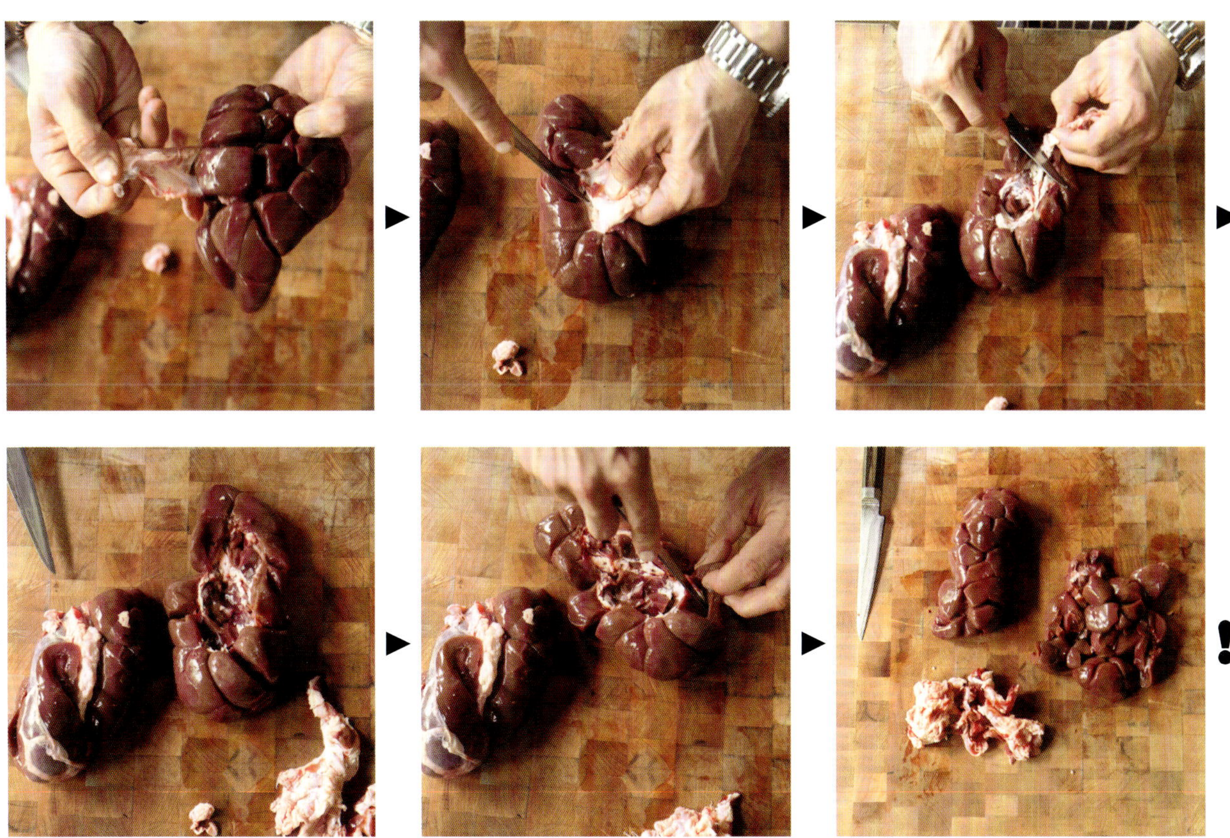

the kidney out too much, or it will easily overcook. I'd stay away from braising pig's kidneys—they usually end up having a weird finished texture—but they're great sautéed or seared.

**SHEEP** Lamb's kidneys are similar to pork, but smaller. Prep them in the same way, and cook them to medium rare.

**FOWL** Weirdly, bird kidneys are on the hollow underside of the thigh, but they're too small to split and clean, and when you eviscerate a bird, most of that stuff gets popped out. It would be funny, and quite dedicated of you, though, to collect a whole bunch and do a chicken-kidney and kidney-bean dish, all braised in rich chicken stock.

❤ **245 likes**

**offalchris** Caul fat & mint wrapped lamb kidneys, Asparagus w/ a meyer lemon vinaigrette

# INTESTINES

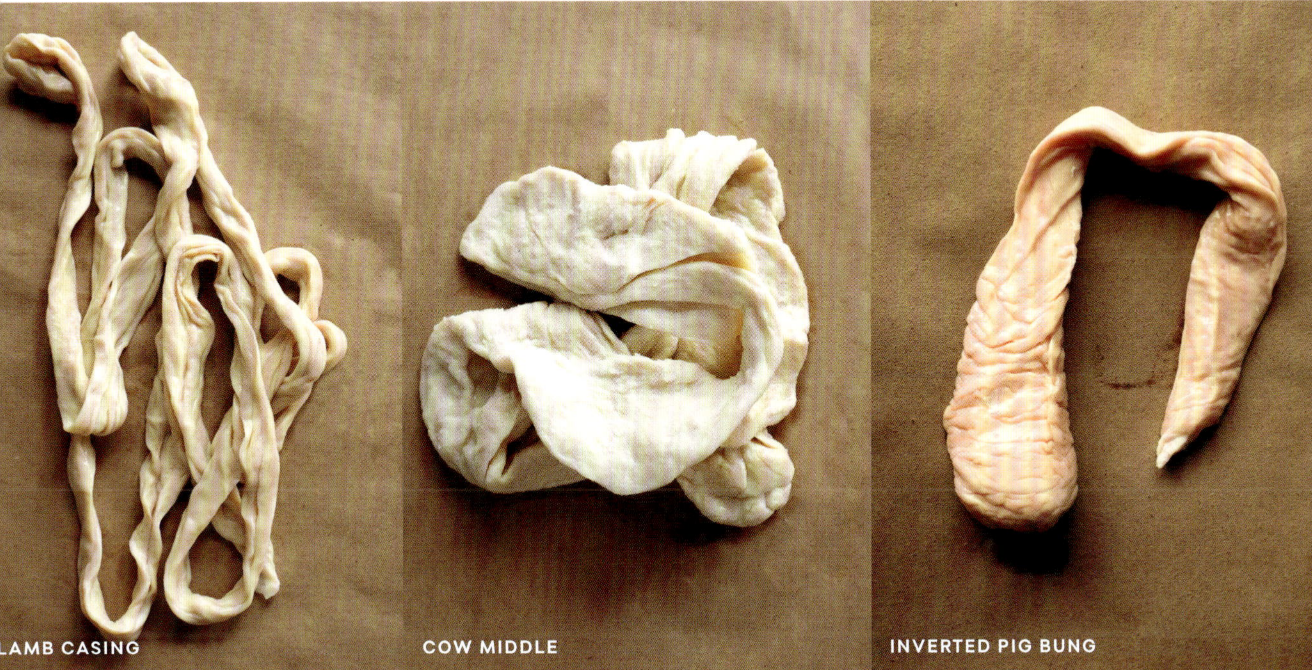


**"I AM CORNHOLIO!!! I NEED HOT SAUCE FOR MY FRIED BUNG HOLES!"**

For all of you who don't know *Beavis and Butt-Head,* a crude cartoon on MTV in the mid-nineties, they said it, and, well, I've fried bung holes and added the hot sauce. But I know the burning question: Why would anyone want to eat the out hole, or the path to it?

I was once in Hong Kong with notorious Alvin Leung (also known as The Demon Chef), whose Bo Innovation restaurant has three Michelin stars. He took me to a place that had an all-intestine menu. This meal exemplified how each type of intestine has its own unique texture, all on the spectrum from soft to chewy. The dish I had was a mix of pig's small and large intestine, cow's small and large intestine, as well as goose and duck intestine, too, all served in a savory sauce on a bed of tofu. I was shocked: How often do you get the same cut from multiple animals on one plate? And how better to really compare and contrast a singular expression of offal? I'd appreciated intestines for years, but that meal really highlighted to me their culinary diversity.

## RINSING CASINGS FOR SAUSAGES

The thing about real casings is that they just plain smell, and unless you buy them pre-cleaned, you'll have to clean them so it's not a nasty experience to eat them.

**For Salted Hog or Beef Casings**

For best results, use this overnight method. Begin with a large bowl of warm water, 90°F.

Open the end of the casing and dip it into the bowl, allowing a bubble of water to enter the casing. Pull the casing out of the bowl, and the water bubble will follow down the casing until it comes out the other end. You can do this by running water from the faucet through as well. After rinsing the casing, allow it to soak in the water overnight, refrigerated.

If you're in a hurry, use the following "Fast Soak" instructions, but understand that you may not get maximum expansion capacity from the casing. Rushing the soaking process can result in the casing being sticky, and it may not slide easily from the horn of the sausage stuffer. This can result in breakage and sausage that is irregular in diameter or too small.

First, rinse the salt from the casings as directed above. Soak them in fresh water at 70°F for 1 hour. Then soak them in a bowl of fresh water at 90°F for 1 hour. Then place them in fresh warm water (90°F) at the stuffing table and use them.

**For Sheep Casings**

Rinse these casings as directed above, but you don't need to soak them overnight. Instead, soak them in fresh water at 90°F for 30 minutes, then place them in a bowl of fresh warm water (90°F) at the stuffing table.

**COW** For the most part, beef bung caps, the first part of the large intestine attached to the small intestine, are used for sausage casings. At four to six inches in diameter and about a foot and a half long, they're used for larger-format salami like bologna and mortadella. Beef middles consist of the rest of the large intestine and are about half the diameter of bung caps; they are made into hard salamis. Beef rounds are about half the size of middles and are actually small intestine, which tend to be used for small-format smoked meat sticks and more delicate sausages like liverwurst. I buy a lot of my casings cleaned, since it's such a laborious process, involving thorough flushing with water and many salt scrubs (sounds like an enema at the spa?), but if you're interested, use the instructions here, or check out a sausage-making book for more detailed guidelines; I've always admired *Great Sausage Recipes and Meat Curing* by Rytek Kutas, a book from the mid-1980s.

**PIG** Pork intestines, while commonly used as sausage casings, are also often prepared to be eaten on their own. They have quite a bit of fat in them, so scrape them out prior to cooking. To do so, turn the intestines inside out and pull off the fat with your hands. Rinse the intestines in cold water and then soak them in a water bath with salt and ice to extract the funk. These intestines freeze well, so you can enjoy them all year round, but try and get them fresh from your butcher, if you can. In Lyon, France, I've dined on andouillette on numerous occasions. It's the city's signature dish, a loosely packed sausage—pork intestines stuffed, basically, with more pork intestines. It has a tender but intriguing, chewy snap. Its scent depends on what part of the intestines is used; obviously the closer to the colon, the stronger the perfume. Braised chitterlings, a pig's small intestines, play a big part in Southern cuisine or soul food.

**SHEEP** Lamb intestines need to be trimmed of their fat, rinsed out, and scrubbed with salt, similar to that of pig intestines. There's not much fat on them, and they're a little more forward in flavor. I like to use them as a mock pasta of sorts in Lamb Intestine, Sheep's Milk Ricotta, Mint, Penne & Black Pepper (page 225).

**FOWL** *Isaw,* a Filipino street food of skewered chicken intestines that are quickly boiled and then grilled, are delicious served with *suka pinakurat* (spicy coconut vinegar). The best way to clean them is to flush them with water, rinse, scrub with salt, then flush with cold water a few more times. Then bring them to a boil in water that's been lightly vinegared, with some salt and pepper, and then simmer for 30 minutes. From there, skewer and grill.

GOOSE INTESTINES

# FAT

My grandmother Helen Easton saved beef fat, or drippings, on top of the stove in a little pot with a handle and a spout. She was constantly filling this pot up as she cooked, and I always keep or find use for my renderings, too. Take all the smoky bacon fat you have left over from breakfast, and make bacon-fat mayonnaise for BLTs. One of my favorite techniques while cooking *poulet roti*, a rotisserie chicken, is to put a tray of plain, starchy potatoes under the bird as it roasts. The fat drips down, transforming the spuds into golden nuggets. This works any time you roast a big piece of meat—just put some vegetables below it.

There's a real range of fats that can be used for all different purposes; I'll list a few of them in particular below. That said, it's rare for fat to be the star of the show, as it tends to be used as a flavor carrier or cooking medium. But a well-cooked and clarified fat is incredible just whipped and spread on bread. Pig's back fat can even be grilled on its own (page 187). Lardo di Colonnata, the Tuscan cured lard, may be featured as proudly as any charcuterie. At Boccalone, my salumi company, we make lardo using Ibérico de Bellota, Spain's famed pata negra pigs, which roam among the groves eating mainly acorns (*bellotas*). Their fat conveys their nutty diet.

**COW** Suet, the hard fat around the kidneys, is best made into tallow by slowly melting it; it liquefies well, whereas intramuscular fat—marbling—tends to become creamy. To render hard suet into liquid tallow, take the fat off the kidney or loin and pull off any membrane or blood clumps. Cut it into small pieces or grind it to make for more surface area, which leads to a more uniform cook. I like to cook it sous vide at 185°F (85°C) for 8 hours; it will render the perfect fat, clean and white as snow, never caramelizing it. Obviously, most people don't have this technology at home, but you can get the same results by putting the fat in a heavy ziplock freezer bag and into a pot of simmering water, just under 185°F, for a few hours. (If you boil it without a bag, eventually the water evaporates, the fat doesn't mix, and the solids sink to the bottom.) Strain out the solids and keep the tallow for cooking or flavoring.

**PIG** Lard is pig fat in its post-rendered state, whether liquid or solidified at room temperature. There is soft lard, though, found in fatty tissues, such as leaf lard that surrounds certain organs like the kidneys. This fat is great for piecrusts and many other baking applications. And there is harder fat, such as fatback, under the skin of the back; this tends to be much denser than most other animal fats, and, while it can be rendered, it can also be cooked or cured to serve on its own.

The rendering process is pretty much the same for both kinds of fat. Follow the instructions for rendering cow's fat, but for this denser fat, use a temperature of 190°F for about 4 hours.

Caul fat is an interior web netting of fat inside the abdomen, which looks like lacy panty hose. It's in cows and lambs, but most often you'll find caul fat from pigs. It's often used as a loose casing for sausages. Cooking *en crépinette* involves wrapping caul fat around a piece of meat, like a ground-meat patty or lean roast. As it cooks, the caul melts away ever so softly.

**SHEEP** Lamb fat imparts a good amount of its own lamby flavor—most of the characteristic "gaminess" of lamb comes from compounds in the fat. Some people may find it has a lanolin quality.

You can certainly render it as you would cow's or pig's fat, but I often simply save the fat from cooking a piece of meat. I really love using this as finishing "oil," in a sense, by heating it up and then drizzling the melted fat on top of cooked greens, grains, and warm dishes. Lamb fat is particularly delicious with artichokes or roasted tomatoes.

**FOWL** Chicken fat, or schmaltz, made from rendering down fatty tissue and skin, is the lifeblood of Ashkenazi Jewish cuisine. If you take the chunks of fat or skin from a bird and simmer them in water, the fat will be rendered and left behind once the water has cooked off. If you keep cooking and stirring these bits over gentle heat, you'll also end up with gribenes, crispy little flavor bombs, the counterpart to the liquid schmaltz. How long this takes varies with the bird, but give it time and cook it at a moderate temperature, as you don't want to scorch the fat. The same process works for most any bird, including duck, but high-quality pre-prepared duck fats are also on the market, which are great for panfrying, confit, and some of the best french fries you'll ever have.

# FEET

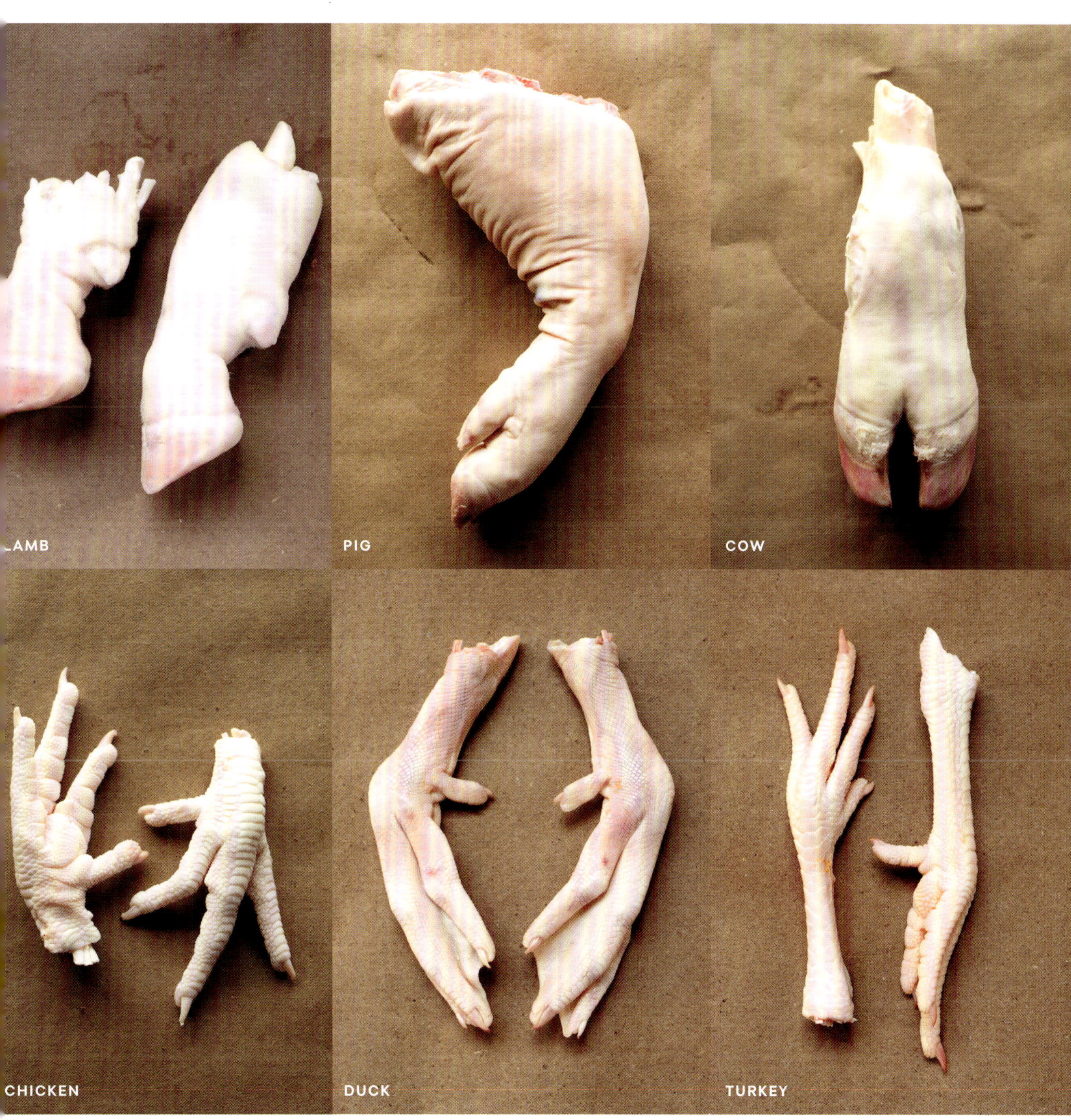

I'm a sucker for pig's trotters. Calf's feet, skin on, are pretty incredible, too. Lamb's feet and the way they stew down . . . Sucking that gelatin off the toes of chickens, ducks, turkeys . . . Okay, okay, I've got a foot fetish. (Well, I actually sort of *hate* feet, but animal feet are delicious!)

I've long loved *zampone*, a stuffed deboned pig's leg and hock, found at many Italian New Year's celebrations. I try to celebrate with one every year during the holidays, if not more frequently. It's really a great share plate—and actually, many "feet foods" are. My mecca for pig's feet is Montreal, where at Au Pied de Cochon, the eponymous dish is stuffed with foie gras and sweetbreads by chef—and legend—Martin Picard.

There's a lot of skin and collagen on feet, and all that gelatinous material can make for some of the richest stocks or broth you've ever tasted. To make these, trotters are usually marinated overnight and then simmered slowly for a long time. Don't roast the feet first, like you do with many bones for stock, as that would render out too much of the delicious fat and make the result cloudy. By gently braising the whole foot, you're able to get a nice clear liquid. This is the base process that many ramen chefs in Japan use to build their broths. A similar broth-based dish called *jokbal*, made from pig's trotter and soy sauce, garlic, ginger, and rice wine, is considered a cure-all in Korea.

I also like to make pig's feet into roulades or shred the meat, collagen, and skin to make crisped trotter cakes, like the Toe Knee Hock (page 193). If I'm going for something with a more unctuous mouthfeel, I'll make my Hot Mess (page 255).

One of my true joys in life is gnawing and sucking on tender chicken feet in Chinese dim sum restaurants. Eating them always makes me wonder why we don't smother turkey feet with gravy at Thanksgiving. I riff on that with my deeply satisfying Confit Duck Feet, Sage & Black Pepper Gravy (page 263).

**COW** Boil cow's feet in lightly salted water for a few minutes to get out the funk. Replace with fresh, well-salted water and aromatics or mirepoix, bring to a boil, and simmer for a couple hours (or more), until the meat and connective tissue are tender and you're able to pick and pull the meat and collagen from the bone.

**PIG** There are a couple of terms that are often confused when it comes to pig's feet. *Pig's trotters* are what most people would think of as the feet of pigs. *Hocks* are a small cut of meat from a front or hind leg just above the foot, and you can get trotters with the hock attached, sometimes called a *long trotter*. These are among my favorite cuts.

Brine pig's trotters in ham brine (page 284) overnight. Rinse them, then cook them in simmering, salted water or stock to pick the meat and skin for dishes like Foot & Mouth Terrine (page 150). Skim the scum off the top as the trotters cook, and save the trotter cooking liquid. I love to make an enriched stock (see page 281) with it, as the trotters provide so much flavor and richness.

I remember the first time I worked with pork trotters: I was a lowly stagiaire at La Tante Claire in London, with multiple Michelin-starred chef Pierre Koffman, who trained (the famous) Marco Pierre White, so I was quite intimidated. I watched him debone a pig's foot and hock in one minute flat. It took me forever, and even a lifetime later, I'm still in awe of his skill and care. In other words, don't be intimidated by the foot, just practice, practice, practice. Have a sharp knife; it's actually only the tip that you'll work with primarily. On the back of the leg, slice lengthwise down the center, all the way to the bone. Start making small strokes, like filleting a fish, separating the muscle from the bone. Pull the skin away, almost inverting it, while holding the exposed bone with a kitchen towel. Work from the joint down to the hoof; when you're at the bottom of the leg, you'll be able to cut the foot away at the ankle, straight through the tendon. The skin and meat should come off as one full piece, and you will be left with a great bone to roast for stock. From here, you can stuff it, then sew it back up for further cooking. This is an involved technique, for sure, but incredibly impressive when it comes to the table.

**SHEEP** Lamb's feet should be rinsed, brought to a boil in water to remove any funk or scum, then placed in a new pot of lightly salted water with aromatics. Simmer until tender.

**FOWL** If need be, give your poultry feet a manicure and clip the claws with kitchen shears. The claws are hollow, so they can carry dirt, and in any case no one needs to get cut by their dinner. Wash the feet well with cold water. If using them for stock, first roast the feet in a 450°F oven for 20 to 30 minutes to brown them. If braising the feet, season them with salt and black pepper, marinate them, and simmer them in stock or water with mirepoix or aromatics until the skin and cartilage are tender but not yet falling apart. Reserve this braising liquid to use for other dishes, as the stock will be very flavorful and gelatinous.

❤ **120 likes**
**offalchris** I wonder how the hell they do this?

# BONES, CARTILAGE & TENDONS

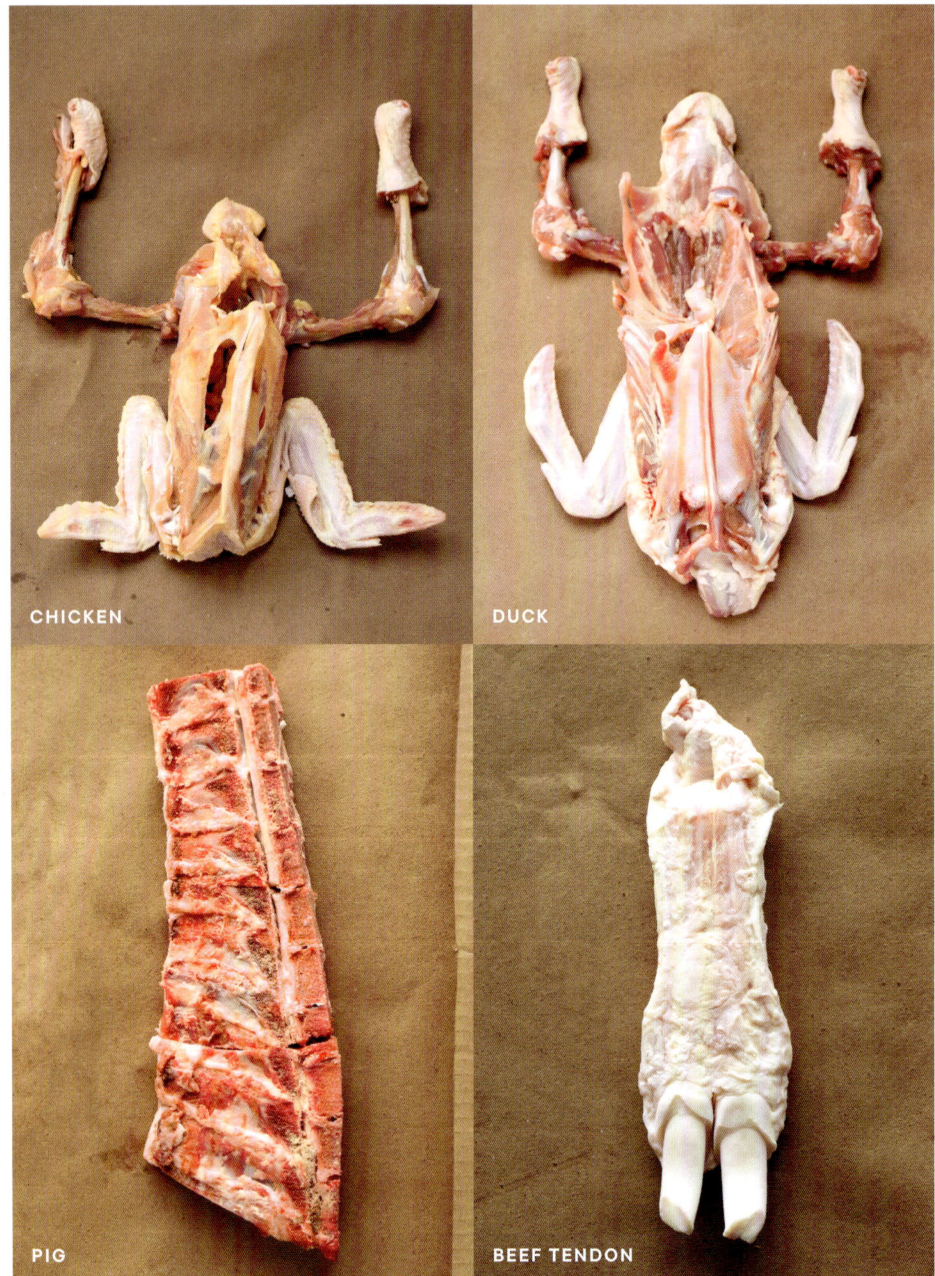

Bones are primarily used for stock, and since the recent bone-broth phenomenon, more people have been interested in the craze than ever before. It's really what's inside the bones that matters. Bone marrow is God's butter. Composed mostly of fat, marrow is where white blood cells are produced, and somehow it has become the most beloved offal of all. Beef bones cut canoe-style—halved lengthwise—and roasted are a menu staple now, diners scooping out the marrow. It's rare to see pork or lamb marrow, but if you do, celebrate it.

Roasting bones before using them to make stock solidifies the proteins and develops great flavor. When I make a stock, I like to let the stock cook overnight. When the stock is done, chill it and let the fat rise to the top, leaving the fat on the top to help preserve the stock until needed. Then skim the fat, keeping that as well to use as a cooking medium or finishing "oil."

After beef stock has been made, I also make a second stock (*remouillage*) by re-covering the bones with water and boiling them again. It will be less flavorful, but it's great to use in braises, or it can be reduced into a flavor-boosting gel.

Can you eat bones? No, not really, you're not a tiger—you don't have a strong enough jaw. But this doesn't mean you can't gnaw on the bits left stuck on them. I take pork neck bones and season them with a spice rub, steam them, then pan-sear them for Chile & Bones with Capers, Garlic & Mint (page 196).

Cartilage, made of bound proteins, is kind of like a softer bone. With poultry, much of the cartilage can be eaten, the best example being the keel bone that you can order grilled until crisp and yielding at many yakitori places. A rooster's crest is also considered cartilage, as is the inside of a pig's ear. If you've ever eaten ribs, there's a likelihood you've chewed on some cartilage.

Tendons attach muscle to bone. They're quite fibrous, tough, and resilient, which means they need time, heat, and moisture to properly soften up. Tendons are best stewed or even cooked in a pressure cooker.

Achilles tendon from beef is popular in Vietnamese pho. *Nervetti* (page 117), a dish from Torino, Italy, is composed of braised tendon from a calf's foot and served with cannellini beans. At Cockscomb, I serve tendon cold in the summer and hot in the winter, or I make it Sichuan-style, in mouth-numbing chile oil, any day of the year (see page 120). I also like to puff up tendons like chicharrones, by simmering, slicing, dehydrating, and frying them (see page 124). I've also been known to pulverize the cooked-and-dehydrated tendons and use this as a thickener for sauces, or grill them, after first simmering them to tenderness in salted water with aromatics.

**COW** Bone marrow can be found in all bones, but you'll want to use bigger ones for a marrowbone recipe. Have your butcher cut them either canoe- (lengthwise) or chimney-style (crosswise). Chimneys are great for baking. I like to use them as pie birds in a crust (see page 114); the marrow cooks and mixes into

**"CLOSER TO THE BONE, SWEETER THE MEAT, LAST SLICE OF VIRGINIA HAM, IS THE BEST THAT YOU CAN EAT."**

—LOUIS PRIMA

the pie filling, plus it's quite a showy and functional centerpiece at that. Canoe cut is way better for allowing an eater to extract marrow, and there's greater visual control when cooking. Before cooking, soak canoe-cut bones overnight in salted ice water to extract any blood; this will leave the marrow pure white and clean.

Cartilage is often used in a recipe involving whole bones but not typically harvested to use on its own.

With beef tendons, season them with salt and black pepper, and let them sit overnight in the fridge. The next day, start them in cold, lightly salted water or stock with mirepoix, and bring it up to a boil. Drop the temperature down to a simmer and cook them until tender—how tender is up to you, as the texture goes from hard to something like a firm gummy candy to a jelly. There are many different textures, as long as you cook it enough to make it soft enough to eat. It depends in part on the culture, as some, like the Vietnamese, prefer it a bit more firm, so it can be put into pho without falling apart. In Italy, it's eaten much more tender and found either sliced and served cold, or in hot dishes where it is very soft and gelatinous. In China, it's also sliced and then marinated, or cooked until gelatinous. In any case, once it's cooked, remove and cool it, and proceed with any recipe.

**PIG** Pork bones can be roasted for stocks for sure, but I like chewing on them once they've been steamed, seasoned, and seared, as seen in Chile & Bones with Capers, Garlic & Mint (page 196).

The cartilage isn't often used on its own, and tendons may be treated as cow's, but they're going to be significantly smaller and will, therefore, cook faster. You usually can't buy pork tendons on their own, but they're there if you buy the whole foot.

**SHEEP** Follow the same procedure as with cow bones and tendons, again adjusting the cooking times to account for their smaller size. Obviously, you'll get a different flavor profile—a bit more gamey, which some folks like to call barnyard, which is pretty consistent in all things lamb. The tendons are typically too small to do anything with separately.

**FOWL** All poultry bones should be rinsed well before cooking. If you're starting with a whole bird, be sure to cut the talons off, as they're hollow and can carry dirt.

Poultry cartilage, like the keel bone or knee joints, may be braised until tender, then fried or grilled. For a crispy crunch, try Fried Rabbit Ears & Carrot Aioli (page 237), which are mainly cartilage.

# TAIL

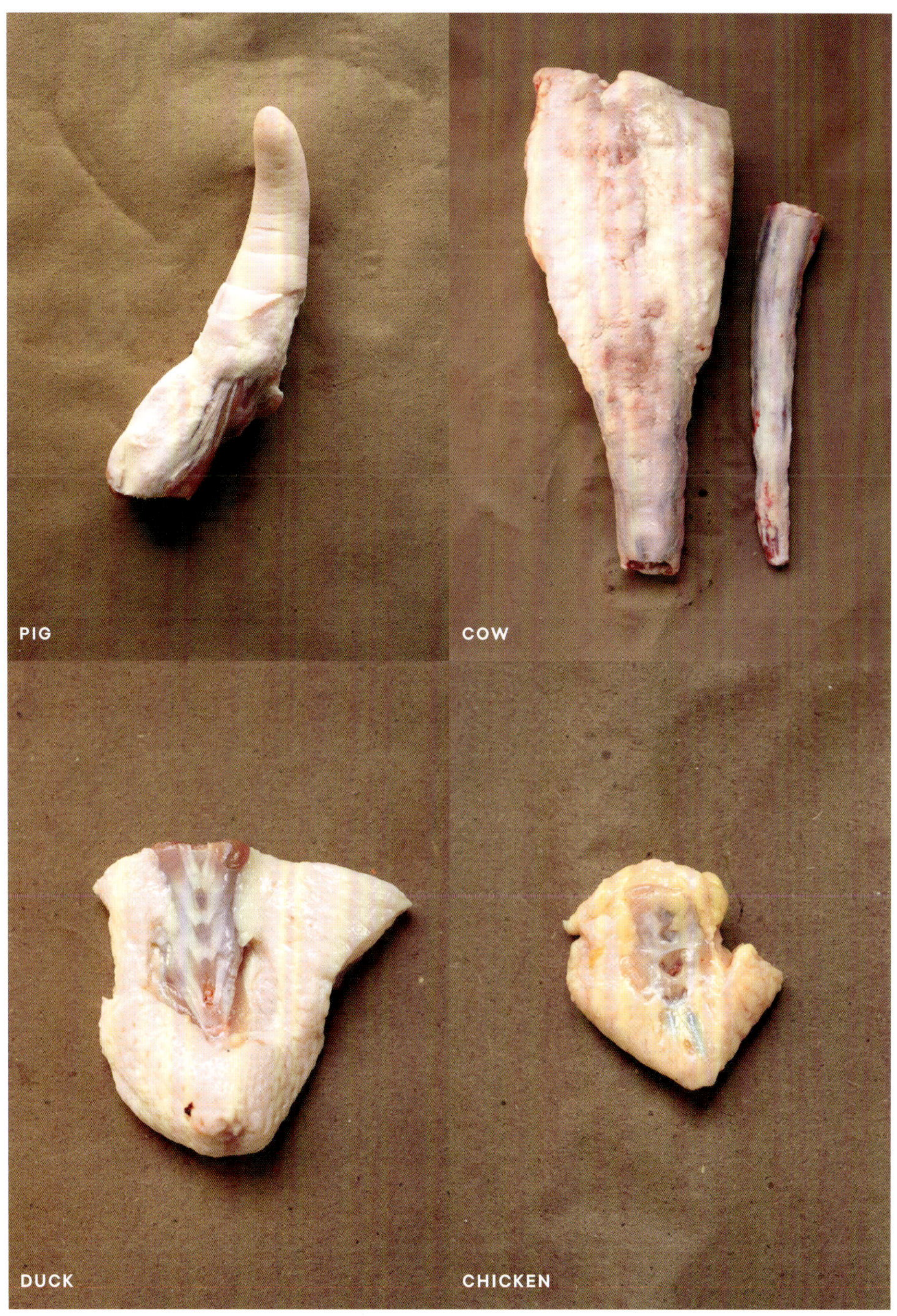

Oxtail, when prepared in the style of osso buco, debunks the idea that tails are mainly skin and cartilage. There's plenty of meat there. (The most tender tail meat is found closest to the body.) Oxtails are typically cooked and served in already separated sections or picked, with the meat turned into marmalades and ragù, but try serving the whole cut, as in Braised Oxtail, Savoy Cabbage, Chanterelle & Puffed Tendons (page 123).

Being well-worked and very cartilage-heavy cuts, tails are usually braised.

**COW** Oxtail usually needs to be trimmed of some of its fat—not too much but enough so that it won't make a greasy braise. Season the oxtail with salt, pepper, mirepoix, and red wine, and let it sit overnight in the fridge. The next day you can sear and braise it in stock as you would a standard braise, or simply simmer it in liquid and pick the meat afterward for terrines and the like.

**PIG** Make sure there's no hair left on the tail, as it will be covered in skin. If there is, torch it off or shave it, then scrub it to release any dirt or bone particles. Rinse the tails in cold water, and season well with salt; marinate overnight with mirepoix and wine. The next day, simmer them in pork or chicken stock until tender, or confit them in gently heated fat, and pick the meat and collagen. After that simmering, you can also deep-fry them until crisp, pan sear them, or serve them braised in a stew.

**SHEEP** Lambs don't have a true tail, just a nub that's been docked for the health and safety of the animal (it prevents fecal matter from accumulating on the tail and hindquarters). If you do get one, though, it's mostly fat, so it's best used for rendering.

**FOWL** The protuberance at the end of a bird, the "pope's nose," is officially called the pygostyle. These nubs have no meat at all, but they are delicious bites of fat and collagen and are great grilled or confited. I just like to call them chicken butts and always order them at my friend Matt Abergel's place Yardbird, in Hong Kong.

# ODD PARTS

## COW'S UDDERS

Udders are most typically thought of as the mammary gland of a cow, but they also exist in many ruminant animals, like sheep. Cattle, however, are the only animals that have two pairs of udders, both of which attach to the milk line. Udders are made of striated muscle that's fatty like bacon and loaded with protein. This cut is served in many South American countries, like Argentina, Uruguay, and Brazil, where it's thrown on a smoking hot grill at a *parrillada* (barbecue).

To clean the udder, start with the skin side of the teat facing up. Hold the skin at one corner. Pulling away from the udder muscle and using the tip of a boning knife, trim the skin away from the udder. Once you get to each teat, you'll need to dig into the muscle a little deeper, removing the base of the teat from the muscle. Continue until all of the skin and teats are removed in one piece.

Take the skin to a tanner, and make a hat or a nice pair of gloves.

Meanwhile, the udder will be in two

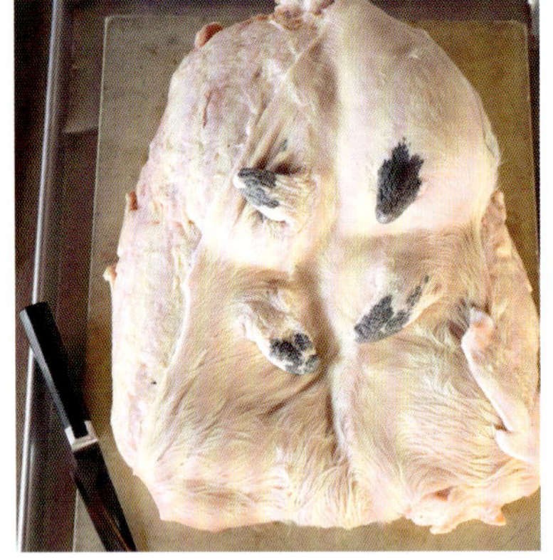

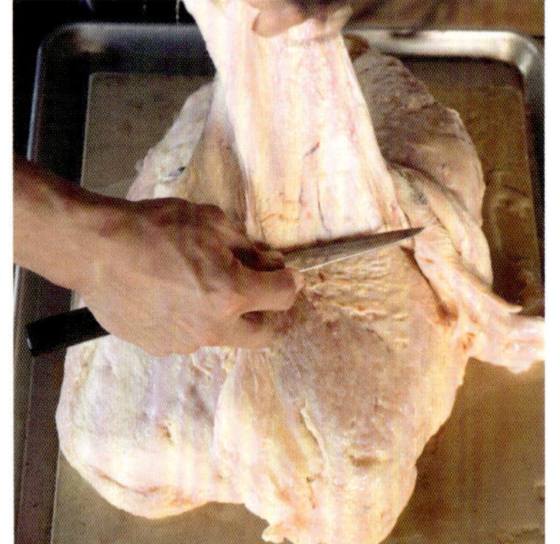

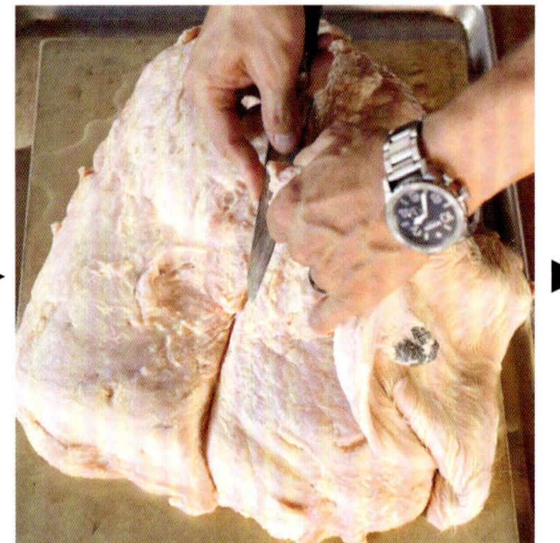

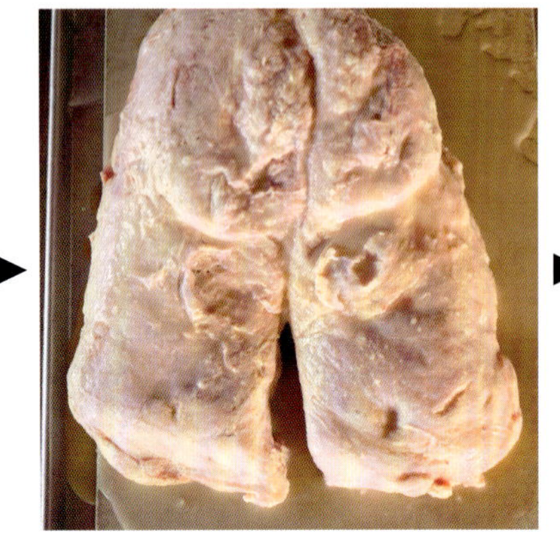

full lobes with seams between. Trim off the thin membranes that look like sinew and any bruises and blemishes. If it is a lactating udder, remove the milk by pressing firmly until it's empty; do this in a pan so the milk doesn't squirt everywhere. Separate the udder into its two lobes. From there you should remove any blood spots and extra membrane. Once that is done, you can simmer it until tender in salted water or stock, but once I tried it in milk, like *maiale al latte* (roast pork in milk; see page 126), I couldn't go back. It's also great for curing like bacon (see page 129); if sliced super thin, this can be used similarly to lardo.

# TESTICLES

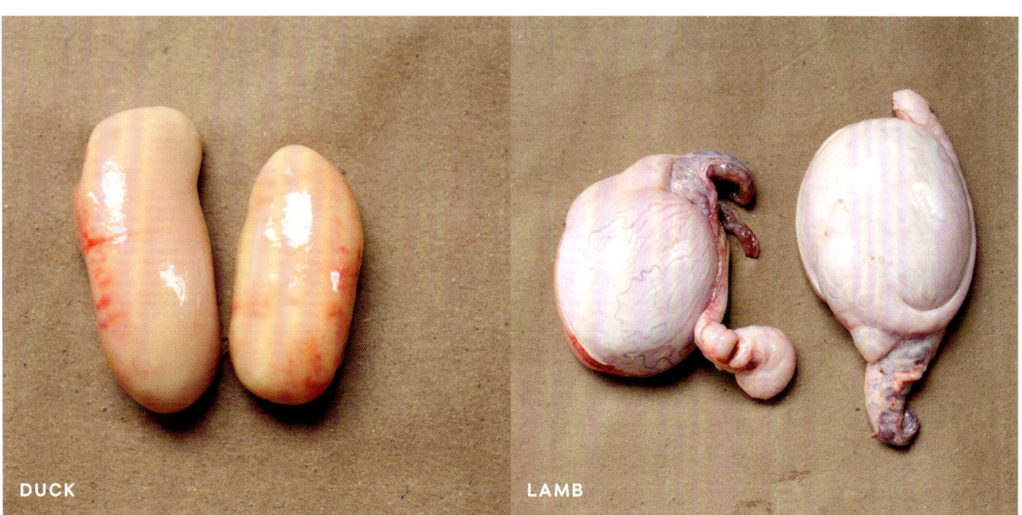


Rocky Mountain oysters—bull's testicles—are a part of the American West and the tradition of cattle ranching, but the custom of eating testicles isn't uncommon around the world. In Spain's Basque country, farmhands castrate lambs in the field and cook their "fries" in a smoking-hot cast-iron pan. In cowboy cuisine, the testicles are often breaded and deep-fried, much more approachable than seeing just-neutered calf balls go from scrotum to skillet. In Big Brain, Little Brain (page 89), I use calf testicles to interplay with calf brain, tied together by a nutty, tart sudachi brown butter. They pair so nicely, and not just as a farce. Sometimes you have to allow for humor to make offal more approachable, but it's not just a punch line!

**COW (well, Bull)** Don't just go to a butcher and ask to see his balls. Bull testicles require a two-step cleaning process after you remove them from the scrotum. Dip them in boiling water to firm up the membrane, then make a shallow incision and carefully peel the balls out, removing the testicles from the membrane. Repeat, as there will be a second membrane. Then poach them in Court Bouillon (page 280) until they're just firm. From here, they can be sliced, seared, breaded, and/or fried.

**PIG** All nuts are the same, so follow the same process as you would for bull's. Treat them gently and with care. I can't stress how important it is to take the testicles out of the membrane; otherwise they'll blow up when you cook them.

**SHEEP** Follow the same two-step cleaning process as with bull testicles, but know that lambs' are a little denser. Be sure to rinse lamb testicles off very well to remove any hair. Lamb often doesn't come with an external skin (scrotum sack). You're usually only getting the nut.

**FOWL** Duck testicles are an internal organ and are very tiny, so you don't usually remove them from the body. If you do, lightly poach them. Otherwise they can explode if they're cooked at too high a temperature. They're slightly creamy, similar to the texture of sweetbreads.

# GIZZARDS

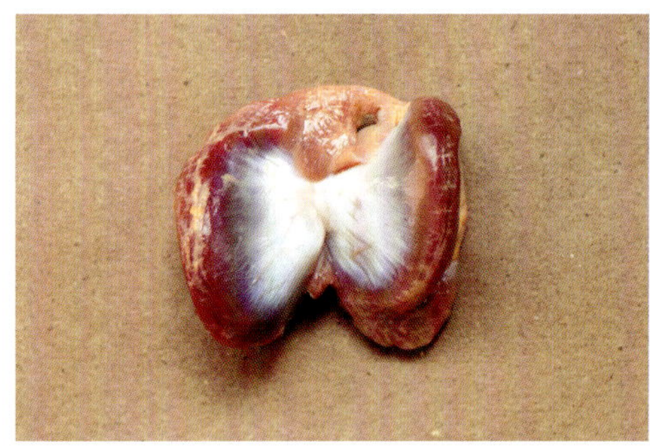

Only found in birds, gizzards from chickens and turkeys are, in my experience, most commonly eaten as snacks by cooks. This organ is comprised of two pyramid-shaped muscles that are attached by silver skin and filled with little stones and pebbles that are meant to grind seeds and feed. The gizzard is considered the "muscular stomach."

My favorite way of eating gizzard is grilled as crunchy yakitori. You see it a lot in Japanese and Korean cuisine. If you confit gizzards, they can become a tender addition to a salad. When well-cooked, gizzard can be tender and toothsome.

To clean gizzards, split them open, wash out the stones, and remove the silver skin.

Lightly season them with salt and either grill, confit, or simmer them.

---

# COCKSCOMB

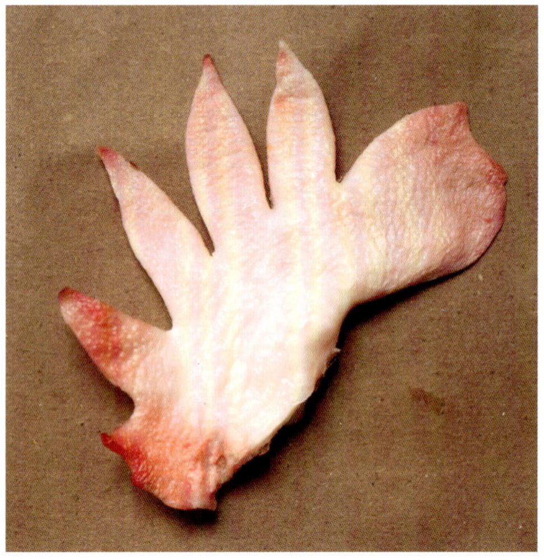

Cockscomb's unique shape and undeniably soft, rich texture make it all too special not to stand out.

You can find cockscombs in many Latin and Asian supermarkets, or just buy the whole bird. Sometimes there's a little feather at the base of the cockscomb that needs to be removed. Use a pair of sharp scissors or a paring knife to remove the base, a hard piece of cartilage that attaches the cockscomb to the top of the head.

Season with salt and black pepper and put them in a pot of water. Bring it to a boil to remove any dirt in the combs, drain, and add fresh salted water or stock with mirepoix and aromatics. After 2 hours or so at a gentle simmer, the cockscomb will be tender enough to eat with a butter knife and fork. Be sure to rinse off any gelatinous stock. From here, cockscomb can be eaten on its own, marinated, or recooked in stock; it takes on other flavors extremely well.

Cockscombs have the texture of warm gummy bears, so why not turn them into a dessert, like Candied Cockscombs, Rice Pudding & Pomegranate (page 266)? If you do this, simmer them in unsalted water with bay leaves and warm spices like cloves and cinnamon, and finish them later by recooking them in flavored syrup.

## CHRIS'S FIRST TIME

These days, few chefs have an opportunity to learn their craft from the killing floor up. But I've met a new wave of cooks who are determined to rediscover all of the traditions of cooking. It's tempting to call these young, gung ho chefs who leap from the grill station to the abattoir "extreme chefs," except that there's nothing extreme about slaughtering animals for meat. What is extreme is the distaste and denial many people have for the natural processes that sustain them.

About a decade and a half ago, when Chris Cosentino learned that I was getting ready to slaughter a goat doe and two kids, he asked to help. From his years in the restaurant trade, Chris knew how to break a whole animal down, but he hadn't learned the slaughter. He asked to bring several members of his kitchen staff along.

While the cooks sharpened their blades, I went to get the first goat. My goats run loose in the canyon and eat brush. They are wary range animals, only half tame, and catching one on the run, in a muddy corral in a rainstorm, can be a bit of a rodeo. It's best to catch the goat quickly, without a lot of scandal and thrashing around. It is cruel to frighten an animal needlessly, and a panicked animal induces a release of adrenaline, too, which lowers the quality of the meat.

I'm a practiced goat snatcher, and I had the doe at the base of the tree before she knew what was happening. Then I shot her at the base of the skull and felt her body go slack. I felt for the esophagus, just behind the jaw and below the ear, and put the point of the knife above it.

I showed Chris where to make the first cut, from heel to heel, down the thighs. He skinned the legs. Working with Chris was a bit like working with a doctor in surgery. He would ask for a boning knife, and one of the other cooks would produce one, razor sharp. Chris finished tying off the intestine and cut the bung end free. The skin came off the goat easily. The body steamed for a moment in the cold rain (see page 6).

Once he had a carcass to work with, Chris was on familiar ground. He pulled out each organ, one by one, and showed us how to handle them in the most sanitary fashion. He showed me the gossamer veil of fat from the internal cavity of the animal that is used to wrap crépinette sausages. He has a recipe for every organ.

The slaughter of the next two goats went more quickly than the first. They were kids and weighed about thirty pounds. Because a kid is so small, it's safest for only one person to work at a time, so that no one gets cut by a helper's knife.

Chris made the cut. There was a bleat, and the kid's eyes went blank. Killing an animal isn't easy, especially the first time. Hunting with a rifle, where the game animal is at a distance, seems easier. With a barnyard animal, it's impossible to distance yourself from the killing—which is fine. The insanity of confinement lots for mass-produced chicken, beef, and pork is only possible because most people are spared from confronting the consequences of their choices. People can only waste food or prepare it carelessly because they don't understand that it's life they're throwing away.

Chris understands that. That's why he cooks the way he does.

—ANDY GRIFFIN, MARIQUITA FARM

BEEF
VEAL
BULL
OX

BRAIN
STOMACH
KIDNEYS
RECTUM
LARGE INTESTINE
SMALL INTESTINE
TONGUE
HEART
SPLEEN
LIVER
UDDER

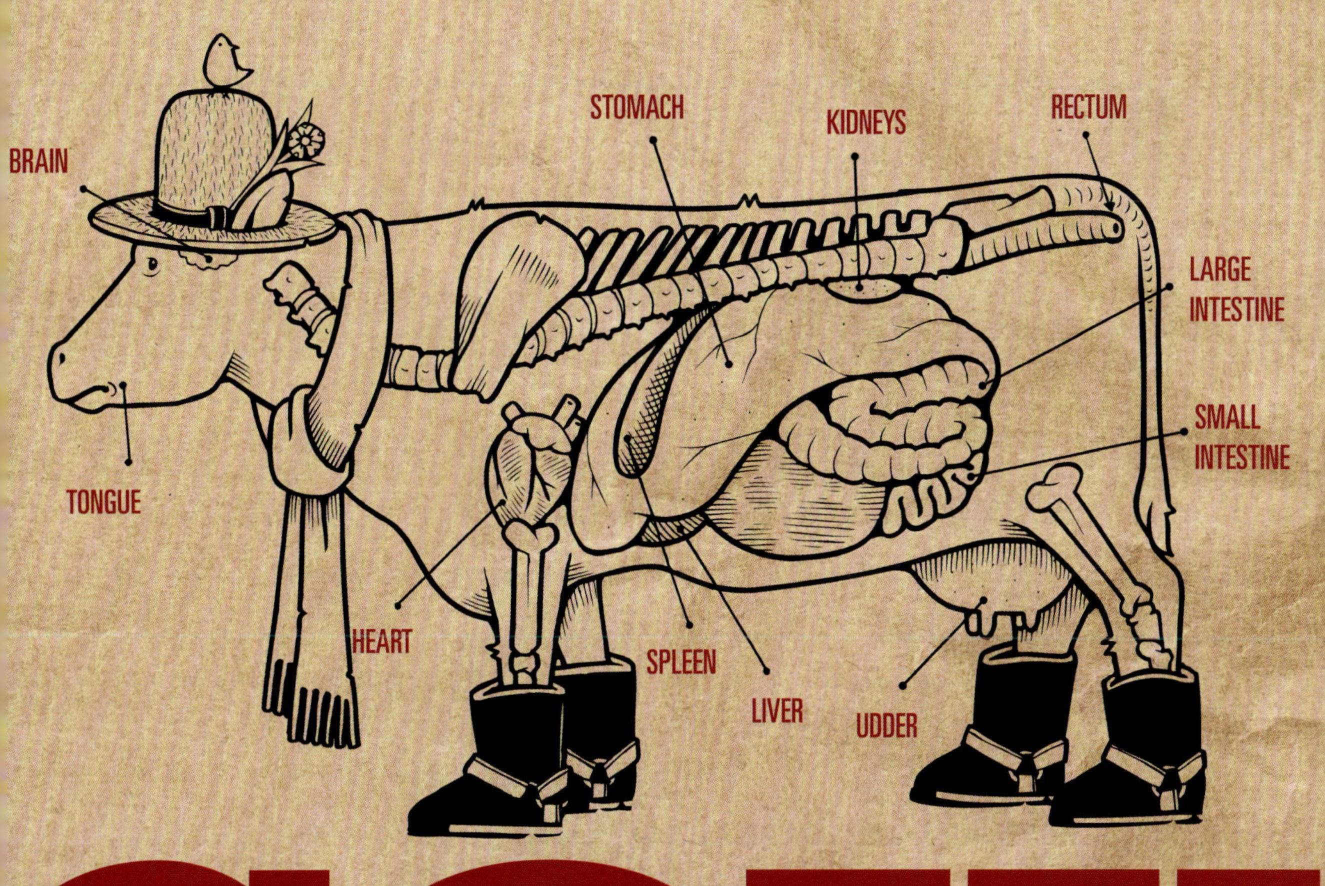

# COW

# "LIPS AND ASSHOLES" BEEF LIPS & OXTAIL TERRINE, ARTICHOKES, TARRAGON

SERVES 12

This terrine doesn't hide what's really in it, nor do many classic sausages, pâtés, and cured meats. It's all about what's really on the inside. These two textures of meat, the lips rich with gelatin and the oxtail meaty and tender, complement each other so well that you'd never know they were on opposite ends of the animal. The sweet, anise-like flavor of tarragon is classically French and makes this terrine very classy.

**1 pound beef lips**
**Sea salt and freshly ground black pepper**
**1 bottle (750 milliliters) red wine**
**1 medium carrot, quartered**
**1 medium yellow onion, quartered**
**2 stalks celery, quartered**
**1 head garlic, split to expose the cloves, plus 12 cloves**
**1 small leek, white and light green parts only, quartered**
**1 bulb fennel, top removed, quartered**
**1 whole oxtail, about 4 pounds**
**2 tablespoons extra-virgin olive oil**
**1½ gallons Roasted Chicken Stock (page 282), or to cover**
**8 baby artichokes, cleaned**
**2 bunches tarragon, leaves and stems separated**
**1 bay leaf**
**3 sheets gold-leaf gelatin**
**1 cup watercress, thick stems removed**
**Zinfandel Vinaigrette (page 272), to taste**
**Tarragon mustard, for serving**

**Equipment: 14 × 4 × 4-inch terrine mold (1½ quarts), blowtorch, wire brush for scrubbing**

**1.** Remove any hair from the lips with a blowtorch; first burn, then scrub with a wire brush. Rinse, being sure to remove any blood. Season the lips with salt and pepper, and place them in a nonreactive container. Cover with a quarter of the red wine and a quarter each of the carrot, onion, celery, split garlic, leek, and fennel. Let marinate, covered, in the fridge for 24 hours. Repeat this with the oxtails, in a separate container, using the remaining wine and vegetables.

**2.** To cook, remove both the beef lips and oxtails from their marinades. Separate the vegetables from the wine and reserve both. Pat the oxtail dry with paper towels.

**3.** Preheat the oven to 350°F. In a large braising pan or Dutch oven over medium heat, add the olive oil and sear the oxtails on all sides until nicely browned, about 16 minutes total, then remove. Add the marinated vegetables to the pan, cooking to get some color on them, about 10 minutes. Deglaze with the red wine, cooking until reduced by three-fourths. Add the chicken stock and bring to a simmer, then cook for 10 minutes to marry the flavors.

**4.** Place the lips and oxtail in separate ovenproof containers, and fully cover both with the wine-stock mixture. Place a piece of parchment paper on top of each, followed by aluminum foil. Braise in the oven until tender, about 2 hours for the lips, 2½ hours for the oxtails. If you only have one pot, cook them together and take the lips out after 2 hours. When the lips are done cooking, inspect them; there are some sections that will have a noticeably thick membrane that you will need to peel off.

**5.** When the oxtails are done, remove them from the braising liquid. Strain the liquid.

**6.** Pick the meat off the bones from both the lips and oxtail and reserve.

**7.** In a separate pot, combine 4 baby artichokes, the garlic cloves, tarragon stems, and bay leaf, and cover with the beef braising liquid. Bring to a simmer and cook until the artichokes are tender, about 10 minutes, then cool in the liquid. Remove the artichokes, and set aside.

**8.** Soak the gelatin sheets in a bowl of cold water.

**9.** In a pot over medium heat, reduce 4 cups of the braising liquid by half, being sure to skim any impurities as it reduces. Taste to make sure it's not too salty; if it is, reduce the seasoning you use for the lips and oxtail later. Once the gelatin is soft, squeeze it dry and add it to the reduced braising liquid. (The remaining braising liquid may be reserved for another use.)

**10.** To prepare the terrine, first spray the terrine mold with cooking spray and lay down enough plastic wrap so it can fold back over the top. Make sure the plastic wrap has no air pockets.

**11.** In a bowl, mix the lips and oxtail meat, and season with salt and black pepper to taste. Remember, the terrine will be served cold, so it will need to be seasoned just a bit more than you normally might, as cold foods hide their seasoning. Mix in the tarragon leaves, reserving 1 teaspoon for the salad. Add some of the gelatin-enriched cooking liquid, just enough to nicely coat the meat, keep it moist, and help bind it when set.

**12.** Cut the cooked artichokes in half. Start layering the terrine mold by first placing a layer of meat about halfway up. Dip the artichokes in the bowl with the braising-gelatin mixture, and make a nice line down the center of the terrine with them. Then layer in the rest of the meat. Wrap the plastic wrap directly over the terrine, and press it down evenly. (A piece of cardboard can help with this, but make sure it's wrapped in plastic before you use it.) If liquid seeps up, you've added too much, but just pour it off. Distribute a little weight on the terrine to help press it evenly. Place it in the fridge overnight to set.

**13.** To serve, remove the terrine from the mold, unwrap, and slice it into ¾-inch-thick pieces. Place them flat on a plate.

**14.** In a mixing bowl, take the reserved artichokes and cut them in quarters, then mix with the watercress and reserved tarragon leaves. Dress with the vinaigrette. Serve the salad on the side of the terrine with small dots of tarragon mustard on each terrine slice.

# "GRASS FED" BEEF TONGUE TARTARE, ALFALFA & HAYAIOLI

SERVES 8

Tongue meat can be extremely well marbled. But it's also toothsome, and the more you chew, the more flavorful the bite; it's one of the most delicious and interesting cuts on any animal, but especially with beef. This dish is like taking an animal back to its feed. Cows graze with their tongues, so we're serving the flavors of their diet in the dish itself.

**1 beef tongue, 4 to 5 pounds**
**¼ cup finely chopped shallots**
**2 tablespoons salted capers, rinsed and chopped**
**¼ cup minced chives**
**¼ cup sprouted grains (see Note)**
**Sea salt and freshly ground black pepper**
**Grated zest of 1 lemon**
**2 teaspoons lemon juice**
**3 teaspoons extra-virgin olive oil, plus more to taste**
**8 thick slices whole-wheat seeded rustic bread, grilled or toasted**
**½ cup Hayaioli (page 276)**
**Wheat grass oil to taste (recipe follows)**
**¼ cup alfalfa sprouts**
**Coarse sea salt**

**Equipment: Meat grinder, parts well-chilled in the freezer**

**NOTE:** You can get sprouted grains at most health food stores, Whole Foods, and many markets. If you'd like to experiment with sprouting them yourself, place grains such as rye berries on a moist towel and cover with another moist towel, then let it sit in a warm area. Spritz with water every other day until the berries sprout, which should take 2 to 4 days. Let them grow as big as you'd like before using, but watch out for molding or rot. Be sure to keep them damp, not soaking wet.

**1.** Freeze the beef tongue just until it holds its shape—not rock hard but frozen enough to peel. Then use a sharp vegetable peeler to peel off the rough skin. Dice the tongue.

**2.** Run the tongue through the meat grinder on a medium setting, about ¼-inch die. Grind the meat into a chilled bowl set over ice to keep the meat cold.

**3.** Add the chopped shallots, capers, chives, and sprouted grains, then mix gently. Season with salt, freshly ground black pepper, lemon zest and juice to taste; mix together. Add the olive oil and mix again.

**4.** To serve, spread the tongue tartare on the grilled bread and dot with hayaioli, drizzle with wheat grass oil, then top with alfalfa sprouts. Finish with a grind of black pepper and some coarse sea salt.

## WHEAT GRASS OIL

MAKES ABOUT 1 CUP

**1½ cups wheat grass**
**Salt**
**1 cup extra-virgin olive oil**

**1.** Blanch the wheat grass until super bright green in a pot of well-salted boiling water, just a few seconds, then shock it in ice water. Drain and pat dry with towels. Place the wheat grass and olive oil in a blender and blend until smooth. Strain the oil through a fine-mesh strainer.

**2.** Store in an airtight container in the refrigerator until needed. This will keep for over a week, but it's best when it's fresh.

# PASTRAMI BEEF TONGUE, LITTLE GEMS, PICKLED RED ONIONS & RYE

SERVES 4, PLUS LOTS OF LEFTOVER TONGUE

This is a play on the classic Jewish deli pastrami sandwich, without the bread. It's heavy on the spice, and leans toward a Quebecois-style smoked meat, like Montreal's famous Schwartz's. At the deli, I usually order the medium because it's the best blend of lean and fat meats, just like the difference between the tip of the tongue and the back end, as in this dish. This recipe makes a lot of leftover tongue, but it can live in the fridge for a week and also freezes well.

**1 gallon Tongue Brine (page 285)**
**1 beef tongue, 4 to 5 pounds**
**1 medium carrot**
**1 medium yellow onion**
**2 stalks celery**
**1 head garlic, split to expose the cloves**
**1 small leek, white and light green parts only**
**1 bulb fennel, tops removed**
**2 bay leaves**
**1 bunch thyme**
**½ cup Pastrami Spice (page 271), plus more, toasted, to garnish**
**4 heads Little Gem lettuce, leaves separated and washed**
**¼ cup Pickled Red Onions (page 286)**
**¼ cup chive batons**
**¼ cup sprouted rye berries (see Note on page 79)**
**¼ cup Mustard Vinaigrette (page 272)**

**Equipment: Smoker or perforated hotel pan; 1 cup Pinot Noir barrel shavings or other aromatic wood chips**

**1.** Combine the tongue and the brine, cover, and refrigerate for 4 days.

**2.** Remove the tongue from the brine and place it with carrot, onion, celery, garlic, leek, fennel, bay leaves, and thyme in a pot with fresh water to cover. Bring the water to a simmer, and cook until the tongue is tender and the skin separates from the meat when squeezed, 2½ to 3 hours (but start checking after 1½ hours, as tongues vary). Peel off the tough skin from the tongue and roll the tongue in the pastrami spice, pressing the spices in. Let cool.

**3.** Set up a cold smoker (see page 175). Smoke the tongue for 45 minutes. Wrap the tongue tightly in plastic wrap, set it in a pan, and return it to the fridge. This allows the meat to fully absorb the smoke; otherwise, it gets sucked out by the air in the fridge.

**4.** To serve, slice the tongue with a sharp knife or on a meat slicer across the grain, thin like a slice of ham you'd find in a tall deli sandwich. For 4 servings, shave about a third of the tongue, reserving the rest for another use.

**5.** Place the tongue slices in a mixing bowl with the lettuce, pickled onions, chives, and sprouted rye berries. Dress the salad with vinaigrette, evenly coating it, then plate. For an extra little flavor boost, dust the top of the salad with some toasted pastrami spice.

# "BEEF ROSSINI" BEEF TONGUE, FOIE GRAS & PORCINI

SERVES 4

Beef tournedos were created for the composer Gioacchino Rossini, probably by French master chef Marie-Antoine Carême. This version of the original dish—served with foie gras, black truffles, and Madeira sauce—replaces the filet mignon with tongue, adds porcinis to the truffles, and, well, leaves the foie well enough alone. I like to think of it as a short-stack order of meat pancakes.

**8 ½-inch-thick slices of beef tongue, cooked and peeled (see page 29)**
**Sea salt and freshly ground black pepper**
**Unsalted butter, as needed for sautéing**
**1 pound porcini mushrooms, sliced ½ inch thick lengthwise, scored on flat side**
**12 ounces foie gras, sliced into 4 servings**
**½ pound Bloomsdale spinach**
**2 tablespoons Madeira**
**½ cup Veal Stock (page 281)**
**1 tablespoon truffle juice**
**1 teaspoon chopped black truffles**
**Black truffles, shaved, as much as you like**

**1.** Pat the tongue slices dry and season with salt and pepper. Heat a large sauté pan over medium heat and add a nice slick of butter. Add the tongue, in batches if necessary, and sear until nicely browned on both sides and heated through, about 2 minutes per side. Reserve warm. Add more butter to the pan, season the porcini mushrooms, and add them to the pan, scored-side down. Cook until golden brown, flip, and cook until tender throughout, about 4 minutes total. Keep tongue and porcini warm.

**2.** Score and season the foie gras with salt and pepper. In a clean medium sauté pan over high heat, add the foie gras and cook until golden brown, flipping it over after about 3 minutes, and cook on the other side until soft throughout; this should take about another 2 minutes. Reserve 2 tablespoons of foie gras fat for the sauce and remove the foie pieces, keeping them warm.

**3.** While the pan is still hot, add the spinach to the pan, season with salt and pepper, and let it wilt off the heat.

**4.** To make the jus, use the pan that the tongue was seared in, and add the Madeira and reduce by half over high heat, scraping the bottom of the pan to pick up any of the fond of the meat. Add the veal stock, bring to a quick boil, then remove from the heat and stir in the reserved foie gras fat, truffle juice, and chopped truffles to make a silky sauce. Season with salt and pepper.

**5.** Put some spinach on each plate, then add a slice of tongue, a slice of porcini, repeat, and then finally add the foie gras. To finish off the dish, top it with a nice spoonful of sauce and sliced truffles.

# BEEF TONGUE, POTATO, PURSLANE & ANCHOVY

SERVES 6 TO 8

Perfect for those meat-and-potato people in your lives, this dish is a cold potato salad with cold cuts, making it a main dish version of an everyday side. The creamy potatoes complement the salty brine of the tongue, while the crispy, succulent purslane makes for a well-rounded bite.

**1 gallon Tongue Brine (page 285)**
**1 beef tongue, 4 to 5 pounds**
**1 medium carrot**
**1 medium yellow onion**
**2 stalks celery**
**1 head garlic, split to expose the cloves**
**1 small leek, white and light green parts only**
**1 bulb fennel, top removed**
**½ bunch thyme**
**½ bunch parsley stems**
**1 jalapeño, split in half**
**1 bay leaf**
**2 pounds small Yukon Gold potatoes**
**Sea salt**
**Freshly cracked black pepper**
**½ pound purslane, thick stems removed**
**1 cup flat-leaf parsley leaves**
**Lemon Anchovy Vinaigrette (page 273) to taste**
**12 white anchovy fillets**

**1.** Combine the brine and tongue and refrigerate, covered, for 4 days, then drain and place the tongue in a pot with the carrot, onion, celery, garlic, leek, and fennel, and a tightly tied cheesecloth sachet containing the thyme, parsley stems, jalapeño, and bay leaf. Add fresh water to cover. Bring the water to a simmer and cook until the tongue is tender and the skin separates from the meat when squeezed, 2½ to 3 hours (but start checking after 1½ hours, as tongues vary). Skim any foam that rises as it cooks. Peel off the tough skin from the tongue while still warm, and store the tongue in the cooking liquid. This will help the tongue stay moist and build flavor while it cools.

**2.** Place the potatoes in a pot, and cover with cold tongue-poaching liquid. Bring to a boil, then turn it down to a simmer and salt the liquid lightly. When the potatoes are cooked through and creamy, about 15 minutes after the water comes to a simmer, remove the potatoes from the liquid and let them cool at room temperature. Once cool, use a paring knife to remove the skins and cut the potatoes in quarters lengthwise. Set aside.

**3.** To serve, slice the tongue into thin pieces across the grain. Toss them in a mixing bowl with the potatoes, seasoning with salt and pepper. Gently toss in the purslane and parsley leaves, dispersing evenly, and dress with the vinaigrette.

**4.** Place the mixture on a platter. Top with the white anchovies and fresh ground black pepper.

# GRILLED BEEF TONGUE, LEMON & BLACK PEPPER

SERVES 8 TO 12 (OR FEWER, RESERVING THE REST OF THE TONGUE FOR TARTARE, SEE PAGE 79)

In the United States, we see a lot of dishes featuring tongue that has been braised, often to a mushy death. Here, we take it from raw, treating the tongue more like a steak and cooking it to medium rare. I got this idea from Japanese robata houses, where they grill meat over hot binchotan charcoal and serve it simply with sides of sesame oil, salt, and pepper, to dip and season. I like slicing the tongue thin, almost like carpaccio, and serving it with olio nuovo for a nice grassy punch.

**1 beef tongue, 4 to 5 pounds, peeled (see page 29)**
**Sea salt**
**Olio nuovo extra-virgin olive oil**
**Freshly ground black pepper**
**2 lemons, cut into wedges**

**1.** Portion the tongue into ¼-inch-thick slices.

**2.** Heat a grill to high heat. Season the tongue slices with salt, and dress with olive oil. Place them on the grill, cooking quickly, and rotate for nice diamond marks on both sides. Be sure the grill is superhot, but also be careful not to overcook, as it will cook really fast—just a minute or so total for medium rare.

**3.** Lay the grilled tongue on a plate with a small pile of sea salt, one of black pepper, and a few lemon wedges. Dip the tongue in the seasonings, use the lemon to freshen your palate, and drizzle with olive oil to add a little grassiness.

# THIS IS YOUR BRAIN ON DRUGS

SERVES 1

I thought the antidrug PSAs that aired on TV in the late 1980s were funny as hell: a deep, dark voice-over, a hand holding an egg, cracking it into a pan and letting it bubble and burn. This dish is an homage to those commercials.

**1 calf's brain, about 1 pound**
**1 quart Court Bouillon (page 280)**
**2 tablespoons unsalted butter**
**Coarsely ground black pepper**
**Coarse salt**
**1 duck egg**
**1 thick slice country bread, grilled or toasted**
**3 parsley leaves**
**3 chervil leaves**
**6 tarragon leaves**
**6 chive batons**
**Sherry vinegar, to taste**
**Black or white truffles, as much as you like**

**1.** To poach the brain, fill a small pot with court bouillon, bring to a boil, and turn it down to a simmer so it's lightly bubbling. Gently place the brain into the water and simmer for 5 minutes. Remove the brain from the court bouillon with a perforated spoon and set it on a plate. Cover and put the plate in the refrigerator to cool for about 15 minutes. (The brain may be stored at this point and finished later.)

**2.** In a sauté pan over medium heat, add 1 tablespoon of butter, season the brain with salt and pepper, then sear the poached brain, presentation-side (a.k.a. the top of the brain) down. Baste with the fat until golden brown, about 4 minutes, then flip over, continuing to baste, until it is hot all the way through.

**3.** In a separate pan over medium heat, add 1 tablespoon of butter and cook the duck egg sunny-side up. Season the top of the egg with black pepper and coarse salt.

**4.** Place the brain on top of the egg white. Top with the herbs and a few drops of sherry vinegar. Shave on as much truffle as you'd like. Serve with a crisp glass of Sancerre and the bread.

# "THE JUNGLE" BRAINS & EGGS

SERVES 4

This dish is a nod to Upton Sinclair's *The Jungle,* where people sometimes fell into rendering tanks at meat processing plants and were "scrambled" in. It's also a dish those workers would likely eat, a proper butcher's breakfast of brains and scrambled eggs. In this case, the brains are cut into cubes and cooked into crispy nuggets.

**2 calves' brains, about 1 pound each**
**1 quart Court Bouillon (page 280)**
**5 eggs**
**2 tablespoons heavy cream**
**1 teaspoon Dijon mustard**
**1 teaspoon chopped chives**
**1 teaspoon chopped tarragon**
**1 teaspoon chopped chervil**
**Sea salt and freshly ground black pepper**
**1 tablespoon unsalted butter, plus more for toast**
**4 ½-inch slices country bread**

**1.** To poach the brains, fill a small pot with court bouillon, bring to a boil, and turn it down to a simmer so it's lightly bubbling. Gently lower the brains into the water and simmer them for 5 minutes. Remove the brains from the court bouillon with a perforated spoon and set them on a plate. Cover and put the plate in the refrigerator to cool for about 20 minutes.

**2.** In a mixing bowl, combine the eggs, cream, mustard, and herbs, and beat with a whisk until light and fluffy; season with salt and black pepper. Set in the refrigerator until ready to use.

**3.** Once the brain is cold and firm, dice it into 2-inch cubes. Heat the butter in a sauté pan over high heat until it starts to brown. Add the cubed brain pieces and season them with salt and pepper. Sear to get some color on one side, then gently stir to brown the other sides, about 4 minutes total. Turn the heat down to medium.

**4.** Pour in the egg mixture and fold the brains and eggs together with a rubber spatula until it's all cooked but still moist, just a couple of minutes. Make sure not to overcook the eggs; just set but a little loose is best.

**5.** While the eggs are cooking, grill or toast the bread so it will be warm when the eggs are finished. Serve the brains on warm plates with buttered toast.

# "BIG BRAIN, LITTLE BRAIN" CALF'S BRAIN & TESTICLES WITH SUDACHI BROWN BUTTER

SERVES 2

Sure, the name of this dish is dirty-minded, but I think it also shows the stark contrast of different offal cuts' textures. Creamy and rich, this dish has just enough chew that it's never one note. Have some brain, and have a ball! I like making people laugh so they don't always need to take food so seriously.

**2 quarts Court Bouillon (page 280)**
**1 calf's brain, about 1 pound**
**2 calf's fries (testicles)**
**Salt and freshly ground black pepper**
**2 tablespoons Seasoned Flour (page 270)**
**1 egg, beaten with a splash of water**
**1 cup fine bread crumbs**
**4 tablespoons unsalted butter**
**1 tablespoon chopped Preserved Sudachi peel (page 286) or preserved lemon**
**2 teaspoons sudachi juice (or use equal parts orange and lemon juice)**
**¼ cup Roasted Chicken Stock (page 282)**
**4 extra-large asparagus spears**
**Ancho cress, a few leaves for garnish**
**Extra-virgin olive oil, to taste**
**Brainaise (page 275), for serving**

**1.** Fill a small pot with the court bouillon and bring to a simmer. Gently lower the brain into the liquid and simmer for 5 minutes. Remove the brain from the court bouillon with a perforated spoon to a plate. Put the plate in the refrigerator to cool for about 15 minutes. When cool, slice the brain in half.

**2.** Poach the testicles in boiling salted water for 1 minute, then shock them in salted ice water. Remove the two membranes by making a slice in the outer membrane and peeling them twice. Bring the court bouillon back to a boil, then turn it down to a bare simmer and poach the fries for 4 minutes. Cool on a plate; do not shock them in an ice-water bath.

**3.** Once the fries are cooled, cut them into 1-inch-thick slices. Season with salt and pepper, then dust each side with seasoned flour. Then dip them in the egg wash and transfer to the bread crumbs.

**4.** In a sauté pan over medium heat, add 2 tablespoons of butter; when it foams, season and add the sliced fries, flip when golden brown, and brown the other side, about 4 minutes total.

**5.** In a separate pan over medium heat, add 2 tablespoons butter. Season the poached brain with salt and pepper and sear the presentation side (a.k.a. the top of the brain) first. Baste with the butter until warm throughout; check the temperature with a cake tester. Add the diced preserved sudachi peel to the brown butter, then add 1 teaspoon sudachi juice. Remove the brain and whisk in the chicken stock.

**6.** Shave the asparagus with a vegetable peeler, and place them in a bowl with the ancho cress. Dress with 1 teaspoon sudachi juice and olive oil to taste, and season with salt and pepper.

**7.** Place the calf's fries on plates, then top each portion with half of the calf's brain. Add some of the brown butter sudachi sauce. Place a nice pile of the asparagus salad on each plate and a dollop of brainaise on the calf's fries. Serve immediately.

# SWEETBREADS, CUCUMBERS & HAZELNUTS

SERVES 4

During a trip to Japan, every time I ordered grilled skewers of meat at an izakaya, there was a side of Japanese cucumbers sprinkled with sesame and salt. It was so simple, but the way the cucumbers counterbalanced the richness of the protein was like having pickles on a deli sandwich. I decided to make a complete dish here, tossed together, that had that same fatty yet refreshing sensation.

**2 quarts Court Bouillon (page 280)**
**2 pounds calf's sweetbreads**
**Sea salt**
**Ice water**
**1 to 2 teaspoons coarsely ground black pepper**
**2 cups Seasoned Flour (page 270)**
**Extra-virgin olive oil, as needed**
**1 pound Persian cucumbers, about 5**
**¼ cup hazelnuts, toasted and cracked**
**2 tablespoons fresh lemon juice**
**1 teaspoon fish sauce, preferably Red Boat**
**1 teaspoon hazelnut oil**

**1.** Bring the court bouillon to a boil, then reduce to a simmer before adding the sweetbreads. Poach them for about 4 minutes until medium rare, then remove them from the liquid and plunge them into a salted ice-water bath.

**2.** Remove the sweetbreads from the ice-water bath. To remove excess liquid, blood, and impurities from the sweetbreads, press them between two plates or sheet trays weighted down by a heavy pan for 5 hours in the fridge. Peel off most of the membrane, keeping enough membrane to hold them together (see page 35), and devein the sweetbreads.

**3.** Break the sweetbreads into 2-inch pieces, season with salt and pepper, then dust them in the seasoned flour. In a sauté pan over high heat, add enough olive oil to generously coat. Shake the sweetbreads to remove any excess flour, and panfry them to golden brown on all sides and crispy, about 5 minutes total. Place them on paper towels to absorb any excess oil.

**4.** Cut the cucumbers into 2-inch lengths and crush them until chunky. In a mixing bowl, combine the crushed cucumbers and toasted hazelnuts, then season with the lemon juice, fish sauce, and hazelnut oil. Adjust the seasoning with salt and a lot of black pepper. Then toss in the crispy sweetbreads, mix well, and place on a platter.

# GRILLED SWEETBREADS & PICKLED GREEN WALNUTS

SERVES 4

I saw Anthony Bourdain go to Argentina for one of his TV shows, where, at the markets, they were grilling whole sweetbreads on the *parilla* (open fire grill), an unusual treatment by American standards, but creamy sweetbreads take well to char. How cool would this be to do at a friend's barbecue? The walnuts are an old-school English condiment—wonderfully acidic, refreshing, and thought to prevent meat spoilage. It takes about 2 months to let them pickle, but they last for a long time. Here, I've turned them into a salsa.

**2 pounds sweetbreads, trimmed of sinew and fat**
**Sea salt and freshly ground black pepper**
**Extra-virgin olive oil**
**Pickled green walnut salsa (recipe follows)**
**Flaky sea salt, for finishing (preferably from Jacobsen Salt Co.)**

**1.** Preheat a grill to medium heat. Season the sweetbreads with salt and pepper, coat with olive oil, and place on the grill. Rotate the sweetbreads every minute or so to get an even amount of heat and well-distributed grill marks.

**2.** The sweetbreads will crisp up and become golden brown in about 10 minutes. Once cooked, let them rest for a few minutes, then slice them into bite-size pieces, like slicing a steak for serving, and place on a plate, topped with the salsa and flaky salt.

## PICKLED GREEN WALNUT SALSA

MAKES ½ CUP

**FOR THE PICKLED WALNUTS:**

**2½ pounds kosher salt**
**50 whole green walnuts**
**2 quarts red wine vinegar**
**4 ounces black peppercorns**
**2 ounces allspice berries**
**10 whole cloves**
**2 sticks cinnamon**
**4 ounces grated ginger**

**FOR THE SALSA:**

**¼ cup pickled green walnuts (recipe follows)**
**2 tablespoons finely sliced chives**
**1 teaspoon freshly ground black pepper**
**3 tablespoons extra-virgin olive oil**
**1 tablespoon walnut oil**

**MAKE THE PICKLED WALNUTS:**

**1.** Dissolve half the salt (1¼ pounds) in 1 gallon water to make a brine. Put on some rubber gloves, because walnut juice will stain your hands for weeks. Trust me. Stab each walnut with a sausage prick in several places; this helps the brine penetrate. Submerge the walnuts in the brine in a nonreactive container, weighting down the walnuts with a plate if necessary, and cover the container with cheesecloth. Let them sit for 2 weeks at room temperature, replacing the brine with a fresh batch of the same mixture (using the remaining 1¼ pounds of salt) after 7 days.

**2.** Remove the walnuts, discarding the brine, and put them on a parchment-lined baking sheet. Leave them outside in the sun for 3 days, or until they turn uniformly black. Be sure to roll them around every few hours for the first day or two, and then daily so that they dry evenly.

**3.** Pack the walnuts into a nonreactive container. In a large pan, bring the vinegar, peppercorns, allspice, cloves, cinnamon, and ginger to a boil, and pour the mixture over the walnuts, again submerging them with a plate if necessary. Seal and keep in a cool place (below 70°F), such as the fridge or a basement, for at least a month before you eat them. They will keep this way for a year.

**MAKE THE SALSA:**

**1.** Chop the pickled walnuts finely, being sure to remove any hard bits of shell. Combine them in a small bowl with the chives and black pepper. Mix in the extra-virgin olive oil and finish with walnut oil. Mix well, then store in an airtight container in the refrigerator. Bring to room temperature before serving.

**❤ 432 likes**
**offalchris** Pickled Green walnuts next to the finished salsa

# SWEETBREADS, PEAS & TARRAGON

SERVES 2

This is inspired by one of the most amazing sweetbread dishes I've ever had, at Paul Bocuse's Brasserie le Nord in Lyon, glazed in a cocotte, stewed with onions, carrots, and other goodies. Prior to this, I had only had crispy sweetbreads, and it was a revelation to have them cooked in a way that shows off their tenderness and creaminess. There's an underlying sweetness to this dish, and it's lighter than it sounds. It pairs so well with a crisp white wine. It's haute offal!

**3 quarts Court Bouillon (page 280)**
**1 pound veal sweetbreads**
**Sea salt**
**Freshly cracked black pepper**
**1 tablespoon extra-virgin olive oil**
**2 tablespoons unsalted butter**
**2 teaspoons lemon juice**
**⅓ cup Roasted Chicken Stock (page 282)**
**1 cup shelled peas**
**1 bunch tarragon, leaves only**

**1.** Bring the court bouillon to a boil and add the sweetbreads. Cook for about 4 minutes, until medium rare, then remove them from the liquid and plunge them into a salted ice-water bath to stop the cooking process.

**2.** Remove the sweetbreads from the ice-water bath and press them under a heavy braising pan or Dutch oven to release excess liquid; overnight is best. The next day, peel off as much membrane as you can without breaking the sweetbreads into tiny bits; ideally the pieces should be 3 inches or larger.

**3.** Season the sweetbreads with salt and pepper. Preheat a sauté pan over medium heat, add the olive oil, and then the sweetbreads. Sauté until the sweetbreads are golden, about 2 minutes. Flip them, then add the butter. Once there is color on the sweetbreads on all sides and the butter is brown, in about 2 minutes, deglaze the pan with lemon juice and chicken stock. Let simmer for 4 minutes, covered. Add the shelled peas and let them cook in the sauce, stirring occasionally. Once the peas are tender and the mixture is emulsified, in about 2 minutes, add the tarragon leaves. Place the sweetbreads on a plate and top with the peas and tarragon sauce.

# BEEF HEART TARTARE CLASSIQUE

SERVES 8

I've always loved raw meat—it's so primal. When I worked at Red Sage in D.C., we made a beef tartare in a cookie cutter that looked like a bull with big horns. I've had horse tartare in Montreal. I've eaten tartare all over Paris. Hanger steaks, New York strip, short ribs, they're all great, but my favorite is heart. It's such a pure muscle, clean, delicious, with very little fat—it makes a very lean tartare. Though I've been known to add some foie gras to mine.

**1 beef heart, about 5 pounds, trimmed (see page 40)**
**6 salted anchovy fillets**
**¼ cup finely diced red onion**
**1 tablespoon finely grated lemon zest**
**¼ cup capers, chopped**
**2 tablespoons extra-virgin olive oil, plus more to finish**
**3 tablespoons Dijon mustard**
**3 teaspoons red wine vinegar**
**2 tablespoons minced chives**
**3 tablespoons flat-leaf parsley, chiffonade**
**Smoked salt**
**Coarsely ground black pepper**
**8 quail egg yolks**
**Grilled baguette slices, for serving**

**1.** After trimming the heart of sinew and gristle, hand-cut the meat into ¼-inch dice or grind on ¼-inch die using a meat grinder for best texture.

**2.** Chop the anchovies into a coarse paste.

**3.** In a mixing bowl, combine the heart with the anchovies, onion, lemon zest, capers, olive oil, mustard, red wine vinegar, and the chives and parsley. Mix the tartare gently. Season with smoked salt and black pepper.

**4.** To assemble the dish, divide the meat among 8 cold serving plates, drizzle with extra-virgin olive oil, top each with an egg yolk, and serve with grilled bread.

# "SURF & TURF" BEEF HEART & OYSTERS

SERVES 6 TO 8

Surf and turf is a dish that usually pairs steak and lobster and speaks to opulence. I like this raw version; the minerality you find in beef heart is similar, to me, to the seawater salinity of an oyster.

**2 pounds trimmed beef heart (see page 40)**
**24 oysters, shucked and coarsely chopped**
**2 tablespoons green peppercorns, chopped**
**2 tablespoons very finely diced shallot**
**1 serrano chile, finely diced**
**2 teaspoons finely grated lemon zest**
**2 tablespoons extra-virgin olive oil, plus more for drizzling**
**1 tablespoon lemon juice**
**2 tablespoons chopped tarragon**
**2 tablespoons minced chives**
**Sea salt and coarsely ground black pepper**
**Oyster crackers, for serving**

**1.** Chop the heart into ¼-inch pieces, or, if you have a meat grinder, cut the meat small enough to put it through the grinder on a medium die (a KitchenAid grinder attachment is the perfect tool for this).

**2.** In a mixing bowl, gently combine the beef heart with the chopped oysters, green peppercorns, shallot, chile, and lemon zest. Add the olive oil, lemon juice, tarragon, and chives. After it is well mixed, season with salt and black pepper to taste.

**3.** To assemble the dish, divide the meat into cold serving bowls. Drizzle with more extra-virgin olive oil, and then sprinkle with the crispy oyster crackers. Finish off the dish with a fresh grind of black pepper and serve.

# CALF'S LIVER CRUDO, BEETS & BALSAMIC

SERVES 6

I had calf's liver sashimi in Japan, and when I came back to the States, I served it immediately at my first Head to Tail dinner in New York City. Raw liver has an unexpected crunchiness and a strong mineral and umami flavor that pairs so well with the raw beets, and their sweetness melds perfectly with balsamic. (If you can find a juniper-infused balsamic, like Cavedoni's Gusto Ginepro, go for it.) All the chew and umami of this dish is like an oyster with mignonette. Just make sure the liver is very fresh.

**½ pound fresh calf's liver, cleaned of membrane and veins (see page 45)**
**1 medium red beet, peeled**
**2 tablespoons balsamic vinegar, plus more for finishing**
**2 tablespoons extra-virgin olive oil, plus more for finishing**
**Coarse sea salt**
**Freshly ground black pepper**
**1 tablespoon chervil leaves**

**1.** Using a sharp knife, slice the liver into thin sashimi-style pieces, about 3 inches long, and place them on a chilled serving platter.

**2.** Using a mandoline with julienne teeth, shave the beet into a mixing bowl. Season it with the balsamic, olive oil, and salt and black pepper to taste. Right before plating, add the chervil to the salad.

**3.** Season the liver slices with sea salt and black pepper. Top them with balsamic, then finish with extra-virgin olive oil. Top with the beet and chervil salad. Serve immediately.

# GRILLED CALF'S LIVER, POLENTA & ARUGULA

SERVES 6

This is a quintessential liver dish. Most people over- or undercook it, but if you just remember to let the liver sit out at room temperature before you cook it, and then remember to let it rest after cooking, you'll help yourself a lot. The fresh herbs, bitter greens, and brown butter sauce tie it all together.

**2 pounds fresh calf's liver, cleaned of membrane and veins (see page 45), cut into 2-inch-thick slices**
**Sea salt and freshly ground black pepper**
**6 branches rosemary**
**1 bunch thyme**
**2 bay leaves**
**12 cloves garlic, crushed**
**¼ cup extra-virgin olive oil**
**½ cup unsalted butter**
**Creamy Polenta (page 289)**
**4 ounces wild arugula**
**½ lemon, plus 2 tablespoons lemon juice**
**4 anchovy fillets, chopped**
**2 tablespoons salted capers, rinsed**

**1.** Season the liver with salt and pepper and lay it in a pan. Lightly bruise the rosemary, thyme, and bay leaves with the side of a knife, and lay them and the garlic on the liver; add the olive oil. Let the liver come to room temperature for 20 minutes before grilling.

**2.** Heat the grill to high; it should be quite hot. Remove the liver from the marinade, keeping it well oiled, and sear for a minute or two on the grill before rotating it to give it diamond-shaped grill marks. Flip it over and repeat. It should take about 2 to 3 minutes per side for medium rare. Set aside to rest for 3 minutes before slicing.

**3.** In a sauté pan over high heat, melt the butter and let it brown with the herbs and garlic from the liver marinade; keep warm.

**4.** To plate, place a pool of polenta on each individual plate, top with some arugula, and squeeze some lemon juice over it. Divide the liver slices among the plates, and add some fresh arugula on top. Deglaze the brown butter with 2 tablespoons of lemon juice and remove the aromatics. Add the chopped anchovies and capers, and sauce the liver plates with this mixture.

# CALF'S LIVER & PORCINI PÂTÉ

SERVES 6 TO 8

Chicken liver pâté is omnipresent, yet for whatever reason calf's liver rarely gets this treatment. But once when I was portioning a calf's liver, there were all these too-small pieces, and I decided to make pâté. Its gigantic flavor got even better daily through a full week. Porcini are meaty mushrooms, and they add a nice earthy, piney touch to the spread.

**1½ pounds calf's liver**
**Kosher salt (see Note)**
**Freshly ground black pepper**
**0.5 grams pink curing salt, such as Instacure #1**
**1¼ pounds fresh porcini, cleaned**
**2 tablespoons tallow or butter, plus more for the bread**
**1 cup sliced shallots**
**2 tablespoons sliced garlic**
**1 tablespoon thyme leaves**
**1 tablespoon nepitella leaves**
**1 pound (4 sticks) cold unsalted butter, cubed, plus 1 tablespoon**
**1 tablespoon sherry vinegar, plus more**
**4 bay leaves**
**Sourdough batard, cut into 1-inch slices**
**Upland cress, for garnish**
**Flaky sea salt, for finishing**

**Equipment: 14 × 4 × 4-inch terrine mold (1½ quarts) or several serving crocks**

**1.** Peel the outer membrane and cut the liver into 3 sections, removing each as a lobe, then cut each into smaller pieces. Remove the large veins and arteries and season well with the kosher salt, black pepper, and the curing salt.

**2.** Cut 1 pound of the porcinis into ¼-inch slices. In a sauté pan over medium heat, add 1 tablespoon tallow, and sauté the sliced porcinis, seasoning with salt and pepper, until lightly browned, 2 to 3 minutes. Add the shallots, garlic, thyme, and nepitella, and cook, stirring, until tender, about 5 minutes. Remove from the heat.

**3.** In another large sauté pan set over high heat, add the rest of the tallow. When very hot, add the liver and 1 tablespoon of butter just as the liver hits the pan. Sear the liver pieces. Be sure to get a nice caramelization, basting the top with the butter. Flip the pieces and cook to medium, 3 to 5 minutes total, being careful not to overcook.

**4.** Place the liver in a food processor, and add the cooked porcini mixture. Process, and add the pound of butter, cube by cube, waiting until the mixture is smooth and even before adding the next. Adjust the mixture with the sherry vinegar, salt, and black pepper to taste. Pass the liver-porcini mixture through a sieve to remove any tough or unblended bits.

**5.** Spray a terrine mold with cooking spray, then line it with a length of plastic wrap that can be folded over the terrine. Pour the liver and porcini mixture into the mold, then place 3 bay leaves on top, folding the plastic wrap over the terrine; place it in the refrigerator to set overnight.

**6.** To serve, brush the bread with some tallow, and toast or grill on both sides. Rub the bread with a fresh bay leaf. Dress some upland cress with sherry vinegar, flaky sea salt, and black pepper; shave the remaining porcini on top. Serve the pâté with the bread, the salad, and a spoon.

# TRIPE CRUDO, HAZELNUTS & SCALLIONS

SERVES 4

The first stomach of a cow, also known as the mino, has a unique muscle lining. It's much more striated, like the wings of skate, and there are ribs of muscle. People who worry that tripe is too funky will be happy to know that mino doesn't taste like a part of the digestive process, because it's where cows store their cud. I first had it served nearly raw at the Japanese offal specialist Takashi in New York City, where they use grated daikon as a natural tenderizer. This technique is often used for octopus in Japan, which has a similar enzymatic reaction with the radish.

**1 large daikon radish, about 12 inches long**
**1 pound mino (a.k.a. blanket or rumen beef tripe)**
**¼ cup toasted hazelnuts, crushed**
**1 cup sliced scallions**
**Coarsely ground black pepper**
**½ cup lemon juice**
**3 tablespoons hazelnut oil**
**2 tablespoons extra-virgin olive oil**
**1 tablespoon fish sauce, Red Boat 40°N brand preferred**
**Flaky sea salt**

**1.** Finely grate the daikon on a box grater into a bowl. Pack the mino in the daikon gratings, cover, and let sit in the fridge overnight.

**2.** Rinse the mino of daikon and bring a pot of well-salted water to boil. Blanch the mino for 15 seconds, then shock it in salted ice water. Drain and pat the mino dry.

**3.** Trim the mino of any tough sinew or membrane, and score it lightly with a sharp knife at ¼-inch intervals.

**4.** Slice the mino against the grain into fine, sashimi-like bite-size pieces.

**5.** Place a mixing bowl over ice, and add the cut mino, hazelnuts, most of the scallions, and black pepper to taste. Dress with the lemon juice and oils. Finish with the fish sauce, salt, and toss.

**6.** Serve portioned into bowls, topping with the remaining scallions and a little more black pepper.

❤ **153 likes**
**offalchris** Blanching mino for 20 seconds

# TRIPE & LOBSTER

SERVES 4

When I was a kid, my great-grandmother Rosalie used to cook tripe. My grandmother Helen made lobster. Back then, I dreaded one dish and loved the other. Of course, I learned to love Rosalie's tripe stewed in tomato sauce, and when I began working in kitchens, I saw lobster pastas with marinara showing up on menus. So this dish is a melding of these two key elements of my childhood.

**2 tablespoons extra-virgin olive oil, plus more to finish**
**½ cup julienned red onion**
**1 pound honeycomb beef tripe, cleaned, cooked, and cut into 2-inch pieces (see pages 48–49)**
**Sea salt**
**2 tablespoons sliced garlic**
**1 cup red wine**
**1 quart Lobster Marinara (page 278), plus lobster meat and roe reserved separately**
**1 teaspoon chopped flat-leaf parsley**
**½ teaspoon oregano leaves**
**1 tablespoon fish sauce, preferably Red Boat, or to taste**
**Lemon juice**
**1 tablespoon grated Lobster Bottarga (page 278)**

**1.** In a large saucepan, combine the extra-virgin olive oil, red onion, and tripe, and cook over moderate heat until the onion takes some color, about 8 minutes. Season with salt.

**2.** Add the garlic, toast lightly, then deglaze with the red wine. Cook until the saucepan is nearly dry. Add the lobster marinara and cook until it turns deep brick red, about 8 minutes, then add the lobster meat and roe and continue cooking just to heat the lobster meat through. Finish with the chopped parsley and oregano, and adjust the seasoning with the fish sauce, some extra-virgin olive oil, and lemon juice to taste. Grate the lobster roe bottarga over the top.

# TRIPE, CLAMS, SERRANO & LEMON VERBENA

SERVES 4

Tripe and clams, when cooked properly, have a nearly identical texture, so bringing them together not only combines my New England past and offal-cooking present, it creates a dish that messes a little with your head (in a good way). Lemon verbena is often found in desserts, but the floral herb helps to bring out the inherent sweetness in the meats here.

**2 tablespoons extra-virgin olive oil, plus more to finish**
**1 pound honeycomb beef tripe, cooked, diced large, and patted dry (see pages 48–49)**
**⅓ cup thinly sliced shallots**
**½ serrano chile, sliced thin**
**48 small clams, preferably savory or Manila, scrubbed and purged (see page 138)**
**¼ cup white wine**
**½ cup Roasted Chicken Stock (page 282)**
**½ cup lemon verbena leaves**
**½ tablespoon lemon juice, plus more to taste**

**1.** In a large braising pan over high heat, add the extra-virgin olive oil and sear the tripe to get a little color. Add the shallots and serrano, and cook, stirring, until softened, about 3 minutes. Add the clams and the wine, let it reduce by half, then add the chicken stock and lemon verbena leaves. Cover the pan and let it steam until all the clams open, about 3 minutes. Stir in some extra-virgin olive oil and the lemon juice. Taste the broth, adjust the seasoning with lemon juice (it will be salty enough from the clams), and divide among bowls.

# SHAVED TRIPE, CITRUS, CELERY, CHILE & PARSLEY

SERVES 8 TO 12

This dish is a riff on a cold tripe salad traditionally served in Tuscany during the summer. Tripe can be really tender when well cooked and shaved thin. When I was on *Iron Chef America,* I paired it with the sweet giant clam called geoduck, and it was fucking amazing! It was just like the cold shaved conch salad, or scungilli, that I grew up on, a surf and turf like no other. Even without the geoduck, this is a great fresh tripe preparation.

**2 pounds honeycomb beef tripe, cooked until very tender (see pages 48–49)**
**1 geoduck clam, rinsed (optional)**
**5 cloves garlic, minced**
**1 tablespoon red chile flakes**
**Zest and juice of 3 limes**
**½ cup extra-virgin olive oil**
**Sea salt**
**1 head celery, light-colored heart only**
**3 tablespoons roughly chopped flat-leaf parsley**

**1.** Shave the tripe, either with a very sharp knife or a meat slicer, to form wafer-thin, ribbon-like strips.

**2.** If using the geoduck, blanch it in boiling Court Bouillon (page 280) or fresh water for 1 minute, then shock it in ice water to loosen the outer membrane from the trunk. Peel this membrane. From there, split the trunk of the clam in half, and shave each half thinly like sashimi.

**3.** Make a vinaigrette by combining the garlic in a small mixing bowl with the chile flakes and lime zest. Add the lime juice and marinate for 5 minutes. Whisk in the extra-virgin olive oil and season with salt to taste.

**4.** Toss the tripe and the geoduck, if using, with the vinaigrette, adding a little at a time until it reaches your desired acidity. (You will have some vinaigrette left). Let the tripe marinate, covered, in the fridge for 2 hours before serving.

**5.** Shave the celery very thin on a mandoline. Dress the shaved celery with some of the remaining vinaigrette to taste. Mix the celery with the marinated tripe and parsley, and serve.

# TRIPE & CHIPS

SERVES 4 TO 6

As the last few recipes have shown, I believe tripe and clams have real similarities texture-wise. I grew up eating fried clams and french fries at New England clam shacks, like Pete and Flo's in Portsmouth, Rhode Island (which moved to Newport and is known just as Flo's). In my mind, it's a short jump from there to frying tripe instead of the clams, and then I think of English chip shops as inspiration for the potatoes—thick chips rather than thin fries. These russets are boiled with herbs, then chunked and fried skin-on for a very rustic effect.

**5 medium russet potatoes**
**¼ cup rosemary needles, stems reserved**
**2 bay leaves**
**1 teaspoon white wine vinegar**
**Peel of 1 lemon**
**Sea salt**
**2 pounds cooked honeycomb beef tripe (see page 49)**
**1 cup Seasoned Flour (page 270)**
**Neutral oil or, even better, tallow, for frying**
**Freshly ground black pepper**
**Basic Aioli (page 274), as much as you like, for serving**

**1.** Place the whole potatoes with the rosemary stems, bay leaves, white wine vinegar, and lemon peel in a pot with cold, well-salted water to cover, and bring it up to boil. Reduce the heat to a simmer and cook for about 25 minutes, until the potatoes are fork tender. Remove the potatoes from the water and let them cool; discard the water and aromatics.

**2.** Cut the cooked tripe into 2-inch squares, shaving any thick edges thin and removing any clumps of fat.

**3.** Break up the potatoes into large bite-size chunks with the skin on.

**4.** Dredge the tripe in the seasoned flour, banging off any excess.

**5.** Preheat a deep fryer or a tall pot filled with several inches of oil to 375°F. Fry the potatoes in batches, cooking until crisp and golden brown, about 5 minutes per batch. Drain on paper towels and season with salt and black pepper while still hot.

**6.** Repeat with the tripe, also frying in batches. During the last 30 seconds or so of the final batch, fry the rosemary needles.

**7.** Combine the potatoes, tripe, and fried rosemary in newspaper cones and serve with a side of aioli.

# GRANDMA ROSALIE'S TRIPE

SERVES 6

When I was a kid, I used to fucking run in fear whenever I smelled this cooking in my great-grandma Rosalie's kitchen. Tripe seemed pretty gnarly back then, and I'd just take off on my skateboard to get away. I started trying tripe at Mike's Kitchen, an Italian VFW hall in Rhode Island. It was served in marinara, with Parmesan, and it somehow became comforting. These days, I may make mine a little spicier, with more acidity, but it's as close as I can get to hers.

**2 pounds honeycomb beef tripe, cooked and cut into 2-inch squares (see page 49)**
**3 tablespoons Salsa Fra Diavolo (page 277)**
**2 tablespoons extra-virgin olive oil, plus more for finishing**
**1 cup julienned red onion**
**1 tablespoon sliced garlic**
**¼ cup red wine**
**1 28-ounce can San Marzano tomatoes, milled**
**Grated orange zest, to taste**
**Red wine vinegar, to taste**
**¼ cup mint leaves**
**Grilled bread, for serving**

**1.** Coat the tripe in the salsa fra diavolo and marinate, covered, in the fridge overnight.

**2.** In a medium braising pan or Dutch oven set over medium heat, combine the extra-virgin olive oil and the onion. Cook, stirring, until softened, about 5 minutes. Add the garlic and tripe and cook, stirring, to bloom the flavors of the fra diavolo, about 3 minutes. Deglaze the pan with the red wine, and reduce until almost dry, about 2 minutes. Add the tomatoes, bring to a boil, turn down the heat to a simmer, and reduce until the sauce is brick red, about 15 minutes.

**3.** Adjust the sauce with orange zest and a splash of red wine vinegar. Tear the mint leaves, add them, and serve immediately in bowls with some grilled bread and a drizzle of extra-virgin olive oil.

❤ **804 likes**

**offalchris** my great Grandmother Rosalie Cosentino who taught me to cook tripe

# LAMPREDOTTO & DANDELION GREENS

SERVES 6

This is a Florentine dish, best enjoyed at the famous market stall restaurant Da Nerbone in Mercato Centrale. One vendor there has vats of simmered tripe for sandwiches. They grab a handful, sauce it with either red (picante) or green (verde), and stuff it into a small hoagie, dripping with braising liquid, like the Italian version of a hot dip. Here I serve it over bread, with plenty of the broth.

**1 pound bible tripe, cooked (see pages 48–49)**
**2 tablespoons extra-virgin olive oil, plus more for drizzling**
**1 medium yellow onion, finely diced, about 1 cup**
**1 head garlic, split and sliced thinly**
**5 dried guajillo or ancho chiles, seeded**
**1 pound dandelion greens, tough stems removed, leaves cut crosswise into wide strips**
**5½ cups Roasted Chicken Stock (page 282)**
**4-inch piece of Parmesan cheese rind**
**Sea salt and freshly ground black pepper**
**6 1-inch-thick batard slices**
**1 lemon**
**Parmesan cheese, for serving**
**¼ cup Salsa Picante (page 279)**

**1.** Cut the tripe into 2½-inch-long strips against the grain.

**2.** In a large pot over medium heat, warm the 2 tablespoons of olive oil. Add the onion and garlic and cook, stirring occasionally, until the onion is translucent, about 5 minutes. Add the chiles and continue to cook, stirring, until lightly toasted, about 5 more minutes. Add the dandelion greens, and toss and stir until wilted. Add the stock and Parmesan rind, and bring to a simmer. Add the tripe and cook at a simmer until the flavors have married, about 30 minutes. Season with salt and pepper, then stir in more olive oil to taste, to balance out the bitterness of the greens. Remove the cheese rind. Mash the soft garlic cloves.

**3.** While the dandelion greens are cooking, grill or toast the bread until crisp. Remove from the heat and rub one side of each slice with the lemon, releasing the natural oils of the zest to flavor the bread.

**4.** To serve, place each batard slice in an individual bowl. Place the lampredetto and dandelion greens over the bread, dividing evenly, and then ladle some liquid over the top. The liquid is the best part. Using a vegetable peeler, shave a few Parmesan curls on top of each serving, and then drizzle with a little extra-virgin olive oil, salsa picante, and a grind of black pepper. Serve right away.

# CALF'S KIDNEYS, RADISH & BLACKSTRAP MOLASSES

SERVES 2

The greatest fear with kidneys is uric acid, which leaves the lingering aroma of urine. If cleaned correctly, though, kidneys' scent is faint and actually inviting, like the allure of biodynamic wines or farmhouse ciders with their barnyard notes. The molasses brings together a sauce with great acidity, sweetness, and tannins, just like a great wine, and the radish adds some spice and bite to the dish. Believe me, this dish will cure you of your kidney anxiety.

**1 whole veal kidney, about 1 pound, cleaned (see page 53)**
**Sea salt and freshly ground black pepper**
**2 tablespoons tallow**
**3 tablespoons unsalted butter**
**2 cloves garlic, crushed**
**1 rosemary branch**
**1 serrano chile, split lengthwise**
**1 teaspoon red wine vinegar**
**1 tablespoon blackstrap molasses**
**2 cups Roasted Chicken Stock (page 282)**
**12 French breakfast radishes, with greens still attached**
**¼ cup tarragon leaves, stems reserved**
**4 red globe radishes, with greens still attached, blanched**
**½ bunch watercress, thick stems removed**
**Zinfandel Vinaigrette (page 272), to taste**
**Freshly grated horseradish, as much as you want, for serving**

**1.** Season the kidney with salt and black pepper, and let sit at room temperature for 5 minutes. Heat a sauté pan over medium heat. Add the tallow and 1 tablespoon of butter to the pan, then the kidney, garlic, rosemary, and chile. Continuously baste the kidney. Once the kidney has a nice color, about 4 minutes, flip and repeat on the other side for about another 4 minutes. Using a cake tester, make sure the kidney is warm throughout and a nice medium rare. Remove from the heat and let rest.

**2.** While the kidney is resting, dispose of the fat in the pan. Add 1 tablespoon of butter and let it brown, then deglaze with the vinegar and add the blackstrap molasses. Once simmering, add ¼ cup of the chicken stock, and cook until the sauce has a nice glaze consistency, about 3 minutes.

**3.** In another sauté pan over medium heat, add the final tablespoon of butter and the French breakfast radishes and their greens. Add the remaining chicken stock, salt to taste, and tarragon stems, and simmer until tender, about 5 minutes. Remove the tarragon stems and add half of the tarragon leaves, then take the pan off the heat.

**4.** To plate the kidney, cut it into 4 pieces, then divide it between 2 plates, along with the braised radishes and a splash of their liquid. Lightly dress the kidneys with the molasses sauce. Shave the red globe radishes on a mandoline, chop their leaves, and add them to a mixing bowl with the watercress and remaining tarragon leaves. Dress the salad with vinaigrette and freshly grated horseradish, season to taste, add to the plate; serve.

# OYSTER & KIDNEY PIE

SERVES 4

Steak and kidney pie is a British essential. In this version, the briny oysters balance the rich meat. Made with an oyster stout beer, this isn't a fancy dish; it's meant to go alongside a pint of beer. Served family-style in the middle of table, it's convivial, marked by a protruding piece of bone marrow in place of a pie bird. Tuck in!

**1 beef marrow bone, 7 inches long, chimney cut**
**Salt and freshly ground black pepper**
**2 whole veal kidneys, 1 pound each, trimmed (see page 53)**
**2 tablespoons unsalted butter**
**2 thyme branches**
**1 clove garlic, crushed**
**2 bay leaves**
**12 pearl onions, peeled**
**1 cup stout beer (preferably oyster stout)**
**3 cups Veal Stock (page 281)**
**2 medium carrots, oblique cut**
**1 cup large-diced celery root**
**24 shucked oysters, juices reserved**
**1 Suet Crust (page 290)**
**1 cup crème fraîche**
**Freshly grated horseradish, to taste**
**¼ cup parsley leaves**
**¼ cup chervil leaves**
**¼ cup tarragon leaves**

**1.** Soak and refrigerate the marrow bone overnight in salted ice water to remove any blood. Before using, remove it from the water and let it come to room temperature. Season the top and bottom of the bone marrow with salt and pepper and set aside.

**2.** Preheat the oven to 400°F. Cut the kidneys into medium dice and season with salt and pepper. In a sauté pan over medium heat, add the butter, and when it bubbles, start to sear the kidneys. Add 1 thyme branch, the crushed garlic clove, and 1 bay leaf. Get a nice golden brown on both sides, cooking it for 4 minutes max, then remove the kidneys from the pan.

**3.** In a separate sauté pan over medium heat, add 1 tablespoon of butter and brown the pearl onions, about 5 minutes. Deglaze with the stout, then add the veal stock, lower the heat to a simmer, season to taste with salt and pepper, and cook until the onions are tender, about 8 minutes. Remove the onions to a sheet tray and set aside. Reserve the rest of the liquid for the pie.

**4.** In a pot, simmer the carrots and celery root in 1 cup of veal stock with a branch of thyme, bay leaf, and salt and pepper to taste until the vegetables are cooked to al dente, about 4 minutes, then remove them to the sheet tray with the onions to cool. Reserve the liquid for the pie, combining it with the onion braising liquid and the remaining 2 cups of veal stock.

**5.** To build the pie, add about ⅓ cup of the veal stock to a heavy braising pan or Dutch oven, then add the pieces of kidney and the vegetables, evenly layering the kidneys and vegetables. Then add the oysters and their juices, and pour in the veal stock mixture. Make sure the pie is filled to at least 1 inch below the rim of the pan.

**6.** Stand the marrow bone up in the center. This will act as the vent for the pie. Roll out the crust to a ¼-inch thickness, then cut out the center for the bone and stick it through. Be sure the dough drapes over the pot, so that when it bakes it won't peel off and slide into the pie.

**7.** Because all the ingredients are warm or at room temp, all you have to do is cook the pie until the crust is baked, the marrow has melted, and the inside is hot; use a cake tester to check. This should take 20 to 30 minutes.

**8.** To serve, place the pan on the table and give each guest a bowl filled with a dollop of crème fraîche, grated horseradish, and mixed herbs. Put some pie in each bowl and mix it all up to eat.

❤ **268 likes**

**offalchris** Kidney & Oyster Pie, Bone marrow Chimney, watercress, herbs, horseradish

# "VITELLO TONNATO" OF MARROW BONES & TUNA HEART

SERVES 4

On the Egadi Islands, during the ancient Sicilian ritual of *mattanza*, tuna are harvested by being led through a series of nets called *isola*, which become smaller and smaller until the tuna arrive at the *camera della morte*, which is a nice-sounding translation of "chamber of death." It's bloody and intense, but also respectful of these animals: every part of the tuna is used, from the flesh to the bones to the heart. This recipe draws from that tradition and plays on a tuna dish from the northern side of Italy: *vitello tonnato*, a pounded veal cutlet topped with tuna mayo. Here, we use nontraditional cuts—but it's still reminiscent of the dish at its core.

**8 beef marrow bones, about 6 inches long, canoe cut (lengthwise)**
**Sea salt and freshly ground black pepper**
**Extra-virgin olive oil, for drizzling**
**⅔ cup flat-leaf parsley leaves**
**⅔ cup mint leaves**
**⅔ cup chervil leaves**
**⅓ cup chive batons**
**Grated zest and juice of 1 lemon**
**Cured tuna heart (see Note), to taste**
**12 pieces grilled bread, ½-inch-thick slices**

**1.** Soak the marrow bones in salted ice water for 24 hours, changing the water multiple times to remove the blood from the bones.

**2.** When you're ready to cook the marrow bones, let them come to room temperature for about 15 minutes. Season with salt and black pepper, then drizzle with olive oil.

**3.** Preheat the oven to 450°F. Place the bones, marrow-side up, on a sheet tray, and roast until soft and warm throughout, about 8 minutes. Remove from the oven and place on a platter. Top the bones with the herbs and the lemon zest and juice. Grate the tuna heart all over the herbs and bones—and don't be cheap, give them a lot! Drizzle the hot bone-marrow fat from the pan over the herbs on top of the bones. This will release the aroma from the herbs and the tuna heart.

**4.** Serve with grilled bread.

**NOTE:** Fresh tuna heart is very hard to find for home-curing, so I recommend buying cured tuna hearts online from FrescaItalia.com or another quality Italian importer. It's wonderful for grating on pasta or other dishes to give them an intense, bottarga-like flavor, with a huge punch of minerality and slight salinity.

# NERVETTI: BEEF TENDONS & BEANS

## SUMMER AND WINTER VERSIONS

SERVES 4

This is a pair of recipes that show how versatile a tendon can be, from a cold, snappy salad with fresh pole beans, to a hot and creamy dish, reminiscent of cassoulet.

**FOR THE TENDONS:**

**3 whole beef tendons (Achilles), about 1½ pounds**
**1 medium carrot**
**1 medium yellow onion**
**1 head garlic, split to expose the cloves**
**2 stalks celery**
**1 bulb fennel, top removed**
**1 cup white wine**
**1 red Fresno chile, split lengthwise**
**2 fresh bay leaves**
**½ bunch fresh thyme**
**2 tablespoons kosher salt**

**1.** Place the tendons in a large pot of water and bring to a boil. Boil for a few minutes to remove the blood and other impurities. Remove the tendons and rinse with cold water.

**2.** Lay a wire rack in the bottom of a clean large pot, and add the carrot, onion, garlic, celery, and fennel. Arrange the tendons on top of the vegetables. Add the white wine, chile, bay leaves, thyme, salt, and water to cover. Place a plate directly on top of the tendons to keep them submerged. Bring the pot to a boil, turn it down to simmer over low heat, and cook until the tendons are tender, occasionally turning the tendons and skimming any scum or fat that accumulates on the surface, 3 to 4 hours.

**3.** To test for tenderness, squeeze the tendons between your fingers; if they glide through, they are ready.

**4.** Remove the tendons from the braising liquid and place them in a clean pan. Strain the braising liquid over the tendons and cool overnight before proceeding with one of the following bean recipes.

### SUMMER BEANS & NERVETTI SALAD

SERVES 4

**1½ cups dried cannellini beans**
**Sea salt**
**1 medium yellow onion**
**1 stalk celery, halved crosswise**
**1 medium carrot**
**Freshly ground black pepper**
**3 tablespoons extra-virgin olive oil**
**1 pound mixed pole beans, such as Romano and yellow wax beans, trimmed**
**8 red radishes, trimmed and cut into ¼-inch-thick slices**
**1 red onion, thinly sliced into rings**
**Zinfandel Vinaigrette (page 272), to taste**
**⅓ cup small basil leaves, preferably Piccolo Fino Verde, bubblegum basil, or Thai basil**
**Cooked tendons (recipe above)**

**1.** Pick over the dried beans, discarding any stones or misshapen beans. Rinse the beans under cold running water, transfer to a large pot, add 1 tablespoon of salt and water to cover by 2 inches, and let stand covered for at least 4 hours at room temperature or refrigerated overnight.

*(continued)*

**2.** Drain the beans and return them to the pot. Add the yellow onion, celery, carrot, and water to cover by 2 inches. Bring to a simmer over medium heat, and cook until tender, about 2 hours. The exact timing will depend on the age of the beans.

**3.** Remove the pot from the heat and let the beans cool in the cooking liquid. Remove and discard the onion, celery, and carrot. Season the beans with salt and pepper and a big splash of olive oil. Cover and refrigerate overnight before serving.

**4.** Prepare a large bowl of salted ice water. Bring a large saucepan three-quarters full of well-salted water to a boil over high heat. Add the pole beans and cook until tender-crisp, about 2 minutes. Drain immediately and immerse in the ice water to cool completely. Drain and pat dry.

**5.** Drain the cannellini beans well, transfer to a large bowl, and add the pole beans, radishes, and red onion. Drizzle with the vinaigrette, season with salt and pepper, and toss to mix. Sprinkle in the basil and taste, adjusting the seasoning if needed.

**6.** Slice the tendons on a meat slicer, ribbon thin. Add the sliced tendons to the beans and mix gently. Adjust final seasoning and serve.

## WINTER HOT TENDON AND CANNELLINI BEANS

SERVES 4 TO 8

**1 pound dried cannellini beans**
**Sea salt**
**1 medium carrot**
**1 bulb fennel, halved**
**1 medium yellow onion, whole**
**1 head garlic, split in half to expose the cloves, plus 2 tablespoons sliced garlic**
**1 bunch sage, stems and leaves separated**
**1 fresh bay leaf**
**3 tablespoons extra-virgin olive oil, plus more to finish**
**1 large yellow onion, diced**
**Zest of 1 lemon zest, or to taste**
**Freshly cracked black pepper**
**Cooked tendons (see page 117)**
**2 cups reserved tendon cooking liquid (see page 117)**
**4 to 8 slices bread, 1 inch thick, grilled**

**1.** Sort through the beans, and remove any stones or misshapen beans. Rinse the beans under cold running water. Place the beans in a large pot, cover with cold water by 2 inches, and add 1 tablespoon of sea salt. Let soak for at least 4 hours or overnight, covered, in the fridge.

**2.** Drain the beans and return them to the pot. Add 4 quarts water, the carrot, fennel, whole onion, garlic, sage stems, and bay leaf. Bring to a simmer over medium heat, and simmer the beans for 1 hour. Reduce the heat so that the beans are barely simmering, and cook until the beans are just tender, an additional 1 to 2 hours. Note that the fresher the beans, the shorter the cooking time. Remove the pot from the heat and let the beans cool in the cooking liquid.

**3.** Drain the beans, reserving the cooking liquid. Remove the whole vegetables, reserving all but the carrot, and place them with some cooking liquid in a blender; squeeze in the split head of garlic. Add 1 tablespoon olive oil and blend until smooth and thick, thinning with cooking liquid if necessary, then pass through a strainer to remove any fibers. Pour this over the beans and season with salt.

**4.** Slice the tendons ¼ inch thick, so when they cook they get nice, soft, and gelatinous.

**5.** In a large, heavy-bottomed saucepan over medium heat, add 2 tablespoons olive oil, sweat the diced onion until translucent, about 7 minutes, and then sizzle the sliced garlic until aromatic, about 2 minutes more. Add the sage leaves and fry them for 1 minute. Be sure not to brown them. Add the beans and ½ cup of their cooking liquid, or more as needed, and let the mixture slowly come to a simmer; add the beef tendons. Stir gently. Watch the beans naturally thicken from the luscious tendon gelatin. If needed, add a bit of tendon cooking liquid to loosen it to the consistency of baked beans. Add a splash of olive oil, grated lemon zest, and season with salt and pepper to taste.

**6.** To serve, place a piece of grilled bread in each warm bowl. Ladle the hot bean and tendon mixture over the bread. Finish it with a drizzle of olive oil and freshly cracked black pepper. Serve immediately.

# MARINATED BEEF TENDONS, CHILE, PISTACHIOS & MINT

SERVES 8

Based on a traditional Sichuan dish, this recipe is a perfect balance of *ma la* ("numbing spicy") with a California twist. Pistachios add crunch to contrast with the chew of the tendon, and loads of scallions and mint are flurried on top.

**4 beef tendons (Achilles), about 2 pounds**
**1 medium carrot**
**1 medium yellow onion**
**2 stalks celery**
**1 head garlic, split to expose the cloves**
**1 small leek, white and light green parts only**
**1 bulb fennel, top removed**
**Sea salt and coarsely ground black pepper**
**1 serrano chile, split in half**
**Peel of 1 lemon**
**1 cup Chile Oil (recipe follows)**
**3 tablespoons chopped pistachios, toasted**
**1 bunch scallions, sliced**
**¼ cup mint leaves**

**1.** Marinate the tendons overnight in the fridge with the carrot, onion, celery, split garlic, leek, fennel, and salt and pepper. Place a wire rack in the bottom of a large pot, add the vegetables and then the tendons, and cover with water. Place a plate on the tendons to keep them submerged, if necessary. Bring the pot to a boil, then turn it down to a simmer. Once simmering, skim any impurities off the top, and cook until the tendons are tender, 2 to 3 hours. Transfer the tendons to a container, cover, and refrigerate overnight before using. Reserve the liquid; it's a great stock.

**2.** The next day, place the beef tendons in the freezer until firm but not rock hard. Slice the tendons lengthwise on a meat slicer or with a very sharp knife, ⅛ inch thick. Lay the slices in a shallow nonreactive pan and season with salt and black pepper. Add the chile oil, cover, and marinate overnight in the fridge.

**3.** To serve the tendons, remove them from the chile oil and toss with the pistachios, scallions, mint, and coarse black pepper to taste.

## CHILE OIL

MAKES 1 CUP

**¼ pound dried chiles, preferably Sichuan**
**2 teaspoons black peppercorns**
**1 tablespoon coriander seeds, toasted**
**1 tablespoon fennel seeds, toasted**
**1 cup olive oil**
**1-inch cinnamon stick**
**2 star anise pods**
**1-inch-piece of ginger, sliced**

**1.** Add the dried chiles and peppercorns to a sauté pan over medium-low heat. Sauté until the chiles become crispy on the surface, about 4 minutes, then transfer the mixture to a food processor and grind it into a powder. In a large bowl, mix the chile powder with the coriander and fennel seeds.

**2.** Place the olive oil in a saucepan over low heat. Add the cinnamon stick, star anise, and ginger slices. Cook until you can see the waves on the surface of the oil. Take out the ingredients, leaving only the oil in the pot.

**3.** Pour the hot oil carefully into the bowl with chile powder and seeds. Cool.

**4.** Filter the oil through a coffee filter. Oil can be kept in a cool place up to a month.

# BRAISED OXTAIL, SAVOY CABBAGE, CHANTERELLES & PUFFED TENDONS

SERVES 2

A whole braised oxtail is quite the sight. Tail meat is constantly worked, swatting flies and such, and it's an inner muscle with a lot of rich connective tissue. It's often ragù-ed, shredded, and served with pasta. Here, you get to take it straight off the bone, which lets it retain all of its moisture. You'll want to pick off every last bit of meat. Because it's got so much connective tissue and fat, it needs something to go with it that's not heavy or burdensome, like a salad.

**FOR THE OXTAIL:**

**1 whole oxtail, about 5 pounds, tip removed and saved**
**Sea salt and freshly ground black pepper**
**1 medium yellow onion, julienned**
**1 bulb fennel, julienned**
**2 large carrots, cut into 3-inch lengths**
**3 stalks celery, roughly chopped**
**6 large cloves garlic**
**1 bottle (750 milliliters) dry red wine**
**Extra-virgin olive oil**
**½ gallon Roasted Chicken Stock (page 282)**
**5 sprigs parsley**
**2 branches rosemary**
**1 bunch thyme**
**2 bay leaves**

**FOR THE SLAW:**

**½ head savoy cabbage (about ½ pound)**
**½ pound chanterelle mushrooms, brushed clean**
**3 tablespoons chopped flat-leaf parsley leaves**
**3 tablespoons chive batons**
**4 tablespoons extra-virgin olive oil**
**2 shallots, sliced paper thin**
**Sea salt**
**1 tablespoon whole-grain mustard**
**1 teaspoon Dijon mustard**
**2 tablespoons champagne vinegar**
**Freshly ground black pepper**

**FOR THE BEEF TENDON PUFFS:**

**1 beef tendon, about ½ pound, cooked (see page 66)**
**Neutral oil, for deep-frying**
**Salt**

**TO COOK THE OXTAIL:**

**1.** Season the oxtail with salt and pepper and put it in a nonreactive container with the onion, fennel, carrots, celery, garlic, and red wine. Cover and refrigerate overnight or for at least 4 hours.

**2.** Remove the oxtail from the marinade and pat it dry, then separate the vegetables from the wine, reserving both.

**3.** Heat a large, heavy soup pot with a lid or a Dutch oven over medium-high heat. Add the oil to slick the pot and then add the oxtail. Sear, turning occasionally, until the meat is uniformly golden brown all over, 10 to 15 minutes. Transfer the oxtail to a plate. Add the reserved vegetables to the pan and cook over medium heat, stirring, until lightly caramelized, about 15 minutes.

*(continued)*

**4.** Preheat the oven to 300°F. Add the reserved wine to the pot and reduce by half, then add the stock. Bring the mixture to a boil, then remove the vegetables. Blend the vegetables with a little bit of stock in a blender, then return them to the pot to create a rich sauce to braise the oxtail in.

**5.** Tie the parsley sprigs, rosemary, thyme, and bay leaves with kitchen twine and drop the bundle into the pot. Return the oxtail to the pot and bring to a simmer. Cover the pot and transfer it to the oven. Cook until the meat is very tender but not yet falling off the bone, about 4 hours.

**6.** Let the oxtail cool in the cooking liquid. The dish will be improved if you let it sit overnight.

**MAKE THE SLAW:**

**1.** Remove the core from the cabbage and then cut the leaves crosswise into thin shreds. Using a paring knife, very lightly scrape the mushroom stems to remove just the outer golden, dirty layer, and then trim off the ends. Cut any larger mushrooms in half.

**2.** In a large bowl, combine the cabbage, parsley, and chives, and toss to combine.

**3.** In a saucepan over medium heat, warm 1 tablespoon of the olive oil. Add the mushrooms and cook, tossing occasionally, until slightly tender and golden, about 4 minutes. Add the shallots and season them lightly with salt (this helps extract some of the flavor), and continue to cook, tossing, until the shallots wilt and the mushrooms are tender, about 4 more minutes. Pour the mushrooms and shallots into the bowl with the cabbage and toss well.

**4.** In a small sauté pan, stir together the mustards and vinegar. Place the pan over medium heat and warm, stirring constantly, for about 1 minute. Add the remaining 3 tablespoons of extra-virgin olive oil and swirl the pan until the ingredients are emulsified. Immediately pour the contents of the pan over the cabbage mixture and toss well. Season to taste with salt and pepper.

**MAKE THE TENDON PUFFS:**

**1.** Slice the tendon with a sharp knife or on the meat slicer as thin as prosciutto, then place it in a food dehydrator at 185°F, or in an oven with the fan and the pilot light on, for 8 hours. Preheat a deep fryer or a pot with several inches of oil to 375°F, and fry a few tendon pieces at a time until they puff. Remove, drain on paper towels, and season with salt.

**SERVE:**

**1.** Reheat the oxtail in a 350°F oven with a few generous splashes of its liquid to keep it moist, basting it occasionally with more juices, until it is hot all the way through, about 45 minutes. Place the whole tail on a platter, and dress with the reduced braising liquid. Place the savoy cabbage slaw next to it, and top with the puffed tendons.

# OXTAIL & SKATE

SERVES 4

As a young cook at Kinkead's, I was surprised by a pairing of skate and oxtail. It's a classic surf and turf, but with some tweaks. The beef is in the form of a ragù, served with skate, which used to be used as the bait to catch lobster, the traditional "surf" in a surf and turf. Here, we go family-style, as if eating with all of your boatmates post-catch.

**3 pounds skate wing, bone in, skin off**
**Sea salt and freshly ground black pepper**
**2 tablespoons extra-virgin olive oil**
**4 tablespoons unsalted butter**
**2 cloves garlic, unpeeled and crushed, plus 2 tablespoons sliced**
**½ bunch thyme, leaves picked, stems reserved**
**¼ cup small diced shallots**
**1 pound savory or Manila clams, cleaned (see page 138)**
**¼ cup red wine**
**1½ cups picked oxtail meat (see Note)**
**2 cups oxtail braising liquid (see Note)**
**¼ cup tarragon leaves**
**¼ cup flat-leaf parsley leaves**
**Lemon juice, to taste**
**1 tablespoon finishing olive oil**

**NOTE:** Prepare an oxtail, either whole or in segments, as on page 68, picking the meat off the bone and reserving the cooking liquid.

**1.** Preheat the oven to 350°F. Pat the skate wings dry and season on both sides with salt and pepper. In a large ovenproof sauté pan over medium-high heat, heat the olive oil until very hot, then sear the skate. Add 2 tablespoons of butter and baste the fish. As the butter browns, add the crushed garlic and thyme stems, and baste some more. Flip the skate over, and place the pan in the oven. Roast until the skate is just cooked, about 8 minutes, then place it on a large platter and keep it warm.

**2.** In a separate pan on the stove, add the remaining 2 tablespoons of butter, the shallots, sliced garlic, and clams. Cook until the aroma of the shallots and garlic blooms, then add the thyme leaves and deglaze with the red wine. Once the red wine reduces by half and the clams are open, add the oxtail meat and braising liquid. Let the mixture simmer for a few minutes so the flavors come together, then add half of the tarragon and parsley leaves. Adjust the flavor with lemon juice. Cover the center of the skate wing with the clam and oxtail ragù.

**3.** To serve, drizzle with the finishing olive oil and top with the rest of the parsley and tarragon leaves.

# MILK-BRAISED COW'S UDDER & SPICY BROCCOLI RABE

SERVES 6

You may have heard of milk-braised pork shoulder (*maiale al latte*). Well, this is teat in milk. The mammary gland is very fatty and renders almost like belly bacon. When using whole milk in the braise, the whey evaporates, and there's a curdling effect, like a self-made cheese sauce.

**1 cow's udder, about 2 pounds, cleaned (see page 69)**
**¼ cup Spice Rub (page 271)**
**Sea salt**
**1 cup white wine**
**1 branch rosemary**
**3 cloves garlic, plus 2 tablespoons sliced**
**Peel of 3 lemons**
**3 large sage leaves**
**2 quarts whole milk**
**1 jalapeño, split**
**Freshly ground black pepper**
**3 tablespoons extra-virgin olive oil**
**1 bunch broccoli rabe, about 1 pound**
**Red chile flakes, to taste**
**2 tablespoons lemon juice**

**1.** Season the cow's udder with the spice rub and salt, and marinate it in the white wine, covered, overnight in the fridge. The next day, drain and pat it dry.

**2.** Preheat the oven to 325°F. In a sauté pan or rondeau over medium heat, sear the cow's udder until golden brown on all sides, about 5 minutes; the udder will render its own fat. Place the udder in a nonreactive pan with the rosemary, 3 cloves garlic, the lemon peel, and the sage. Cover with the milk, add the jalapeño, and place the pan in the oven. Braise until tender, about 2½ hours. Remove from the oven, cool, and refrigerate overnight in the milk, covered.

**3.** Preheat the oven to 350°F. Remove the udder from the braising milk (reserving the milk for later), pat dry, and slice it into 6 portions. Season with salt and black pepper. Slick an ovenproof sauté pan over high heat with 2 tablespoons of the olive oil and sear the udder until golden brown, about 3 minutes. Flip it over and place in the oven for 5 minutes, or until it's hot and fully rendered. Warm 1½ cups of the reserved braising milk.

**4.** Blanch the broccoli rabe in salted boiling water until al dente, about 4 minutes. Cut the stems into thin rings and leave the nice florets whole. In a sauté pan over high heat, add the remaining 1 tablespoon of olive oil. Sauté the stems and florets with the sliced garlic and chile flakes. Season with salt and black pepper, and adjust with the lemon juice.

**5.** To serve, remove the seared cow's udder and place it on a plate. Cover with ¼ cup of the warmed braising liquid, then add the broccoli rabe on top. Serve immediately.

# JEWISH BLT

SERVES 1; MAKES 2 POUNDS UDDER BACON

I feel bad for a whole sect of people with religious or dietary restrictions that deprive them of eating of the world's most perfect sandwiches: the BLT. This is a play on the BLT that non-pork eaters can enjoy. Do I dare say, it's *udderly* delicious?!

**FOR THE UDDER BACON:**

**2 pounds cows' udders, cleaned (see page 69)**
**3 fresh bay leaves**
**½ cup sea salt**
**5 grams pink curing salt, such as Instacure #1**
**2 tablespoons freshly ground black pepper**
**2 teaspoons red chile flakes**
**¼ cup dark brown sugar, packed**

**FOR THE BLT:**

**2 ½-inch-thick slices sourdough bread**
**1 tablespoon Basic Aioli (page 274)**
**2 leaves Little Gem or butter lettuce**
**2 thick slices heirloom tomato**
**Sea salt and freshly ground black pepper**
**4 slices Udder Bacon**

**Equipment: Smoker or perforated pan, wood chips of your choice**

**MAKE THE UDDER BACON:**

**1.** Rinse the udder under cold water, then pat dry. Set aside.

**2.** Bruise the bay leaves with the back of a knife to release the natural oils. Mix with the salts, black pepper, chile flakes, and brown sugar. Season the udders well, rubbing them all over with the salt mixture. Place the udders in a nonreactive pan, cover, and refrigerate for 7 days, flipping them over every 2 days, until they are firm.

**3.** Once the udders are cured, remove the pan from the fridge, rinse the udders with water, and pat them dry. Set the udders on a pan of ice, and cold smoke (see page 175) for 3 hours, replacing the ice when it melts so as not to soak the udder. (If the smoker is cool enough, the ice is not necessary.) Once the bacon is smoked, store it in the refrigerator until you're ready to use it.

**4.** Cook the udder bacon as you would any other bacon, either on the stove or in the oven, but don't cook it too brown; you'll still want a little chew.

**MAKE THE BLTS:**

Toast the bread and spread aioli on one side of each slice. Start layering the sandwich: lettuce first, tomatoes next, season with salt and pepper, then add the udder bacon and top with the other slice of bread, as you do with sandwiches.

PORK

STOMACH
SPLEEN
KIDNEY
RECTUM
BRAIN
TONGUE
HEART
LIVER
SMALL
INTESTINE
LARGE
INTESTINE

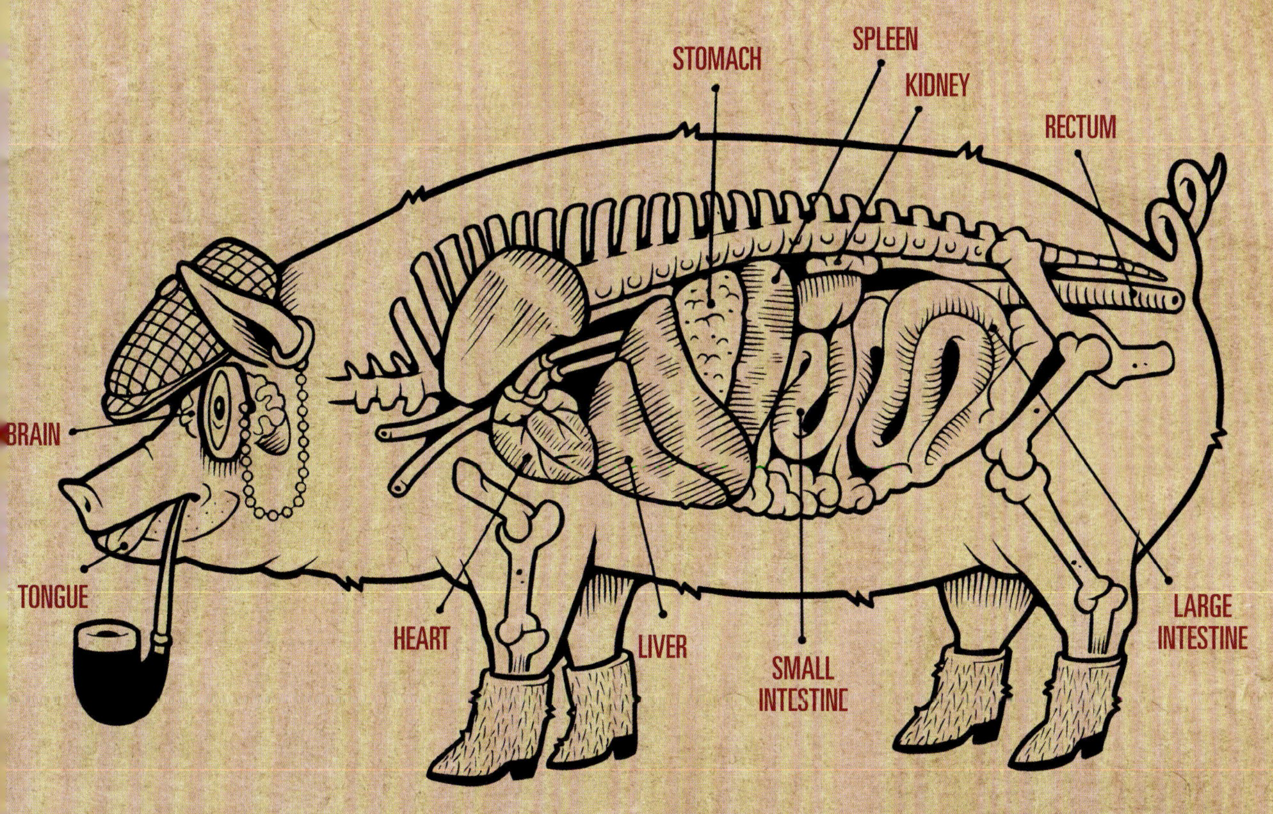

# PIG

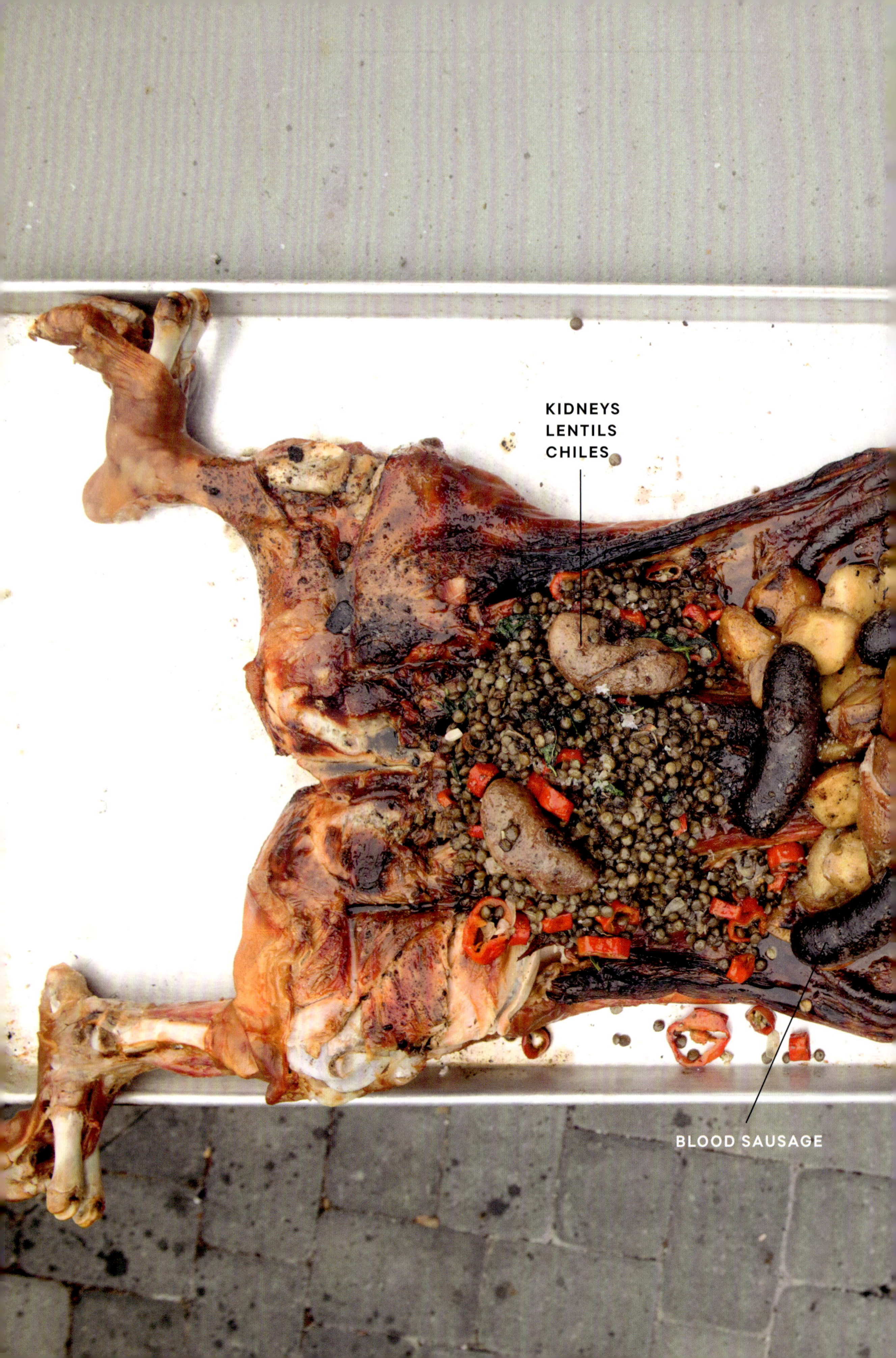
KIDNEYS
LENTILS
CHILES
BLOOD SAUSAGE

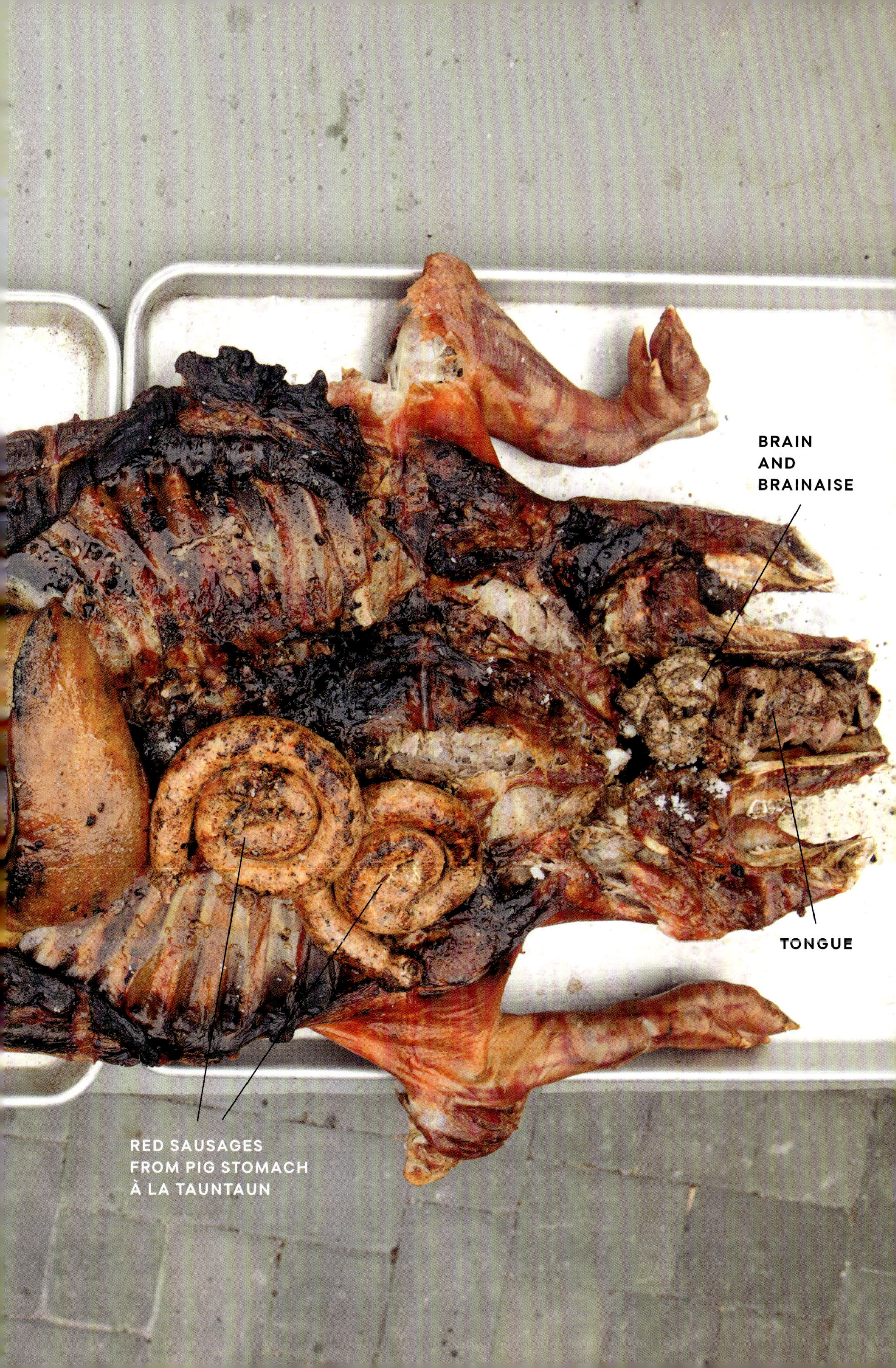
BRAIN
AND
BRAINAISE
TONGUE
RED SAUSAGES
FROM PIG STOMACH
À LA TAUNTAUN

# PIG SKIN SPAGHETTI TWO WAYS

SERVES 12 (EXTRA SPAGHETTI FREEZES WELL)

The night before cooking a Head to Tail dinner in Montreal with my friend chef Derek Dammann, I found myself dining at the epic Joe Beef. It's a legendary bistro in the Little Burgundy district, owned and operated by Fréderic Morin and Dave McMillan. Dave, a mountain of a man, walked up to the table, stared me down, and said, "I hear you're an Italian chef," dropping a bowl in front of me that I thought was simply spaghetti. It was a perfectly cooked gluten-free pasta, albeit richer, with a glisten. I almost wept when I realized it was pig skin—and that I had never thought of this process before. Their version is hand-cut and cooked with marinara. I use a pasta machine to portion mine and have served it a few different ways. Here are two of my favorites: as puttanesca, which I call Porca Puttana, as well as with white wine and small clams, a riff on a classic New England dish of my childhood.

**1 bulb fennel, top removed, quartered**
**1 large onion, quartered**
**2 stalks celery, quartered**
**1 head garlic, split to expose the cloves**
**2 pounds pig skin**
**½ cup white wine**
**½ cup kosher salt**
**¼ cup freshly ground black pepper**
**1 bunch thyme**
**2 fresh bay leaves**
**1 teaspoon whole black peppercorns**
**1 teaspoon fennel seeds**
**1 teaspoon coriander seeds**

**Equipment: Pasta machine / cutter**

**1.** Place the fennel, onion, celery, and garlic in a nonreactive container that will also accommodate the pig skin.

**2.** Season the skin by first rubbing it with the white wine, then the salt and black pepper. Place it in the container with the fennel, onion, celery, and garlic, cover, and marinate for 24 hours in the refrigerator.

**3.** Place the thyme, bay leaves, whole peppercorns, fennel seeds, and coriander seeds in a sachet of cheesecloth and tie it tightly with twine.

**4.** Place a rack on the bottom of a large, heavy-bottomed pot, then layer in the vegetables and the skin. Cover everything with water and weigh down the skin with a plate or bowl filled with weights. Bring the water to a gentle simmer, skimming off any scum or foam that rises to the top, and cook for about 1 hour, or until the skin is soft enough that you can pinch through it, but not so overcooked that it tears when you pick it up; it should have a nice al dente feel.

**5.** Gently remove the skin, keeping it whole, and place it flat on parchment-lined sheet trays in a single layer. Cover the trays and refrigerate the skin until cool. Discard the vegetables.

**6.** Once the skin is cold, after about 2 hours, use a bench scraper to remove all the fat from the underside of the skin, then rinse the skin with hot water to remove any residue. Pat dry and cut the skin into widths that will fit a pasta roller.

*(continued)*

**7.** Set up a pasta machine and wrap the base in plastic so the only thing to clean afterward is the cutter. Using a tagliatelle cutter, roll the sheets through, only once, leading them a bit—they'll need help getting started—and pulling them through as they come out the other side. Once all of the skin is cut, wash the cutter and pasta machine, making sure they're dry before you put them away.

**8.** Divide the skin into 2½-ounce portions, since the pig skin can be very rich. If it's vacuum-packed or stored in heavy plastic ziplock bags with the air pushed out, it can keep in the freezer for a month. In the refrigerator, it can be stored for up to 4 days.

## PORCA PUTTANA

SERVES 4

**3 tablespoons extra-virgin olive oil, plus more for finishing**
**½ cup finely diced red onion**
**8 cloves garlic, pounded into a paste**
**2 tablespoons capers**
**4 salt-packed anchovy fillets**
**4 boquerones (pickled anchovies) fillets**
**Red chile flakes, to taste**
**Aleppo chile flakes, to taste**
**½ cup red wine**
**3 cups whole San Marzano tomatoes, chopped or milled**
**¼ cup San Remo or other green olives, whole, pitted**
**10 ounces Pig Skin Spaghetti (page 134)**
**Fish sauce, to taste, preferably Red Boat**
**Orange zest, to taste**
**1 teaspoon fresh oregano leaves**
**2 tablespoons fresh mint leaves**
**Freshly cracked black pepper, to taste**

**1.** In a large non-reactive sauté pan, heat the olive oil over medium-high heat, then add the red onion and garlic. Let sizzle until aromatic, about 1 minute. Add the capers and both anchovies, breaking them up with a spoon to bloom the flavor. Add both chile flakes, then deglaze the pan with the red wine before the chile flakes burn. Reduce the wine by three-fourths, then add the tomatoes, crushing them with a spoon if chopped, and let the mixture cook until it has reduced by just over a half.

**2.** Add the olives and pig skin spaghetti, adjusting the seasoning with fish sauce and orange zest to taste. Once warm throughout, finish the pasta with fresh-torn mint and oregano.

**3.** Divide the pasta among 4 bowls. Top with extra-virgin olive oil and cracked black pepper.

## CLAMS, GARLIC & WHITE WINE

SERVES 4

**2 teaspoons extra-virgin olive oil, plus more for finishing**
**2 tablespoons sliced garlic**
**2 tablespoons sliced green garlic**
**3 dozen Manila clams, cleaned (see box)**
**½ cup white wine**
**1 cup Rich Pork Stock (page 280)**
**10 ounces Pig Skin Spaghetti (page 134)**
**Lemon juice, to taste**
**1 cup flat-leaf parsley leaves, coarsely chopped**
**¼ cup garlic chives, chopped**
**Kosher salt**
**Grated lemon zest, for finishing**

*(continued)*

## CLEANING CLAMS

I use ground oatmeal to clean clams, as my grandmother Helen Easton did. Grind oatmeal in a spice grinder or a blender until fine. You'll need about 1 tablespoon of ground oatmeal per one dozen clams.

Wash the clams by putting them in a pan with well-salted ice water and shaking the pan back and forth; the ice and salt will scrub the shells of the clams clean. (This is an old fisherman's trick.) Drain the clams, and then submerge them in fresh water with the ground oatmeal and a teaspoon of salt. Let them soak for 15 to 30 minutes, agitating them every 5 minutes. This makes them spit out the sand as their bellies fill with the powdered oatmeal, and it will also make them a bit sweeter.

Rinse the clams of the oatmeal before use, and drain.

**1.** In a large sauté or braising pan over medium heat, warm the olive oil. When the oil is hot, add the garlic and green garlic, releasing their flavor. When the garlic is fragrant, after about 1 minute, add the clams and deglaze the pan with the white wine. Let the clams cook until they're open and the alcohol is cooked off, about 3 minutes; discard any stubborn clams that won't open. Add the pork stock and spaghetti. Let the sauce reduce a bit, a minute or two, and then adjust the seasoning with lemon juice. Add the parsley, garlic chives, and salt to taste.

**2.** Portion the spaghetti and clams among 4 bowls. Finish the dish with extra-virgin olive oil and lemon zest.

❤ **104 likes**

**offalchris** Cutting pig skin on the pasta machine makes it consistent

# CICCIOLI

SERVES 10 TO 16

A specialty of Emilia-Romagna, ciccioli is a gelatin-rich terrine made of a mixture of skin, sinew, tendon, and all the stuff that's too tough and chewy to eat without marinating and cooking for a long time. When it's warm, it's often fried or served with potatoes and beans, but it can also be made as a cold terrine, served sliced on bread.

I like it on bread, but I love it baked *into* bread. When seared, Ciccioli Brioche (page 140) is crispy and delicious, like French toast with built-in bacon. Use this bread to make your favorite egg sandwich. I prefer an over-easy egg, aged Cheddar and Gruyère cheeses, a nice ripe, juicy heirloom tomato, and some crunchy butter lettuce. If you go the French toast route, find yourself a nice dark maple syrup.

**1¼ pounds pork skin**
**Sea salt**
**½ tablespoon freshly ground black pepper, plus more as needed**
**¾ tablespoon toasted fennel seeds, ground**
**1 small onion**
**1 small bulb fennel**
**1 small carrot**
**1 stalk celery**
**1 bay leaf**
**1 tablespoon rosemary needles**
**2 cloves garlic, whole**
**¼ cup white wine**
**1¼ pounds pork trim, sinew, tendon, and gristle**
**1 pint warm lard, or as needed to cover**

**Equipment: 14 × 4 × 4-inch terrine mold (1½ quarts)**

**1.** Season the pork skin well with salt, the black pepper, and the fennel seed. Place it in a nonreactive container with the onion, fennel, carrot, and celery, which are left whole so they don't cook into nothing and cloud the meat with vegetable scraps. Add the bay leaf, rosemary, and garlic cloves, mix well, and add the wine. Cover and let marinate overnight in the refrigerator.

**2.** Preheat the oven to 250°F. In a large braising pan or Dutch oven, combine all of the vegetables. Layer the skin and pork trim on top, and cover all this with warm lard. Cover the pot with parchment paper and a lid, put it in the oven, and cook until the skin and meats are tender, about 2½ hours.

**3.** Spray the terrine mold with cooking spray, and line it with enough plastic wrap to fold back over the top. Strain the warm fat from the meat and reserve it for other uses. Remove all the vegetables, leaving the rosemary and garlic cloves in with the meat. Taste, and adjust the seasoning of the skin and meat with salt and black pepper. Place the skin and meat into the terrine molds. Don't add too much fat, as it will prevent the natural gelatin in the skin from binding the terrine together. Fold the plastic over the top of the mold, and press the meat with a heavy weight. Let cool for 2 hours at room temperature, then place in the fridge overnight.

# CICCIOLI BRIOCHE

MAKES 2 LARGE PULLMAN LOAVES

In my curing and baking recipes, where precision is important, I always work with measurements as weights (and, in some cases, only in grams).

**430 grams bread flour**
**313 grams whole eggs**
**23 grams fresh yeast**
**10 grams salt**
**43 grams sugar**
**230 grams unsalted butter, at room temperature**
**200 grams Ciccioli (page 139), shaved ¼ inch thin, then cut into 1-inch squares**
**Olive oil, to coat the bowl**

**Equipment: Two 13 x 4 x 4-inch Pullman loaf pans**

**1.** In a stand mixer fitted with a dough hook on low speed, combine the flour, eggs, yeast, salt, and sugar until fully incorporated. Scrape the sides of the bowl as necessary.

**2.** Turn the mixer up to medium and add the butter, a little bit at a time, giving the butter time to emulsify into the dough before the next addition. Add the ciccioli in small additions, again allowing time for it to incorporate.

**3.** Turn the mixer speed up to high and mix until the dough pulls away from the sides of the bowl and forms a tight ball around the hook. The dough should pass the so-called windowpane test, meaning you can stretch a piece of dough until it's translucent without ripping. (This means the gluten is well-formed, which will allow the bread to develop a nice crumb.)

**4.** Put the dough in a lightly oiled bowl, and wrap with a large plastic bag or cover with plastic wrap. Refrigerate overnight.

**5.** Remove the dough from the fridge, and let it sit at room temp for at least an hour, or until it nearly doubles in size. Form it into 2 loaves and place them in loaf pans, filling about half of the loaf pans. Cover the loaves with the plastic again, and proof for at least 2½ to 3 hours, or up to 5 hours, depending on the room temperature. The dough is ready when you can push it lightly with a finger and it barely springs back.

**6.** Preheat the oven to 350°F. Bake until the crust is deep golden brown and the loaf sounds hollow when tapped, 35 to 40 minutes; oven temperatures vary, so keep an eye on it. Remove the loaves from the oven and let them cool in the pans for 20 minutes, then turn them out onto a wire rack and cool completely before slicing.

# SWEET CRACKLINS "CHICHACHURROS"

SERVES 8

Who said cracklins had to be a savory snack? I've served them with smoked chocolate pudding (see page 171) and called it Pig in a Mud Bath. I like to dust cracklins with confectioners' sugar, cocoa powder, and ground fennel seeds, a flavor combination that reminds me of the pizza fritta (fried dough) my grandmother Rosalie used to make.

As with the savory version, the pre-fried skin may be stored at room temperature in an airtight container for weeks.

**2½ pounds pig skin**
**2 teaspoons sea salt**
**½ pound granulated sugar**
**4 fresh bay leaves, bruised**
**Peel of 2 whole lemons**
**Peel of 2 whole oranges**
**4 vanilla beans, scraped, seeds reserved for another use**
**¼ cup white wine**
**½ cup confectioners' sugar**
**2 tablespoons cocoa powder, for dusting**
**2 tablespoons fennel seeds, toasted and ground, for dusting**
**Neutral oil, like canola or rice bran oil, for frying**

**1.** Season the skin liberally on both sides with the salt and granulated sugar, then lay it in a deep pan. In a cheesecloth sachet, wrap the bay leaves, lemon and orange peels, and vanilla beans, being sure to tie it tightly, and place it in the pan. Let marinate, covered, overnight in the refrigerator.

**2.** Place a wire rack in the bottom of a large, heavy pot so the skin won't stick. Add the skin and enough water to cover. Add the white wine and the cheesecloth sachet and bring the water to a boil, then reduce the heat to a simmer. Cook until the skin is tender, about 2 hours. Check its doneness by tearing the skin by hand; it should have just the slightest bit of resistance.

**3.** Lay the skin out in a single layer on parchment-lined sheet trays to cool for 2 hours in the fridge, or until very firm. Using a bench scraper, remove all the fat from the bottom of the skin, and then cut the skin into strips about as long and as thick as a pencil. Dehydrate for 24 to 36 hours, either in a dehydrator or in an oven with just the pilot light on and the fan running, until dry and brittle. (At this point, the skin may be stored for weeks in an airtight container at room temperature, with a silica gel pack if available.)

**4.** Stir together the confectioners' sugar, cocoa powder, and ground fennel. Preheat a deep fryer or a large pot with several inches of oil to 375°F. Fry a few pieces of skin at a time, just until puffed. Be sure not to let them get golden brown, as pure white is what you're aiming for. Remove them from the oil and drain on paper towels. To finish, dust with the confectioners' sugar mixture.

# CRACKLINS CACIO E PEPE

SERVES 8

Cracklins, dried and puffed pig skin, are like the pork rinds you see in a bodega. You can find a range of ratios of fat to meat in these snacks, and sometimes, as here, it's just skin. In this recipe, we flavor them with cheese and pepper, like the Roman pasta dish cacio e pepe. It's a great snack, even better if you grate Pork Liver Bottarga (page 288) on top of it. The ultimate is making coronets (cones) of cracklins filled with pork liver mousse.

This recipe makes a generous quantity, but it scales up and down readily. It may make sense to prep a lot of it at once, as the cooked and dried skin can be kept for weeks in an airtight container at room temperature before frying.

**2½ pounds pig skin**
**Sea salt and freshly ground black pepper**
**1 large yellow onion**
**1 large carrot**
**1 stalk celery**
**1 bulb fennel**
**1 bay leaf**
**1 bunch thyme**
**1 teaspoon black peppercorns**
**1 teaspoon coriander seeds**
**1 teaspoon fennel seeds**
**½ cup white wine**
**Neutral oil, like canola or rice bran oil, for frying**
**Pecorino cheese, for shaving**
**Aleppo pepper, for dusting**
**Parsley chiffonade, for garnish**

**1.** Season the pig skin liberally on both sides with salt and black pepper. Lay it in a deep pan with the onion, carrot, celery, and fennel. In a cheesecloth sachet, wrap the herbs and spices, and add it to pan. Mix in the wine, cover, and let marinate overnight in the fridge.

**2.** Place a wire rack in the bottom of a large, heavy pot. Add the marinated vegetables, white wine, and skin, and salted water to cover generously. Bring it to a boil, reduce the heat to a simmer, and cook until the skin is very tender, about 2 hours. Check its doneness by seeing if the skin tears by hand, with just the slightest bit of resistance; we're actually trying to overcook it.

**3.** Lay the skin out flat in a single layer on parchment-lined sheet trays. Cover and refrigeratate for 4 hours, or until very firm. Using a bench scraper, remove all the fat from the bottom of the skin, and dehydrate the skin for up to 36 hours, either in a dehydrator or in an oven with just the pilot light on and the fan running, until dry and brittle. Break these into small, snack-size pieces. (At this point, the skin may be stored for weeks in an airtight container at room temperature, with a silica gel pack if available.)

**4.** Preheat a deep fryer or large pot with several inches of oil to 375°F. Fry just a few pieces of skin at a time; they should triple in size as they fry and look like puffy, white edible Styrofoam when cooked. Drain the skin in a large bowl lined with paper towels and season with salt. Let the skin rest for a few minutes; otherwise it will be chewy. Toss with shaved pecorino and black pepper to taste. Top with Aleppo pepper and parsley.

# WHOLE FRIED PIG'S HEAD, ENDIVE, CAPERS, PARSLEY & LEMON-ANCHOVY VINAIGRETTE

SERVES 8

There's no denying what you're presenting here: a whole fried pig's head is a statement on a table, but a delicious one, with so many different flavors and textures among the different muscles of the cheek, the jowls, and the bits in between. On average, pig heads weigh 25 pounds, so I split them in half; each side serves four people. You can ask your butcher to split the head lengthwise, but you will likely have to buy both sides of the head.

I like using rice bran oil for frying, as it doesn't mask the flavor and it won't burn as quickly as olive or vegetable oil. A nice bite of a bitter salad with white and red endive and bracingly sharp lemon-anchovy vinaigrette makes this both a visually striking plate and palate pleaser.

**1 pig's head, 20 to 25 pounds, split lengthwise (see Note)**
**2 gallons Ham Brine (page 284)**
**About 2½ gallons lard, or to cover**
**1 head garlic, split to expose the cloves**
**1 medium white onion, halved**
**1 bunch thyme**
**6 bay leaves**
**Rice bran oil or other neutral oil, for frying**
**Sea salt and freshly ground black pepper**
**6 heads of endive, red and white, whole leaves separated**
**2 tablespoons salted capers, rinsed**
**¼ cup flat-leaf parsley leaves**
**3 tablespoons Lemon-Anchovy Vinaigrette (page 273), or to taste**

**NOTE:** If splitting the head yourself, remove it from the fridge and bring it to room temperature before working with it. Saw the pig's head lengthwise, between the snout holes to the center of the skull. Remove the brain and reserve it for another recipe, storing it in an airtight container in the refrigerator for a day or two. Rinse the split head with water, washing off any bone dust or excess blood.

**1.** Place the two sides of the pig's head in the ham brine for 3 days in the refrigerator.

**2.** To confit the heads, preheat the oven to 225°F. Remove the head from the brine, discarding the brine, and dry the head with kitchen towels. Place each half in a large deep pan or Dutch oven, dividing the garlic, onion, thyme, and bay leaves between them. (You can cook the halves together if your pan is large enough.) Heat the lard just enough to liquefy, and cover the head halves with it. Bake until the meat and skin become very soft and tender, 4½ to 5 hours. Remove the pan from the oven, cover, and refrigerate overnight, keeping it in the lard.

**3.** To remove the pig's head from the lard, place the pans in a 300°F oven for about 10 minutes, just enough to loosen up the lard. Once the lard starts to melt, put on rubber gloves and pull the head halves from the pan, then place them on a wire rack over a sheet tray. Scrape the lard from the head halves and return the head halves to the pans; remove the large aromatics and strain the lard through a fine strainer. Keep the lard refrigerated in a covered container for another use.

**4.** Preheat a large, tall pot or deep fryer filled with oil to 375°F, making sure there is plenty of clearance, as the head halves will cause the oil level to rise a lot. Carefully lower a head half in slowly, until completely submerged, and fry over high heat until it is hot throughout and the skin is crispy and bubbled, 10 to 15 minutes. Check the temperature by inserting a cake tester in the thickest part of the jowl; the meat is ready when the tester comes out hot. Remove the head to a wire rack and season with salt and pepper. Repeat with the other half.

**5.** In a mixing bowl, toss together the endive, capers, and parsley. Season to taste with salt, pepper, and the lemon-anchovy vinaigrette.

**6.** Place the pig's head on a cutting board or large platter, and serve with the salad.

❤ **104 likes**

**offalchris** pigs head, Gilded snout, Brainaise, Chicories & lemon Anchovy Vinaigrette

# PIG'S HEAD & SNAILS

SERVES 6

When I was eating at Gramercy Tavern in New York City as a young cook, Tom Colicchio said to me, "What grows together, goes together." It was a powerful moment for me, as back then I thought I already knew it all, but that thought changed my cooking a lot. This dish takes that saying to another place. Pigs root around to find snails to eat, and snails munch on watercress, so why not serve the whole food chain in one dish?

**1 cup precooked canned Helix snails**
**2 cups Court Bouillon (page 280)**
**½ pig's head confit (see page 144)**
**Sea salt and freshly ground black pepper**
**3 tablespoons lard**
**2 tablespoons sliced garlic**
**2 cups Rich Pork Stock (page 280)**
**½ pound baby dandelion greens**
**1 cup whole shallots**
**3 tablespoons lemon juice**
**3 tablespoons extra-virgin olive oil**
**2 cups croutons**
**¼ cup chives, cut into 1-inch lengths**
**1 cup flat-leaf parsley leaves**
**2 tablespoons salted capers, rinsed**

**1.** Rinse and drain the snails. Place them in a saucepan with the court bouillon, and simmer them until tender, about 30 minutes. Remove the snails, and let cool.

**2.** Remove the meat and skin from the pig's head in large pieces, and cut into 2-inch cubes; don't worry if they aren't all perfectly square. Season the pig's head with salt and pepper. In a large sauté pan over high heat, melt the lard. When it's very hot but before it's smoking, sear the head pieces on all sides until they are golden brown. Remove all but 1 tablespoon of the lard from the pan and add the sliced garlic to bloom, about 30 seconds. Add the snails and pork stock; reduce the heat to a simmer and let the liquid reduce by half, about 7 minutes, until it's slightly viscous.

**3.** Place the baby dandelion greens in a large mixing or serving bowl. Using a mandoline, slice the shallots into very thin rings straight into the bowl. Add all the contents from the sauté pan to the bowl and toss with the lemon juice and olive oil. Toss the salad with the croutons, herbs, and capers and adjust the seasoning with sea salt and black pepper. Serve.

# WHOLE ROASTED JOWL, CLAMS & ESCAROLE

SERVES 4

Pork and seafood are magic together—just ask the Spanish and Portuguese, whose cuisines are filled with combinations of the two. Roasting the jowl at high heat allows the skin to bubble, so the outside becomes puffy like cracklins and the inside has a wonderful chew, like the clams. The whole dish bastes itself as it cooks in the oven, so all you have to do is wait.

**FOR THE JOWL:**

**1 whole pork jowl, from a large pig's head, about 5 pounds**
**Sea salt and freshly ground black pepper**
**1 red Fresno chile, cut in half**
**1 branch rosemary, needles only**
**1 bunch thyme**
**1 bay leaf**
**Peel of 1 lemon**

**FOR THE DISH:**

**Extra-virgin olive oil**
**1 cup sliced shallots**
**4 cloves garlic, crushed**
**2 dozen Manila clams, cleaned (see page 138)**
**1 bunch thyme, leaves only**
**½ cup white wine**
**3 cups Roasted Chicken Stock (page 282)**
**1 serrano chile, sliced thin**
**1 head escarole, washed and dried, cut into 4-inch pieces**
**Lemon juice, to taste**
**Fish sauce, to taste, preferably Red Boat**
**8 slices bread, grilled, for serving**

**1.** Season the jowl liberally with salt and black pepper, and place it in a Cryovac bag with the Fresno chile, rosemary, thyme, bay leaf, and lemon peel. Seal the bag, dip it in a pot of boiling water, then cook it in a water bath at 175°F (79.5°C) for 12 hours. Alternatively, you can place all the same ingredients in a braising pan and roast them, uncovered, in a 275°F oven for 3½ hours, or until the jowl is soft.

**2.** Cool the bag in an ice-water bath (for vacuum-packed jowl) or at room temperature (if roasted) until you can handle it with your hands. Open the bag over a pan, removing the jowl and reserving any liquid that comes out of the bag. Remove all the herbs from the jowl, and pat it dry.

**3.** Preheat the oven to 400°F. Heat a large, heavy braising pan or Dutch oven over medium heat; add enough olive oil to coat it lightly. Score the skin of the jowl, then place it in the pan, skin-side up. Put it in the oven and roast the jowl until hot throughout, 15 to 20 minutes. (A convection oven will help produce a crispy skin, but it will also speed up the process as a whole, so shave some time off accordingly if using one.) Remove the pan from the oven and place it back on the stovetop over medium heat. (If the jowl doesn't leave room in the pot for the clams and escarole, remove it to a cutting board.) Add the sliced shallots and crushed garlic to the pan, and let them sizzle and bloom. Add the clams and thyme, cook for 1 minute, then deglaze with the white wine. Cook until the wine is almost evaporated, then add the stock, serrano chile, and escarole. Cover, let the escarole wilt and the clams open, then season to taste with lemon juice and fish sauce.

**4.** Serve with grilled bread on the side.

# FOOT & MOUTH TERRINE

SERVES 4 TO 8

It seems like I'm putting my foot in my mouth by naming a pork dish after a cow disease, but even if the joke doesn't work for you, the terrine will. It's a mixture of head and foot meat inlaid with carrots. Serve it thinly sliced, cool but not cold, with mustard and bread for a rustic treat.

**1 small pig mask (see Note), minus ears and jowls, about 1½ pounds**
**2 pig's feet (aka trotters), fresh, not cured**
**1 gallon Ham Brine (page 284)**
**3 large carrots**
**2 large onions**
**2 fennel bulbs, tops removed**
**3 stalks celery**
**3 baby leeks, washed well**
**2 bay leaves**
**1 bunch thyme**
**1 bunch parsley stems**
**Sea salt and freshly ground black pepper**
**Grated zest of 1 lemon**
**3 tablespoons chopped tarragon**

**Equipment: 14 × 4 × 4-inch terrine mold (1½ quarts)**

**NOTE:** You can debone a pig's head yourself (see page 25) or ask your butcher to debone it for you as a mask. Be sure to take the bones, though, as they make for fantastic broth.

**1.** Place the pig mask and the trotters in the brine for 12 hours in the refrigerator, then drain.

**2.** Place a wire rack in the bottom of a large, heavy pot, then add the carrots, onions, celery, leeks, and a sachet filled with the bay, thyme, and parsley. Place the pig mask in the pot. Top it with the trotters and cover with water. Bring the liquid to a boil, skimming the scum. Reduce the heat to a simmer and cook until very tender, about 3 hours. Remove the pig mask and trotters and strain the liquid through a fine strainer. Keep the carrots, quartering them lengthwise.

**3.** Remove 2 cups of the braising liquid to a saucepan, and reduce it over medium heat, skimming any fat. When the liquid is silky and rich, strain it through a tea towel or cheesecloth. Taste, and if it's salty, don't season the terrine with salt.

**4.** Pick the trotters and place the meat and skin in a large mixing bowl. Add a little bit of the reduced cooking liquid, just enough to keep it moist. (If you press down on the meat and the stock pools at the top, you've added too much; pour off the extra.) This will be the natural "glue" for the terrine.

**5.** Cut the mask into bite-size pieces and combine with the trotter. Season the meat to taste with salt, black pepper, lemon zest, and tarragon.

**6.** Spray the terrine mold with cooking spray, and line it with plastic wrap. Start by putting a layer of meat on the bottom, add carrot pieces to create inlays, then add more meat and repeat layering. Finish with a top layer of meat, then fold over the plastic wrap and press the terrine with weights overnight in the refrigerator, making sure the meat sets firm enough to slice.

**7.** To serve, remove the terrine from the refrigerator and unmold. This terrine may be simply sliced and eaten slightly cool with grilled bread, mustard, and pickles. It's also great breaded and panfried.

# PICKLED PORK TONGUE GIARDINIERA

MAKES 4 QUARTS OF PICKLES

Giardiniera is a pickled vegetable condiment, an Italian American tradition found as a topping on Italian beef sandwiches in Chicago, among many other uses. It is also called *sotto aceto*, which literally means "under vinegar," and is a great way of preserving a farmer's bumper crops for year-round use. In this preparation, we take the same liquid for the pickling process and apply it to tongue, whose richness and texture take particularly well to pickling. It's served in a mason jar with the traditional giardiniera mix of vegetables punched up with spice and a fresh acidic taste.

**4 pig tongues, about 1¼ pounds each**
**Sea salt and freshly ground black pepper**
**¼ cup white wine**
**1 large yellow onion**
**1 large carrot**
**1 stalk celery**
**1 bulb fennel**
**1 bunch thyme**
**1 fresh bay leaf**
**4 carrots, oblique cut**
**1 head cauliflower, cut into small florets**
**12 pearl onions, blanched and cut in half lengthwise**
**3 stalks celery, cut into half-moons**
**12 baby Tokyo turnips, quartered, stems on**

**FOR THE PICKLING LIQUID:**

**½ bunch thyme**
**2 tablespoon toasted coriander seeds**
**1 tablespoon toasted fennel seeds**
**1 tablespoon toasted black peppercorns**
**1 quart cider vinegar**
**1 quart champagne vinegar**
**4½ tablespoons kosher salt**
**1⅓ cups sugar**
**1 dried Calabrian chile or red chile flakes to taste**
**12 fresh bay leaves**

**1.** Lightly season the pig tongues with salt and pepper, and combine them in a non-reactive pan with the wine, onion, whole carrot, celery, fennel, thyme, and bay leaf. Marinate, covered, overnight in the refrigerator.

**2.** The next day, place all the ingredients in a pot, add water to cover, and bring to a boil, skimming the scum. Turn the heat down and simmer gently until the tongues are tender with some chew, about 1 hour. Remove the tongues from the cooking liquid and peel the membrane off each tongue while it's still warm. (When it gets tough, use the back of a paring knife to scrape any stubborn parts.) Dip the tongue back in the hot cooking liquid to help this process. Rinse the tongue under water to remove any loose proteins and membrane. Discard the cooking liquid and aromatics.

**3.** Combine the thyme, coriander, fennel, and peppercorns in a cheesecloth sachet, and tie it tightly. In a stockpot, mix the vinegars with the kosher salt, sugar, chile, and bay leaf. Bring the vinegar solution to a simmer, add the sachet to bloom the flavors, and then turn off the heat. Remove the sachet after the liquid is cold.

**4.** Evenly divide the cut vegetables among 4 quart-size mason jars, adding 1 tongue per jar. Cover with the cold pickling liquid; be sure the tongue stays submerged. Marinate the jars in the refrigerator at least 6 days before serving; they will keep for a month.

# PIG'S EAR TERRINE, CHILE & FENNEL

SERVES 4 TO 6, WITH LEFTOVER TERRINE

Everything in this dish is sliced paper thin, from the terrine (on a meat slicer) to the fennel (on a mandoline), then tossed together, more like a salad than a charcuterie plate. It's light, bright, and has an array of textures, from chewy to crisp. The leftover terrine can be wrapped in plastic or vacuum-packed and refrigerated for up to a week.

**3 pounds pig ears, scrubbed and cleaned (see page 31)**
**1 gallon Hay Brine (page 284)**
**1 large yellow onion**
**2 large bulbs fennel, fronds picked and reserved for garnish**
**1 large carrot**
**1 head garlic, split to expose cloves**
**1 stalk celery**
**Sea salt and coarsely ground black pepper**
**1 teaspoon orange zest**
**1 tablespoon Aleppo chile flakes**
**1 small red onion**
**5 large Cara Cara oranges, supremed or sectioned**
**1 cup San Remo or other green olives, pitted but left intact**
**Zinfandel Vinaigrette (page 272)**

**Equipment: Brush, 14 × 4 × 4-inch terrine mold (1½ quarts)**

**1.** Combine the ears and brine in a nonreactive container, and place in the refrigerator, covered, for 2 days, making sure the ears are fully submerged.

**2.** Spray the terrine mold with cooking spray, then line with enough plastic wrap to fold over the top, and spray the interior of the wrapped mold.

**3.** Place a wire rack in the bottom of a large stockpot. Remove the ears from the brine and place them on top of the rack; cover with water. Set the pot over high heat, bring to a boil, then dump the water. Rinse the ears in cold water and refill the pot with fresh water. Add the onion, 1 bulb of fennel, the carrot, garlic, and celery, and place the ears on top. Bring to a boil, reduce to a simmer, and simmer until the ears are tender, about 2½ hours. While still hot, carefully remove the ears from the cooking liquid, making sure not to tear the skin. Lay them on a sheet tray and season with salt, black pepper, the orange zest, and the Aleppo chile.

**4.** Working quickly while they are still warm, layer the ears in the prepared terrine, pressing them in and making sure to fill all the gaps. Cut the ears to fit if necessary. Once the terrine mold is filled just over the top, cover it with the plastic wrap.

**5.** Place the terrine in the refrigerator overnight, pressing the meat down with weights and allowing the natural gelatin to set.

**6.** To serve, remove terrine from the mold and, using a meat slicer or a very sharp knife, slice it about three baseball cards thick on a meat slicer; cut about 6 slices per serving. With a mandoline and keeping the base intact, shave paper-thin lengthwise slices of the remaining fennel bulb into a mixing bowl. Shave the red onion, and add the orange supremes, cracked olives, and terrine slices. Season the salad with salt and coarse black pepper, dress with vinaigrette to taste, and toss well. Divide the salad among plates, forming mounds. Top with fennel fronds and sea salt.

# PIG NEWTONS

ABOUT 40 COOKIES

These are kind of a fuck-around with Fig Newtons. Pig ears are cooked in a sweet marinade and braised with lemon peel and vanilla beans, then mixed with figs until the filling turns into something that resembles a sticky, gooey date. It's an unlikely update on the childhood cookie.

**FOR THE COOKIE DOUGH:**

**1½ cups all-purpose flour, plus more for rolling**
**1 teaspoon baking powder**
**¼ teaspoon kosher salt**
**8 tablespoons (1 stick) unsalted butter, at room temperature**
**2 tablespoons lard**
**⅔ cup dark brown sugar, packed**
**1 large egg**
**1 vanilla bean**
**Zest of 1 orange**

**FOR THE FIG FILLING:**

**1 pound pig ears, scrubbed and cleaned** **(see page 31)**
**1 cup granulated sugar**
**1 good rasp of lemon peel**
**1 vanilla bean pod, split and scraped (from above)**
**1 teaspoon sea salt**
**1 pound dried figs, cut into small pieces**

**TO MAKE THE DOUGH:**

**1.** Whisk the flour, baking powder, and salt together in a mixing bowl, and set aside.

**2.** In a large bowl or the bowl of a stand mixer fixed with the paddle attachment, beat the butter, lard, and brown sugar until light and fluffy, about 3 to 5 minutes. Split the vanilla bean and scrape out the seeds, reserving the pod. Add the egg, vanilla seeds, and orange zest to the mixer bowl, and beat until combined. Incorporate the flour mixture into the butter mixture until well blended. Place the dough on a large piece of plastic wrap, shape into a disk, wrap, and refrigerate for at least 4 hours or overnight.

**MAKE THE FILLING:**

**1.** Place the ears in a pot, add water to cover, and bring to a boil. Dump the water, and rinse the ears in cold water. Place a wire rack in the pot to keep the ears from resting on the bottom. Return the ears to the pot with 1 gallon of water, sugar, lemon peel, vanilla, and salt, and slowly simmer until very tender, about 2 hours. Let the ears cool in the liquid, remove the ears from the water, and chop them into small pieces.

**2.** Combine the figs and ½ cup water in a medium saucepan over medium-high heat. Bring the water to a boil and cover. Allow the water to boil until the figs have absorbed all the water, about 10 minutes. Transfer the figs to a food processor and pulse until the mixture is completely smooth; let cool. Fold in the ears, mixing well.

**3.** Preheat the oven to 325°F. Place a large piece of parchment on your work surface and flour it liberally. Divide the chilled dough into 4 pieces, place one piece on the parchment, and return the other 3, wrapped in plastic, to the refrigerator.

**4.** Shape the piece of dough into a rectangle, then roll the dough into a long rectangle about 4 × 12 inches, stopping frequently to make sure it isn't sticking to the parchment. Be vigilant about lifting and re-flouring the dough as you roll to further prevent sticking.

**5.** Scoop the fig filling into a pastry bag, or a plastic ziplock bag with one corner cut off. Pipe the filling in a 1-inch strip down the center of the dough rectangle. Fold one side of the dough over the filling, then the other. Press down on the seam to close it. Using the parchment, flip the cookie roll over, seam-side down. Transfer it gingerly to a baking sheet and refrigerate while you repeat this step with the other 3 pieces of dough.

**6.** Bake the logs of dough until the dough is no longer tacky and has begun to brown around the edges, about 16 minutes. While the cookie logs are still warm, cut them into 1½ to 2-inch pieces. Immediately place the cookies in a single layer inside a plastic ziplock bag and close the bag. This seems counterintuitive, but in order to keep the cookies soft, like the real thing, they need to steam.

**7.** Cool the cookies completely on the counter while still in the bags, then remove them from the bags and place them in an airtight container. They can be kept at room temperature for up to 2 days.

# CRISPY PIG'S EARS

SERVES 6 TO 10

This is the french fry of offal, dusted with seasoned flour and served with Brainaise (yes, a brain-based mayonnaise). You can also use them on a salad instead of croutons. Or dress them with lime juice and chile. Crisp and rich, they are amazingly versatile.

**2½ pounds fresh pig ears, scrubbed and cleaned (see page 31)**
**½ gallon Hay Brine (page 284)**
**Rice bran oil or other neutral oil, for frying**
**3 cups Seasoned Flour (page 270)**
**Sea salt and freshly ground black pepper**
**Aleppo chile flakes, to taste**
**Brainaise (page 275), for serving**

**1.** Brine the ears in a large, nonreactive container overnight in the refrigerator.

**2.** Remove the ears from the brine, pat them very dry, and slice them lengthwise into julienne strips so they look like french fries. Place them in a non-reactive pot and cover with water. Bring to a boil, lower the heat to a simmer, and cook until tender, about 2 hours. Drain the ears, let them cool, and pat them dry with paper towels.

**3.** Preheat a deep fryer or a large pot with several inches of oil to 375°F. Dredge the julienned ears in seasoned flour, knocking off any excess. Deep-fry a handful at a time until crispy and golden brown, about 4 minutes. Transfer to a paper towel–lined bowl. Season with salt, black pepper, and Aleppo chile.

**4.** Serve with a side of Brainaise.

# "THREE LITTLE PIGGIES" PIG'S BRAIN & PORCINI ON TOAST

SERVES 4

*Porcini* literally translates into "little piggies." The brain's creamy richness pairs so well with the earthy nuttiness of these mushrooms, which is reinforced by brown butter. This is a delicate tartine, but if you want to blow it up, think "pigs root for truffles"—why not shave a load of truffles on top to make it *très soigné*?

**6 cups Court Bouillon (page 280)**
**Sea salt**
**2 whole pigs' brains, about 1 pound total**
**1 pound grade A small fresh porcini**
**4 ½-inch-thick slices crusty sourdough batard**
**Extra-virgin olive oil**
**Black pepper**
**3 tablespoons unsalted butter**
**1 bunch thyme**
**Pinch of nepitella leaves (or a mix of mint and oregano)**
**Lemon juice, to taste**
**1 tablespoon salted capers, rinsed**
**1 cup Roasted Chicken Stock (page 282)**
**2 tablespoons chopped flat-leaf parsley**
**Small handful of cress**
**2 large shallots, sliced into thin rings**

**1.** Bring the court bouillon to a boil in a large saucepan, then turn the heat down to a gentle simmer and season with salt. Lightly salt the brains, then poach them in the court bouillon until just cooked through, about 5 minutes. Remove the brains, place them on a plate, and cool in the refrigerator, about 20 minutes. Once cooled, carefully peel off any membrane, and if there are any blood spots, remove them with the tip of a paring knife.

**2.** Separate the brains into 2 lobes, reserving the cerebellum (the stem and 2 knobs at the back of the brain) for Brainaise (page 275).

**3.** Cut the porcini into quarters, reserving one to shave over the finished dish.

**4.** Season both sides of the batard slices with olive oil, salt, and pepper, then grill or toast them until golden and crisp. The key here is to not burn the bread; carbon shouldn't be part of the dish.

**5.** In a sauté pan, melt the butter over high heat. Once it starts to brown, add the brain lobes. Add the thyme and begin basting the brains. Add the porcini and shallots, and cook until the brains are nicely caramelized, 2 to 3 minutes.

**6.** Remove the brains and place a whole lobe on each slice of bread; divide the porcinis and shallots equally on top. Add the nepitella to the pan, sauté for a second, then deglaze with lemon juice to taste, add capers, and whisk in the chicken stock to emulsify. Adjust the seasoning with salt and pepper, then add the parsley. Reduce the sauce to ¼ cup, then spoon it on the toasts.

**7.** Top with shaved raw porcini and cress.

# CORNED PORK HEART, ONIONS & LARD BRUSCHETTA

SERVES 8

This is a tribute to Takashi-san's beef heart and schmaltz on the menu at his eponymous West Village yakiniku restaurant, where he serves nothing but beef, and primarily offal. Substituting pork, I treat it like beef for St. Patty's Day. I corn the heart through a brining process, which helps tenderize the lean meat and adds a savory character. If you are feeling especially festive, this could even be served with cabbage.

**4 pig hearts, about 1 pound each, trimmed (see page 40)**
**1 gallon Corning Brine (page 283)**
**2 medium yellow onions**
**1 medium carrot**
**1 stalk celery**
**1 head garlic, split to expose the cloves**
**2 fresh bay leaves**
**1 bunch thyme, leaves picked**
**Neutral oil, for the grill**
**Sea salt and freshly ground black pepper**
**4 ½-inch-thick slices of rye bread**
**3 tablespoons lard (or strutto, flavored lard, page 168), plus more for the bread and drizzling**
**2 cups scallions, cut very thin on the bias**
**Onion sprouts, for garnish**

**1.** Place the hearts in a container with enough brine to cover. Leave for 2 to 3 days in the refrigerator.

**2.** Drain the hearts and put them in a nonreactive pot along with the spices from the brine, 1 onion, the carrot, celery, garlic, bay leaves, and thyme leaves. Cover with water and bring to a boil, then reduce the heat to a simmer, skimming off any impurities that rise to the top. After 15 minutes, cover the hearts with a cartouche (a piece of parchment cut to fit the pot) and cook until tender, about 1½ hours. Remove the pot from the heat and let the hearts cool.

**3.** Preheat a grill to high and brush the grates with oil. Slice the remaining onion on the horizon into ½-inch slices, season them with salt and pepper, and grill them on both sides until charred and three-quarters cooked. Place them in a bowl and cover with plastic wrap to let them steam and finish cooking. Slice the hearts ham-sandwich thin, on a meat slicer, reserving any corning spices that fall off the hearts for garnish.

**4.** Lacquer the rye bread with a little lard, and season with salt and black pepper. Grill the bread on both sides until toasted.

**5.** Working in batches, melt the 3 tablespoons lard in a large sauté pan over high heat. When it's hot but not smoking, add the sliced corned hearts, some grilled onions, and some of the reserved corning spice. Toss all the ingredients in the pan together just to heat through. Be careful not to burn the lard; you don't want the heart meat to get crispy, you just want to let it pick up a little color.

**6.** Divide the heart slices among the grilled bread, top with scallions, and drizzle with fresh lard. Garnish with onion sprouts and reserved corning spices. Serve hot.

# PIG'S BLOOD SOUP, 'NDUJA-STUFFED DATES & HERBS

SERVES 6 TO 8

This dish came to be because of a Twitter conversation with chef René Redzepi of Noma in Copenhagen. He talked of a Danish-style black soup, and when I introduced the idea of making an Italian version to the staff, all my Filipino cooks started laughing. *Dinuguan,* also known as "chocolate meat," is a traditional dish served in the Philippines, which most children get tricked into eating because they think it's made of cacao. It is more like a murky stew, and the traditional preparation uses pork, blood, and vinegar as the three main ingredients. We use caramelized onions, like in French onion soup, and then add blood to give it body. Its intense minerality is offset by the addition of fresh herbs and sweet seared dates.

**2 tablespoons pork fat, plus more as needed**
**1 medium yellow onion, julienned**
**1 medium carrot, cut into large dice**
**1½ stalks celery, cut into large dice**
**½ bulb fennel, cut into large dice**
**6 cloves garlic, chopped**
**½ bunch fresh thyme, leaves picked**
**1 cup red wine**
**2 quarts Rich Pork Stock (page 280)**
**1 cup pork blood**
**1 tablespoon balsamic vinegar, or to taste**
**12 to 16 whole Medjool dates, pitted**
**2 ounces 'nduja (spicy spreadable salami)**
**½ cup croutons, for garnish**
**2 tablespoons mint leaves**
**2 tablespoons cup celery leaves**
**2 tablespoons cup chervil leaves**
**¼ cup flat-leaf parsley leaves**
**1 bunch chives, cut into 1-inch batons**

**1.** In a large Dutch oven or soup pot over medium heat, melt the 2 tablespoons of pork fat and cook the onion, carrot, celery, fennel, garlic, and thyme, stirring regularly, until caramelized, about 20 minutes. The vegetables should be well colored but not dark. Deglaze with the red wine and cook until the vegetables are dry, about 5 minutes. Add the pork stock and simmer until the vegetables are very tender, about 20 minutes. Add the blood and cook for 5 minutes. Transfer to a blender, and pulse until smooth. Let cool.

**2.** Strain the soup through a fine strainer to remove any fibers, and place it back in the pot. Season with the balsamic vinegar.

**3.** Split each date and stuff it with a little 'nduja, pressing them back together to seal them up as best you can.

**4.** Warm up the blood soup over medium heat.

**5.** Coat a sauté pan with more pork fat over medium heat, and toast the croutons until they are golden brown, crispy, and warm. Remove to a bowl. Slick the pan again with pork fat and sear the dates for a couple minutes to achieve a nice caramelization.

**6.** To serve, pour the hot blood soup in bowls, adding 2 hot seared dates per bowl. Drizzle with a little pork fat to finish, and top with croutons and the herbs.

# BLOOD SAUSAGE

MAKES TWELVE 8-OUNCE SAUSAGES

This is a proper northern Italian blood sausage, using heart as the lean meat and a straightforward binder (*panade*) of bread and dairy. You'll taste the blood here, mild but mineral and slightly sweet.

As with many of my curing and baking recipes, precision is vitally important, and you'll need to use a scale and work in grams for this recipe. The sausages may be frozen for up to a month after cooking.

**65 grams fine white bread crumbs**
**50 grams milk**
**45 grams salt**
**2 grams dark brown sugar**
**250 grams heavy cream**
**56 grams lard**
**500 grams pork back fat, diced small**
**500 grams onions, finely chopped**
**15 grams garlic, crushed**
**8 grams thyme leaves**
**5 grams savory leaves**
**1 fresh bay leaf**
**4 grams black pepper, freshly ground**
**3 grams fennel seed, ground**
**3 grams coriander seed, ground**
**4 grams Aleppo chile flakes**
**1 gram pink curing salt, Instacure #1**
**14 grams red wine**
**1,000 grams fresh pig's blood**
**500 grams pork heart, ground fine**
**Bundle of natural casings (see Note), rinsed (see page 56)**

**NOTE:** Use beef-middle casings for large-diameter sausages that can be cut into wide slices, or large sausage-size hog casings for individual sausages.

**1.** In a small bowl, make a panade by soaking the bread crumbs in the milk. Mix the salt, sugar, and cream in another bowl.

**2.** In a large pot over medium heat, melt the lard and sweat one-fourth of the back fat, adding the onions, garlic, thyme, savory, bay leaf, black pepper, fennel, coriander, Aleppo chile, and pink curing salt. Cook until the onions are translucent and the back fat is cooked through but not mushy, about 8 minutes. Deglaze with red wine. Add the rest of the diced back fat, the blood, the cream mixture, and the panade. Fold in the ground heart meat. Mix together using a wooden spoon, quickly breaking up the panade mixture and making sure the meat is evenly distributed.

**3.** Immediately remove the blood sausage mixture from the heat and get ready to stuff your casing. Fit the casing over a funnel, then ladle the blood sausage mixture into the funnel. Don't tie off the ends yet; you first need to push the air out of the casing as you fill it. Once the filling is almost at the end, tie off the end of the casing.

**4.** Using a sausage prick, remove any air pockets and air bubbles while twisting the sausage every 6 inches to make individual links. Repeat with the remaining sausage mixture and casings.

**5.** In a large pot of salted water, poach the blood sausages at 165°F, keeping the sausage submerged with a clean kitchen towel. Keep the temperature constant. Cook the sausage until firm, about 45 minutes. To test, prick the sausage. When it doesn't leak blood, it's finished.

**6.** Cool sausages in a salted ice-water bath until cold. Then set in the refrigerator to cool overnight before use.

# BLOOD SAUSAGE WITH GUINEA HEN EGG, MORELS, PEAS & SUGAR SNAPS

SERVES 4

Guinea hens lay in the spring, which also happens to be the season for morels, peas, and sugar snaps. This dish combines those bright springtime ingredients with the wintry richness of blood sausage, a bridge between seasons.

**2 pounds fresh morels**
**2 tablespoons champagne vinegar**
**4 Blood Sausages (page 164)**
**¾ cup (12 tablespoons) unsalted butter**
**2 medium shallots, cut into thin rings**
**Sea salt and freshly ground black pepper**
**2 cups Rich Pork Stock (page 280)**
**4 cups shelled fresh peas**
**4 guinea hen, chicken, or duck eggs**
**1 cup julienned sugar snap peas**
**1 cup pea tendrils**
**1 cup pea sprouts**
**½ cup mint leaves**
**Lemon juice, to taste**
**Extra-virgin olive oil, to taste**

**1.** Clean the morels by agitating them in water with the vinegar. This will remove any dirt or possible worms. Spin the morels dry in a salad spinner, and place them on a towel on a plate in the refrigerator.

**2.** Preheat the oven to 400°F. Place the blood sausages in a cold, medium-size ovenproof sauté pan with 4 tablespoons of the butter over medium heat. (If you put the sausages in a hot pan, they may burst.) Once the sausages turn black, in about 5 minutes, flip them and roast in the oven until they are very hot but not bursting, about 4 minutes more. Remove the sausages from the oven and keep them warm.

**3.** In a large sauté pan, melt 4 tablespoons of the butter over medium heat, then add the shallots and sweat until tender, about 5 minutes. Add the morels, season with salt and pepper, and cook until tender, about 5 minutes. Deglaze the pan with the stock, add the peas, and cook until tender, about 3 minutes. Season to taste with salt and keep warm.

**4.** Heat another large sauté pan over medium heat with the remaining 4 tablespoons of butter, and, when the butter is foaming, cook the eggs sunny-side up.

**5.** Divide the eggs and sausages among 4 bowls, and distribute the morel and pea mixture on top.

**6.** In a small mixing bowl, dress the snap peas, pea tendrils, pea sprouts, and mint with lemon juice, olive oil, and salt and pepper to taste. Place some salad to the side of each sausage. Season the eggs with salt and black pepper and serve.

# HANGTOWN FRY BURGER

SERVES 1

This is an ode to a bacon and oyster omelet made during the California Gold Rush of the 1850s and popularized by the Tadich Grill, a San Francisco landmark, for over 150 years. I've transformed it into a luxurious "burger," using blood sausage as the pork. We slice it thick, sear it, and serve it on a buttered sesame-seed bun. Don't forget the fried egg, fried oysters, herbs, and zingy mayo. It's quite a mouthful.

**1-inch slab of large-format Blood Sausage (see Note), casing removed**
**3 tablespoons unsalted butter**
**Neutral oil, for frying**
**3 oysters, shucked**
**3 tablespoons Seasoned Flour (page 270)**
**Sea salt and freshly ground black pepper**
**1 duck egg**
**1 sesame-seed bun**
**A few leaves arugula**
**A few leaves mint**
**A few leaves parsley**
**Remoulade (page 277), to taste**
**A few thin slices of red onion**
**Tomato slices, in season**

**1.** Sear the blood sausage on a flat top or in a sauté pan over medium heat with 1 tablespoon of the butter. Remember, the blood sausage is cooked, so it just needs to be caramelized and heated through, about 2 minutes per side.

**2.** While the burger is cooking, preheat a deep fryer or a large saucepan with several inches of oil to 350°F. Dredge the oysters in the seasoned flour and fry until crispy and golden brown, about 3 minutes. Remove to a paper towel, and season with salt and pepper.

**3.** In a small sauté pan, cook the egg sunny-side up in 1 tablespoon of butter over medium heat. Remove the egg to a plate, and then toast the bun in the remaining tablespoon of butter.

**4.** Start building the burger with a layer of remoulade, arugula, and herbs on the bottom bun, then the blood sausage. Top with the fried oysters, red onion, tomato, and the fried egg. Season the fried egg with salt and pepper. Cover with the top bun.

**NOTE:** To make large-format blood sausage, double the recipe on page 164, and use large beef bung casings, the diameter of mortadella.

# SPAGHETTI, BLOODTARGA & EGG YOLK

SERVES 4

Spaghetti with grated bottarga—a cured, dried sac of fish roe—is a simple classic; the bottarga gives the pasta a briny, creamy, almost cheese-like flavor. This is a riff on that dish, using "bloodtarga." The cured blood grates beautifully, and it works just like bottarga, but with a more mineral flavor. There's no need for cheese; the bloodtarga and egg yolk give the dish all the richness it needs.

**Sea salt**
**½ cup pork fat**
**1 tablespoon Aleppo chile flakes**
**2 cloves garlic, thinly sliced**
**1 pound spaghetti, preferably Italian**
**½ cup finely chopped flat-leaf parsley**
**1 tablespoon coarsely chopped oregano leaves,**
**Grated zest of 1 lemon**
**4 egg yolks**
**1 to 2 ounces Bloodtarga (page 287)**

**1.** Bring 6 quarts of water to a boil over high heat and salt it well.

**2.** In a large sauté pan, heat the pork fat, Aleppo chile, and garlic over low heat, just until very fragrant. This flavored lard is also known as *strutto*. Remove from the heat.

**3.** Cook spaghetti until al dente according to the package instructions. Once the pasta is cooked, put it in the sauté pan with the seasoned pork fat over medium heat. Add parsley, oregano, and lemon zest. Toss well to mix, and pour directly into 4 warm serving bowls.

**4.** Top each portion with one egg yolk. Grate on a generous amount of bloodtarga, and serve immediately, instructing guests to mix it all together.

# PIG'S BLOOD PAPPARDELLE, TROTTERS, FOIE GRAS & DATES

SERVES 4

The dish is rich, rich, on rich, and a bit more involved than the blood-based pasta dish that precedes it. It's also beyond luscious, with trotter meat and seared foie gras tucked throughout the pasta. Caramelized dates add another level of almost gratuitous richness, but once you taste it, you'll know it's happily welcome.

**FOR PIG'S BLOOD PASTA:**

**1 cup "00" flour**
**1 cup fine semolina**
**A pinch of pink curing salt, such as Instacure #1**
**5 egg yolks**
**½ cup pork blood**

**FOR THE DISH:**

**1 lobe foie gras, about 1½ pounds, cleaned (see page 252)**
**Sea salt and freshly ground black pepper**
**4 large shallots, thinly sliced**
**6 cloves garlic, thinly sliced**
**12 Medjool dates, pitted and cut lengthwise into quarters**
**1 cup Rich Trotter Stock (page 281)**
**1 pound braised trotter meat (see page 62)**
**1 teaspoon sherry vinegar, or to taste**
**Snipped chives, for garnish**
**Chive flowers or onion flowers, for garnish**

**Equipment: Pasta machine**

**TO MAKE THE PASTA:**

**1.** Combine the flours and salt in the bowl of a stand mixer and, using the paddle attachment, mix at medium-low speed. Slowly add the egg yolks and pork blood. Once mixed well, wrap the dough in plastic and let it rest in the fridge for about 15 minutes. When you're ready to roll it out, remove it from the fridge to take the chill off a little.

**2.** Roll the pasta out with a pasta machine using progressively smaller settings until it reaches your preferred thickness. Cut the sheets into pappardelle by hand, one inch wide. Divide the pasta into 4 portions.

**TO MAKE THE DISH:**

**1.** Preheat the oven to 350°F. Season the foie gras with salt and black pepper. Preheat a medium sauté pan over medium-high heat; when the pan is hot, sear the foie until golden brown on all sides, then transfer it to a baking sheet and place it in the oven until cooked through, about 4 minutes. Remove and set aside to cool, reserving all the fat to use in the dish. Cut the foie into ½-inch cubes.

**2.** Start a large pot of boiling water, seasoning it with salt.

**3.** In a large sauté pan over medium heat, add the reserved foie gras fat and sauté the dates, shallots, and garlic. Deglaze the pan with the trotter stock, then add the cooked chunks of trotters and let simmer until tender and loose, about 4 minutes.

**4.** Place the pasta in boiling water, and cook until just a little underdone, 2 to 3 minutes.

**5.** Add the diced foie to the sauté pan with the trotter stock, and then add the pasta. Toss well. Adjust the seasoning with sherry vinegar, salt, and fresh black pepper.

**6.** Serve immediately, topping with chive batons and chive flowers.

# SMOKED CHOCOLATE BLOOD CREMEUX

SERVES 12 TO 18

This isn't your grandmother's Christmas pudding (unless she's Sardinian, where they use goat blood instead of pig blood as a thickening agent). Think warming holiday spices highlighted by the minerality of blood and smoke from the chocolate. One taste and you'll see it's pure deliciousness with just a hint of mystery.

**3 sheets gold-leaf gelatin**
**1 vanilla bean**
**1 cinnamon stick**
**2 cups whole milk**
**2 cups heavy cream**
**1½ cups pork blood**
**1 cup sugar**
**1 teaspoon grated nutmeg**
**¼ teaspoon freshly ground black pepper**
**½ teaspoon sea salt**
**6 ounces egg yolks**
**14 ounces 72% bittersweet chocolate, coarsely chopped**
**4 ounces smoked chocolate, coarsely chopped (see Note)**

**Equipment: Stick blender**

**NOTE:** Smoked chocolate may be ordered online from specialty purveyors, or you can cold smoke your own using the method on page 178.

**1.** Place the gelatin in a bowl of cold water to bloom; set it aside until ready to add to the mixture. Split the vanilla bean open with a sharp paring knife, scrape out the seeds, and reserve them. If you'd like, grill the cinnamon stick until it starts to unroll and has a nice flavor of smoke; this adds so much depth to the dish.

**2.** In a mixing bowl set over a simmering double boiler, combine the milk, cream, blood, sugar, cinnamon, nutmeg, pepper, and salt, and stir. Let this come to 176°F; it will start to thicken at this point. Mix together the egg yolks in a medium mixing bowl, and whisk in a thin stream of the hot milk mixture until it's loose, about the texture of cream. Remove from heat, and whisk the yolk mixture back into the bowl of the hot milk and let cool to 140°F. Drain the gelatin and squeeze it dry. Remove the cinnamon stick from the milk mixture, then stir in the chocolates, gelatin, and vanilla seeds.

**3.** Blend the mixture with a stick blender until smooth and all the chocolate is dissolved. Strain the mixture through a chinois or fine-mesh strainer, and pour into one large or individual serving bowls. Cover the top with plastic wrap, pressing gently onto the surface of the pudding and gently smoothing it, and chill in the refrigerator until set, 3 to 6 hours.

# BLOOD MOUSSE, POLENTA, EGG & PORK LIVER BOTTARGA

SERVES 6

Every culture has a porridge. The United States has Cream of Wheat, China has congee. This is my Italian version, elevated by technique. It's one of the more precise, equipment-intensive recipes in the book, as you need the steady heat of an immersion circulator to pasteurize the blood to keep it from turning brown, and an iSi siphon to whip it. But what comes out is both comforting and surprising: warm polenta with soft boiled egg and an airy mousse whose flavor is much richer and meatier than you'd expect.

**FOR THE MOUSSE:**

**50 grams pig's blood**
**10 grams egg white powder**
**500 grams Rich Trotter Stock (page 281)**
**1 bunch thyme**
**1 bay leaf**
**½ teaspoon juniper berries, ground**
**½ teaspoon black peppercorns, ground**
**15 grams agar agar**

**FOR THE DISH:**

**6 large eggs**
**3 cups Creamy Polenta (page 289)**
**Pork Liver Bottarga (page 288), for garnish**
**1 cup sliced scallions**
**Chile oil (see recipe on page 120), to finish**

**Equipment: Bain marie, immersion circulator, hand blender, blender, small iSi or other foaming canister**

**TO MAKE THE BLOOD MOUSSE:**

**1.** Place the blood in a bain marie or a relatively tall metal container and cover with plastic. Place it in a water bath kept at 65°C (149°F) with an immersion circulator to pasteurize the blood and set its red color, 15 minutes.

**2.** Meanwhile, heat the trotter stock to a simmer and add a cheesecloth sachet of the thyme, bay leaf, juniper, and black pepper. Turn off the heat, letting it infuse for 15 minutes, then remove the aromatics.

❤ 335 likes

**offalchris** Blood Mousse, polenta, poached egg and pork liver Bottarga a true peasants dish

**3.** Remove the blood from the circulator, add the egg white powder to the blood, and buzz with a hand blender to bring together.

**4.** Bring the trotter stock to a boil, then blend it in a blender with the agar agar. (Don't put the lid on tight, as blending hot liquids can cause the lid to fly off; protect your hand with a towel.) Chill it in the fridge until it's set (30 minutes to an hour), then blend again until smooth.

**5.** Add the warm blood to the stock mixture.

**6.** Strain the mixture into an iSi canister, filling it to the marker, and charge the canister twice. Keep warm in a circulator at 144.5°F (62.5°C).

**TO FINISH THE DISH:**

**1.** Bring a large saucepan of water to a boil. Place the cold eggs in the pot and cook, uncovered, for 6½ minutes. Remove the eggs, and chill them in cold water. When ready to use, peel.

**2.** To serve, spoon ½ cup of polenta in a bowl, place one big charge of blood mouse in the center, and slide an egg right on top. Cover the egg with the scallion rings, then shave a generous amount of pork liver bottarga with a microplane over the whole dish. Finish the dish with a drizzle of the chile oil and serve immediately.

# I'LL HAVE A SMOKED LIVERWURST WITH A BAG OF CHIPS

SERVES 1 TO 2, MAKES ABOUT 3½ POUNDS LIVERWURST

This is like salad posing as an open-faced sandwich. It really is "all that and a bag of chips." The trick here is to use frozen liver when you're making the emulsified meat. This keeps the temperature cold, helping you hold the emulsion for a smooth product.

Since this is a curing recipe that uses a precise amount of pink curing salt, I measure the ingredients in grams. Any extra liverwurst freezes well.

**FOR THE SMOKED LIVERWURST:**

**793 grams lean pork, cut into 1-inch cubes**

**453 grams pork back fat, cut into 1-inch cubes**

**312 grams pork liver, cut into 1-inch cubes**

**9 grams crushed garlic**

**34 grams kosher salt**

**15 grams dark brown sugar**

**2 grams ground fennel seeds**

**2 grams ground coriander**

**2 grams ground cinnamon**

**2 grams cayenne**

**2 grams Aleppo chile flakes**

**3 grams pink curing salt, such as Instacure #1**

**3 grams whole black peppercorns**

**1 beef bung casing, 10 to 12 inches**

**Equipment: Cold smoker, meat grinder**

**FOR THE DISH:**

**¼ to ½ pound smoked liverwurst**

**2 heads Little Gem lettuce, washed, leaves separated**

**1 tablespoon Pickled Red Onions (page 286)**

**1 cup flat-leaf parsley leaves**

**Mustard Vinaigrette (page 272), to taste**

**Sea salt and freshly ground black pepper**

**Rye sprouts, for garnish**

**A small bag of your favorite potato chips**

**MAKE THE SMOKED LIVERWURST:**

**1.** Using the cold-smoking method of your choice (or see opposite page), smoke the lean pork, back fat, and liver for about 45 minutes while set on a pan of ice. I like using Pinot Noir barrel shavings, but any wood you like will do.

**2.** Once you've finished smoking, place the pork, fat, and liver in the freezer until frozen. Grind the frozen pork using an ⅛-inch die, then grind the frozen fat, keeping them chilled in separate containers.

**3.** Place the ground meat in a food processor, and pulse with the garlic, salt, brown sugar, fennel seeds, coriander, cinnamon, cayenne, Aleppo chile, and curing salt until smooth. Then, with the machine running, alternate adding the frozen smoked pork liver and ground fat, which keeps the mixture cold and helps to best emulsify the mousse. Scrape down the sides of the bowl as needed. It will first look like the meat is almost curdling, then it becomes a paste, and finally a smooth mousse. Once the mixture is fully combined, stop the machine and scrape down the bowl. Chill the mixture by placing it in a mixing bowl, set it in an ice-water bath, then fold in whole black peppercorns.

## COLD SMOKING

Traditionally, cold smoking is used as a form of preservation; the recipes in this book use it for flavoring, not preserving, and the process is relatively quick. For food safety reasons, handle your cold-smoked food the same way you would if it was not smoked.

The best way to cold smoke depends on your kitchen and preference. To make it really easy, you can use a smoking gun, which will produce all the smoke you need. If you have a smoker or smoking box, consult your manufacturer's instructions.

To smoke in a grill, soak your wood chips in water, about ¾ cup of chips for 30 minutes of smoke. Start a small fire with just a few pieces of charcoal on one end of the grill, then let it burn to embers; remember, you're not trying to heat the chamber, just provide a little heat for the chips to smolder, so keep the fire small. Smother the embers with the drained wood chips and remove any air by closing all the vents on the lid and then closing the lid. Once the smoke is billowing, add the food, preferably in a pan on ice to keep it cold, all the way on the opposite side of the embers and smoke, so it's away from any heat. Close the top of the grill, and check the food every 10 minutes with a thermometer to make sure the temperature doesn't go over 68°F. Once smoked, refrigerate your food or use it immediately in the next step of the recipe.

**4.** To stuff the mixture into the casing, fold the sides of the beef bung over like a paper bag, insert your hand into the fold, and scoop the mixture out of the bowl and into the casing. Press and massage it gently to force out any air bubbles, then tie one end, twist the other end to form a taut sausage, and tie that end off.

**5.** Place the liverwurst in a pot with cold water to cover, and submerge it with a plate. Slowly bring the water to 165°F over a medium-low flame; never let it boil. Cook the liverwurst to an internal temperature of 165°F, then plunge it into an ice-water bath to cool before use.

**6.** The liverwurst has a good shelf life and can last up to 7 days in the fridge, or for weeks frozen. It can be used as a spread as well, almost like a pâté.

**ASSEMBLE THE DISH:**

**1.** Slice the liverwurst ⅛ to ¼ inch thick on a meat slicer or with a sharp knife. Arrange the slices in an overlapping fashion on one side of a plate.

**2.** In a mixing bowl, combine the lettuce leaves, pickled onions, and parsley. Toss it all with vinaigrette, salt, and black pepper. Place the salad on top of the meat, then garnish with rye sprouts. Serve with the chips.

# LIVER & KIDNEY PIE WITH A SUET CRUST

SERVES 12

This may be a cold dish, but it's a heartwarming meal. Slice this pie into wedges, serve them with some pickles and whole grain mustard, and have yourself a mighty ploughman's lunch. Or take it on the road! It's made to be transported, the crust a vehicle to carry the meat wherever life may take you.

**13 ounces fresh pork liver, cleaned (see page 46)**
**13 ounces fresh pork kidney, trimmed (see page 53)**
**1 teaspoon sea salt**
**1 large onion, finely diced**
**4 fresh bay leaves**
**1 tablespoon unsalted butter**
**⅔ cup whole milk**
**1 tablespoon heavy cream**
**7 tablespoons bread crumbs**
**½ teaspoon freshly ground black pepper**
**1 teaspoon thyme leaves**
**8 sage leaves, chopped**
**Pinch of cayenne**
**9 ounces pork heart, ground**
**1 tablespoon red wine**
**2 Suet Crusts (page 290)**
**36 thin slices of smoked bacon, (preferably Benton's bacon)**
**3 sheets gold-leaf gelatin**
**2 cups Rich Pork Stock (page 280), heated**
**Grilled bread, for serving**
**Pickles, for serving**
**Whole-grain mustard, for serving**

**Equipment: Nonstick springform pan, meat grinder**

**1.** Roughly chop the liver and kidney. Season the meat with salt and grind it with an ⅛-inch die before placing it in a food processor.

**2.** In a large saucepan, sweat the onion and bay leaves in the butter over medium heat, until the onions are soft and translucent, about 8 minutes. Remove the pan from the heat and discard the bay leaves.

**3.** Warm up the milk and cream to just above room temperature, stir in the bread crumbs, and soak for 5 minutes. Add this mixture to the onions.

**4.** Place the bread crumb mixture in the food processer with the livers and kidneys. Add the pepper, thyme, sage, cayenne, heart meat, and wine to the food processor, and pulse until thoroughly mixed.

**5.** Preheat the oven to 450°F. Line a large springform pan with one suet crust, making sure there is a ½-inch overhang to attach the top crust. Line the crust with bacon slices, such that you will be able to fold the bacon over to cover the filling. Pile the filling into the pie and fold the bacon slices over the top of the meat.

**6.** Cut a small hole in the top of the pie crust for the chimney before laying the top crust on. Place the top crust on, making sure the hole is in the center, then crimp the edges all the way around to make a nice fluted edge. Make a chimney with a piece of foil so the pie has a steam vent.

**7.** Bake until the top crust is golden brown, about 15 minutes, then reduce the temperature to 250°F and continue to bake for 2 hours. The pie is cooked when it comes to an internal temperature of 165°F.

Remove the pie from the oven and let it cool on a cooling rack.

**8.** Place the gelatin in a bowl of cold water to bloom; set aside until ready to add to the mixture. When the pie is fully cooled, squeeze the gelatin sheets dry and place them in 2 cups of hot stock to dissolve. When the gelatin mixture has cooled to room temperature, pour enough of it into the pie through the chimney to fill the interior space. This might take multiple pours, as you need to wait for the liquid to distribute throughout the filling. Let the pie set in the fridge so there's a nice layer of delicious pork gelée.

**9.** Slice the pie into wedges; serve with whole-grain mustard, some pickles, and grilled bread.

❤ **676 likes**
**offalchris** cooking with my friend Derek Dammann

# PORK LIVER, ONIONS & SAGE

SERVES 6

There's something to be said for a classic: if it's not broken, don't fix it. That said, the traditional caramelized onions are replaced here with whole cipollinis, which are wonderfully sweet and will keep their textural integrity, and a combination of both charred and raw onions; the layers of onion flavor give the dish a wonderful balance. Make sure you have all your mise en place ready to go; this moves pretty quickly once you start.

**1 whole pork liver, about 3 pounds, peeled and deveined (see page 46)**
**2 large yellow onions**
**Sea salt and freshly ground black pepper**
**1 bunch thyme, leaves picked, 2 full branches reserved**
**6 tablespoons balsamic vinegar, plus more as needed**
**¼ cup pork fat**
**16 cipollini onions, peeled, left whole**
**8 sage leaves**
**3 tablespoons unsalted butter**
**½ cup Rich Pork Stock (page 280)**
**2 cups arugula**
**1 small red onion, shaved thin**
**Extra-virgin olive oil, to taste**

**1.** Divide the liver into 3 sections, separating it by lobe. Dry the liver on a towel and set it aside, letting it come to room temperature.

**2.** Cut the yellow onions into 1-inch-thick rings, season with salt and pepper, then combine with the picked thyme leaves and 2 tablespoons of the balsamic vinegar and let them marinate for 15 minutes.

**3.** In a cast-iron pan over high heat, brûlée the onions, which means caramelize them over high heat without fat, getting a hard char on both sides, about 5 minutes per side. Place the onions in a mixing bowl, cover with plastic wrap, and keep them warm to let them steam themselves through.

**4.** In a large sauté pan over medium heat, add half the pork fat. When hot, add the cipollini onions and a thyme branch. Once the onions are caramelized on one side, about 3 minutes, flip them over and caramelize the other side, another 3 minutes. Deglaze the pan with 2 tablespoons balsamic vinegar, then turn off the heat, cover the pan, and let the onions cook through with carryover heat, about 15 minutes.

**5.** Preheat oven to 350°F. Season the liver with salt and a lot of black pepper. In a large ovenproof sauté pan over high heat, add the rest of the pork fat. Once the fat is very hot but not smoking, add the liver and sear, adding a thyme branch and basting with the fat while caramelizing. When lightly browned, flip the liver and caramelize the other side, then place the pan in the oven. The liver is done when warmed to medium rare throughout, 5 to 8 minutes. Cooking times depend on the thickness of the liver, though, so keep an eye on it.

**6.** Remove the liver and let rest in a warm area. Add the brûléed yellow onions, cipollinis, and sage leaves to the pan. Heat through on medium-high heat, add 2 tablespoons of butter, then 2 tablespoons balsamic vinegar. Add the pork stock, and whisk together. Whisk in the last knob of butter and remove the pan from the heat.

**7.** Place the onions on a large platter, laying the liver on top of them. In a mixing bowl, toss the arugula and red onions. Dress with olive oil and balsamic, salt and pepper, then drape this mixture over the liver.

# FRIED CHITTERLINGS & ARTICHOKES WITH BRAINAISE

SERVES A SERIOUS PARTY

You're at a county or state fair; it's a hot sticky day, and you're walking from ride to ride with a cold beer in hand. If you're underage, maybe it's a Cheerwine. You're watching the Ferris wheel go round and round, and you need a snack. You might not find fried chitterlings at the fair, but one bite of these and you'll feel like you're right there. Fried, fatty, and satiating in the best of ways, these snacks make your time at the fair complete.

Chitterlings often come frozen in large quantities, and this recipe reflects that, but of course you can scale it down. Keep in mind, though, that chitterlings shrink significantly when cooked, nearly by half.

**10-pound bucket of chitterlings (thawed if frozen)**
**1 cup cider vinegar**
**5 bay leaves**
**2 large onions, coarsely chopped**
**2 medium carrots,**
**3 cloves garlic, minced**
**Salt**
**2 red Fresno chiles**
**Freshly ground black pepper, to taste**
**2 cups Seasoned Flour (page 270), or as needed**
**Neutral oil, for frying**
**12 baby artichokes, trimmed**
**2 lemons, cut into wedges**
**½ cup flat-leaf parsley leaves**
**Your favorite hot sauce**
**Brainaise (page 275), for serving**

**1.** Using a small, soft brush, clean the chitterlings thoroughly, then rinse them in several changes of cold water, removing any fat found in the intestines. This will remove the aroma associated with uncleaned chitterlings.

**2.** Cut the chitterlings into 2-inch pieces. Place the cleaned chitterlings in a large pot, cover with water, and add the vinegar. Add the bay leaves, onions, carrots, garlic, salt, and chiles. Bring this to a boil, then reduce the heat to low and simmer for 2½ to 3 hours, or until the chitterlings are tender. Remove from the heat; drain well, discard the vegetables and bay leaves, and let cool. Pat dry with paper towels to remove as much of the moisture as possible.

**3.** Season the chitterlings with salt and pepper, then dust with the seasoned flour.

**4.** In a large pot or deep fryer, preheat several inches of oil to 350°F. Drop in the baby artichokes and fry until crispy and nicely browned, about 4 minutes. Transfer to a bowl lined with paper towels and season to taste with salt and pepper. Turn up the oil to 375°F. Fry the chitterlings in batches for about 5 minutes at a time, being sure not to overcrowd the oil, until they're lightly golden. Transfer to paper towels to drain; season to taste with salt and pepper. Quickly fry the parsley, and toss it with the chitterlings. Serve on a brown paper–covered plate with a few lemon wedges, hot sauce, and brainaise.

# PIG STOMACH À LA TAUNTAUN

SERVES 8 TO 10

You know that scene in *The Empire Strikes Back* when Han Solo stuffs Luke Skywalker into the stomach of a tauntaun on the ice planet Hoth to avoid hypothermia? We're making our version of it, with a pig's stomach as the poor departed tauntaun, three types of sausages—red, white, and green—as the organs, and lobster-infused marinara sauce, because I love surf and turf. All of these spill out when you split the stomach and present the dish to your nerdy offal-eating friends.

When stuffing, use as much of the sausages as will fit; any leftover sausages freeze well.

This dish is a project, for sure, and you'll have to start it several days in advance to properly marinate the meats and chill the sausages, but it will be epic, I promise.

**FOR THE STOMACH:**

**12 pearl onions**
**1 tablespoon unsalted butter**
**¼ cup Rich Pork Stock (page 280)**
**6 medium carrots, cut obliquely, 1 inch thick**
**Sea salt**
**1 pork stomach, scrubbed and rinsed**
**Freshly ground black pepper**
**Green, red, and white Sausages (recipes follow)**
**1 batch Lobster Marinara (page 278)**
**A few large handfuls of mixed herbs of your choice**
**1 small red onion, shaved**
**Lemon juice, to taste**
**Extra-virgin olive oil, to taste**
**1 batch Creamy Polenta (page 289)**

**Equipment: Meat grinder, sausage stuffer, large soup terrine, large cutting board or platter, tongs for serving, trussing needle, butcher's twine**

**FOR THE GREEN SAUSAGE:**

**1 pound pork butt, cubed**
**½ pound pork belly, skin off, cubed**
**½ bulb fennel, diced**
**2 teaspoons sea salt**
**½ teaspoon sugar**
**½ teaspoon coarse-ground black pepper**
**3 stalks green garlic, tops included, chopped**
**½ cup flat-leaf parsley leaves**
**3 shallots, sliced**
**1 tablespoon white wine**
**½ pound lacinato kale, stems removed, leaves coarsely chopped, about ½ pound**
**½ tablespoon ground fennel seeds**
**1 sleeve of long hog casings, rinsed and soaked (see page 56)**

**1.** Combine all the green sausage ingredients except the casings in a large mixing bowl; and cover and marinate overnight in the refrigerator. Chill a meat grinder and medium plate in the freezer.

**2.** Grind the meat mixture. Be sure to keep the meat cold at all times. Once the meat is ground, return it to the refrigerator to cool the meat down again.

**3.** Rinse the hog casings by attaching one end to the water faucet and running the water through to flush out the salt brine.

**4.** Slide the casings onto a wet stuffing tube and begin the stuffing process. When all of the meat has been put into the casings, it's time to "prick and twist" to create the links. The green sausage is meant to represent an intestine. Here we'll pinch them into 1½-inch balls, leaving a two-finger gap in

*(continued)*

between each one. When making sausages, it's important to remove any air bubbles; you can use a sausage prick or a sewing needle. Just prick the sausages where you see air bubbles, not all over. After that, the twisting process is very easy: squeeze the sausage to get the meat into a section, and use that first sausage size as a guide for the rest. Repeat the process again, spinning the middle sausage. Repeat twice, but always skip a sausage when spinning, or you will untwist the sausage you just twisted. Once this is complete, refrigerate them overnight.

**FOR THE WHITE SAUSAGE:**

**½ teaspoon whole fennel seeds**
**2 tablespoons white wine**
**1 pound pork butt, cubed**
**½ pound pork belly, skin off, cubed**
**2¼ teaspoons sea salt**
**½ teaspoon coarsely ground black pepper**
**5 cloves garlic, crushed**
**½ teaspoon thyme leaves**
**3 shallots, sliced**
**¼ teaspoon ground fennel seeds**
**Grated zest of 1 lemon**
**1 fresh bay leaf**
**1 sleeve of long hog casings, rinsed and soaked (see page 56)**

**1.** In a small saucepan over medium heat, cook the whole fennel seeds in the white wine until nearly dry, about a minute, then let cool.

**2.** Combine all ingredients except casings in a large mixing bowl, cover, and marinate overnight in the refrigerator. Chill a meat grinder and medium plate in the freezer.

**3.** Before grinding, remove the bay leaves. Grind the meat mixture. Be sure to keep the meat cold at all times. Once the meat is ground, return it to the refrigerator to cool the meat down again.

**4.** Rinse the hog casings by attaching one end to the water faucet and running the water through to flush out the salt brine.

**5.** Slide the casings onto a wet stuffing tube and begin the stuffing process. When all of the meat has been put into the casings, it's time to "prick and twist" to create 4-inch links. When making sausages, it's important to remove any air bubbles; you can use a sausage prick or a sewing needle. Just prick the sausages where you see air bubbles, not all over. After that, the twisting process is very easy: squeeze the sausage to get the meat into a section, and use that first sausage size as a guide for the rest. Repeat the process again, spinning the middle sausage. Repeat twice, but always skip a sausage when spinning or you will untwist the sausage you just twisted. For this sausage, shape the links into a long string of little balls to look like beads. Once this is complete, refrigerate them overnight.

**FOR THE RED SAUSAGE:**

**1 pound pork butt, cubed**
**½ pound pork belly, skin off, cubed**
**1 tablespoon red wine**
**¼ teaspoon ground fennel seeds**
**½ teaspoon red chile flakes**
**½ teaspoon Aleppo chile flakes**
**½ teaspoon pimentón de la Vera picante**
**2 teaspoons sea salt**
**½ teaspoon sugar**
**½ tablespoon coarsely ground black pepper**
**½ cup pig's blood**
**4 garlic cloves, crushed**
**1 red Fresno chile, thinly sliced**
**3 shallots, sliced**
**Grated zest of 1 orange**
**1 sleeve of lamb casings, rinsed (see page 57)**

**1.** Place the pork in a large mixing bowl. Mix the wine with the spices to make a paste and rub it into the pork. Add the remaining ingredients, except for the casings; cover and marinate in the refrigerator overnight. Chill a meat grinder and medium plate in the freezer.

**2.** Grind the meat mixture. Be sure to keep the meat cold at all times. Once the meat is ground, return it to the refrigerator to cool the meat down again.

**3.** Rinse the lamb casings by attaching one end to the water faucet and running the water through to flush out the salt brine.

**4.** Slide the casings onto a wet stuffing tube and begin the stuffing process. When all of the meat has been put into the casings, it's time to prick. When making sausages, it's important to remove any air bubbles; you can use a sausage prick or a sewing needle. Just prick the sausages where you see air bubbles, not all over. After that, the twisting process is very easy: squeeze the sausage to get the meat into a section, and use that first sausage size as a guide for the rest. Repeat the process again, spinning the middle sausage. For this sausage, we won't be making links but instead coiling the lengths of sausage into 4-inch diameter wheels, twisting off the wheels as you would links. Once this is complete, refrigerate them overnight.

**TO STUFF THE STOMACH:**

**1.** In a sauté pan over medium heat, caramelize the pearl onions with the butter, then deglaze with ¼ cup pork stock. Remove the pan from the heat.

**2.** Place the carrots in a large pot, cover them with salted water, and bring to a boil. Lower the heat and simmer until nearly tender, 5 to 8 minutes. Drain and cool the carrots.

**3.** Preheat the oven to 250°F. Open the stomach and stuff it with as many sausages as you can, placing them in clusters as if they're organs. I've found 4 white links, 1 foot of green balls, and 2 coils of red sausage is a great amount. Add the pearl onions and carrots, distributing them throughout as best you can. Using a trussing needle and butcher's twine, stitch the stomach shut. Leave an air hole so it won't pop while cooking.

**4.** Place the stomach in a large, nonreactive braising pan or large Dutch oven, season it with salt and pepper, cover with warmed lobster marinara sauce (not the meat), and bake, covered, for about 4 hours, until the air hole you left on the stomach is very tender when squeezed and the internal temperature of the sausages has reached 165°F. Baste the stomach occasionally along the way. When the baking is nearly completed, add the cooked and cleaned lobster meat to the marinara sauce to gently warm it.

**5.** In a bowl, toss the herbs and onions with salt, pepper, lemon juice, and olive oil to taste.

**6.** To serve, place the hot stomach and sauce in a beautiful soup terrine and cover it. On a large cutting board, place a nice pool of loose polenta, about 2 cups, reserving the rest on the side. Present this to the table. Bring the soup terrine tableside, and remove the stomach from the terrine with a pair of tongs. Hold it just above the polenta, then, using a very sharp knife, slit open the bottom of the stomach, letting the sausages fall out. Lay the stomach down on the board, and spoon over the sauce. Top with the herb salad.

# CULOMARI

SERVES 4 TO 6

Did you ever hear that episode of *This American Life* about dopplegängers, where a meat-processing plant in China was selling pig bung as fake calamari? Well, if that ever happens to you, here's how to make the most of it: simmer, dredge, and fry it. Thanks Ira Glass, this one's for you!

**10 pounds boneless inverted pig's rectum (aka bung)**
**3 gallons ice water**
**Sea salt**
**1 tablespoon white wine vinegar or champagne vinegar, plus more as needed**
**2 bay leaves**
**Peel of 1 lemon**
**1 vanilla bean, split and scraped (seeds saved for another use)**
**4 cups Spicy Dredge (page 270)**
**Rice bran or another neutral oil, for frying**
**Chopped parsley, for garnish**
**Lemon wedges, for serving**
**Basic Aioli (page 274), for serving**

**1.** Pull the outer membrane and fat off the bung with your hand. Don't use a rubber glove; it's too slippery, and then you won't have that lovely smell to share with your family and friends. Scrape off all the fat with a bench scraper. Invert and repeat the pulling and scraping.

**2.** Soak the bungs in a large bowl with ice water, 2 tablespoons salt, and the tablespoon vinegar. Cover and refrigerate for 24 hours, agitating the bungs every so often.

**3.** Take the bungs out of the water and smell them. They should smell pretty clean, with a slight odor of the barn but not that strong. If they still smell strong, repeat the soaking process with fresh salted, vinegared ice water.

**4.** In a pot, bring enough fresh water to cover the bungs to a boil. Add the bay leaves, lemon peel, and vanilla pod. Add the bungs, and reduce the heat to a gentle simmer for about 30 minutes, until the bungs are tender and tear easily.

**5.** Remove the pot from the heat and let the bungs cool in the liquid. Make sure there's no extra fat on them; if there is, you may have to clean them again. (Smell and see.) Cut the bungs into ½-inch rings and pat them as dry as possible with paper towels.

**6.** Preheat a deep fryer or a large pot filled with several inches of oil to 375°F.

**7.** Coat the bungs in the spicy dredge and fry them in batches, making sure the fryer isn't overcrowded, until they're crispy and golden brown, about 3 minutes. Flash-fry the parsley just until crisp, about 30 seconds. Drain everything on a towel. Season with salt.

**8.** Garnish with the fried parsley, and serve wedges of lemon and aioli on the side.

# GRILLED BACK FAT, BUDDHA'S HAND CITRON & PARSLEY

SERVES HOWEVER MANY CAN STAND AROUND THE TABLE

The first time I got to work with a Mangalitsa pig I realized there was equal fat to meat ratio. It's a breed from Hungary that has curly, wooly hair, and it looks like a pig and sheep went to screw in the woods. This pig was so fatty that I had to come up with ways just to use the fat, so I marinated pieces in spices, grilled them to get a crisp crust all around, and served them like spiedini, little Italian skewers.

Any good-quality back fat can work in this recipe, but the Mangalitsa has a creamy mouthfeel that makes it special.

**¼ cup fennel seeds**
**¼ cup black peppercorns**
**¼ cup coriander seeds**
**¼ cup Aleppo chile flakes**
**2-pound slab of pork back fat**
**¼ cup white wine**
**Sea salt**
**1 Buddha's hand citron (use a lemon if you absolutely must)**
**½ cup whole flat-leaf parsley leaves**
**6 large shallots**
**3 tablespoons lemon juice**
**3 tablespoons extra-virgin olive oil**
**Freshly ground black pepper**

**1.** Coarsely grind the fennel seeds, peppercorns, and coriander seeds, add the chile flakes, and then place the spice mixture in a small bowl.

**2.** Rub the fat slab with the white wine, then season it well with salt and the spice rub.

**3.** Vacuum-pack the slab to impart the spices' flavor into the fat. Let it sit in the refrigerator for at least 2 hours. You can also cover and marinate the fat and spices overnight, refrigerated, if you don't have access to a Cryovac. Before cooking, let the fat come to room temperature.

**4.** Preheat a grill to medium. Grill the back fat, making a nice seared crust of spices and fat on all sides, 5 minutes per side. The key is to be able to create this crust without melting all the fat.

**5.** Once the fat is hot throughout and well crusted, let it rest in a warm place.

**6.** Using a mandoline, shave the Buddha's hand citron paper thin into a mixing bowl. Add the parsley. Shave the shallots into thin rings. Dress the salad with the lemon juice, olive oil, and salt and black pepper to taste.

**7.** Slice the fat and place it on a warm plate, then distribute the salad over top. Finish with a little more sea salt. Serve warm.

# BRAISED BACK FAT, POTATOES & CAPERS

SERVES 4 TO 6

Years ago, I was fortunate enough to go on a culinary tour of Spain with chef José Andrés. We went to a beef restaurant where they served braised back fat family-style. We all stood up at a high-top table and wore aprons while eating it, and the liquefying fat reminded me of dipping clams in warm drawn butter, except we were chewing something closer to salty, briny butter itself! I thought, "How cool would it be to do this with Ibérico fat?" Ibérico pigs are one of Spain's great national treasures. The flavor of the fat is nutty and luscious, but if you can't get it, use a very good-quality pork back fat instead.

**2-pound slab of pork back fat (preferably Ibérico)**
**Sea salt and freshly ground black pepper**
**1 cup white wine**
**1 small yellow onion, roughly chopped**
**1 medium carrot, roughly chopped**
**1 leek, white part only, roughly chopped**
**1 stalk celery, roughly chopped**
**4 bay leaves**
**1 bunch thyme**
**1 jalapeño, split but still intact, seeds removed**
**Peel and juice of 1 lemon, or to taste**
**2 quarts Roasted Chicken Stock (page 282)**
**12 baby Yukon Gold potatoes**
**3 tablespoons salted capers, rinsed**
**¼ cup flat-leaf parsley, chopped**

**1.** Season the back fat all over with salt and black pepper. Cut it in half and place it in a container with the white wine, onion, carrot, leek, celery, 2 bay leaves, thyme, jalapeño, and lemon peel. Cover and let marinate overnight in the fridge.

**2.** Preheat the oven to 300°F. Place the fat and aromatics in a large braising pan or Dutch oven. Bring the chicken stock to a boil in a saucepan and pour it over the fat. Cover the pot and place it in the oven. Depending on the thickness of the back fat, it will cook for 45 minutes to an hour. It's done when the fat is very tender but not falling apart; be sure to catch it on the early side, as overcooked fat won't be solid enough to serve.

**3.** Remove the pot from the oven and let the back fat cool in the liquid. (If the fat is on the verge of overcooking, remove it and cool it outside of the liquid, then replace it once it's room temperature.) Chill, covered, overnight in the fridge.

**4.** To serve, remove the fat slabs from the pan, strain out the aromatics, and reserve the liquid. In a separate pot, cover the potatoes with cold salted water, add the remaining 2 bay leaves, and bring the liquid to a boil. Turn the heat down and simmer until the potatoes are fork tender, about 20 minutes. Drain and peel off the skins with a paring knife.

**5.** Cube the back fat into 1-inch squares.

**6.** To serve, heat up the fat braising liquid to a simmer and add the fat cubes and potatoes. Cook until hot throughout, then add the capers. Adjust the seasoning with lemon juice. Divide the fat and potatoes evenly among bowls, and fill with just enough broth to cover. Top with parsley leaves.

# FRIED PORK KNUCKLES, GARLIC & BLACK PEPPER

SERVES 4

This recipe was inspired by a visit to a Hong Kong beer garden called Tung Poa, where all the waitresses wear color-coordinated shirts that signify what specific beer they serve, and where garlicky, peppery pork knuckles are the snack of choice. We ate these with our hands while drinking beers, like a crawfish boil, picking the tender meat and glistening skin with our teeth. To serve, feel free to dump the pork knuckles on a table or put them in a galvanized bucket lined with day-old newspaper.

**5 pounds pork knuckles, skin on**
**Sea salt and coarsely ground black pepper**
**1 bulb fennel**
**2 medium yellow onions**
**1 head garlic, split to expose the cloves**
**1 bunch thyme**
**Peel of 1 lemon**
**3 bay leaves**
**½ gallon pork fat, or to cover**
**Mixed animal fats (tallow, lard, duck, etc.) or oil, for frying**
**2 tablespoons crushed garlic**
**¼ cup fish sauce, preferably Red Boat**
**1 jalapeño, thinly sliced**
**1 medium red onion**
**½ bunch scallions**
**½ bunch mint, leaves picked**
**½ bunch garlic chives**

**1.** In a large, nonreactive braising pan or Dutch oven, season the pork knuckles well with salt and pepper. Add the fennel, yellow onions, garlic, thyme, lemon peel, and bay leaves, and let sit, covered, overnight in the refrigerator.

**2.** Preheat the oven to 250°F. Remove the pan from the refrigerator. Heat the pork fat in a pot until very warm, then pour it over the knuckles and aromatics in the pan. Make sure everything is submerged, then place a circle of parchment cut to fit the pot on top and place it in the oven and cook, confiting them until tender, about 2½ to 3 hours. If the meat easily comes off the bone with the poke of a fork, it's finished.

**3.** Remove the pot from the oven and let cool to room temperature. Chill overnight in the fridge before removing the knuckles from the fat.

**4.** Preheat a deep fryer or large pot with several inches of fat or oil to 375°F. In a large mixing bowl, combine the crushed garlic, fish sauce, sliced jalapeño, and 1 tablespoon of coarsely ground black pepper.

**5.** Fry the pork knuckles a few at a time until crispy and hot throughout, 5 to 8 minutes. Remove and toss them in the bowl with the seasonings, then remove and hold them in a warm place as you finish frying the rest. Julienne the red onion, slice the scallions on the bias, tear the mint leaves, and mince the garlic chives. Place the knuckles on a platter, then top them with the red onion and herbs. Serve with some moist towelettes—it's going to be a bit messy.

# HAM HOCK & PARSLEY TERRINE

SERVES 12

This is my play on *jambon persillé*, a classic French jellied ham with parsley. You take ham hocks, brine them like a ham, and slow cook the meat with the skin on. Press it all in a terrine mold, and voilà, some French guy will tell you it's better than his mom's.

**1 gallon Ham Brine (page 284)**
**4 large, skin-on fresh ham hocks, about 5 pounds in total**
**1 medium carrot**
**1 medium yellow onion**
**2 stalks celery**
**1 head garlic, split to expose the cloves**
**1 small leek, white part only**
**1 bulb fennel, top removed**
**2 sheets gold-leaf gelatin**
**1 cup parsley leaves, roughly chopped**
**Sea salt**
**Lemon zest, to taste**
**2 tablespoons whole-grain mustard**
**1 bunch watercress**

**FOR SERVING**
**Whole-grain mustard**
**2 handfuls watercress**
**1 pound boiled potatoes, peeled and cut into bite-size pieces**
**3 tablespoons crème fraîche**
**1 tablespoon minced chives**
**Freshly ground black pepper**

**Equipment: 14 × 4 × 4-inch terrine mold (1½ quarts)**

**1.** Combine the ham hocks and brine, and refrigerate, covered, for 4 days. To speed up the process, you can vacuum-pack the hocks with brine to cover and let them sit for 2 days in the refrigerator.

**2.** Remove the hocks from the brine solution, and place them in a pot with the carrot, onion, celery, garlic, leek, fennel, and fresh water to cover. Bring the liquid to a simmer and cook until the hocks are tender, 2 to 3 hours. The meat should be nearly falling off the bone, but not shredding by itself. Don't let it overcook or the texture of the terrine will be horrible and mealy. Let the hocks cool in the liquid.

**3.** Remove the hocks from the pot while still a little warm, reserving the cooking liquid, and pick the meat, skin, and collagen off the bone and into a mixing bowl; set aside any large chunks. Use your hands so you can feel and discard any hard gristle.

**4.** Reduce 2½ cups of the cooking liquid to 1 cup, then pass it through cheesecloth and a fine-mesh strainer to remove any impurities. Meanwhile, soak the gelatin sheets in cold water for 5 to 10 minutes, then drain and squeeze them dry.

**5.** Place the gelatin sheets in the reduced cooking liquid to dissolve, and let it cool to room temp. Mix the parsley with the hock meat and just enough of the gelatin liquid to cover the meat. Season the mix with salt and lemon zest. Spray the terrine mold with cooking spray and line it with plastic wrap, enough to fold over the top of the terrine. Pack the meat mixture into the mold. Cover the terrine with plastic, then weigh down the terrine overnight to set. Be sure to put heavy weights on it, so it compacts.

**6.** When cold and set, slice the ham terrine into 1-inch-thick slices. Serve with whole-grain mustard, watercress, and potatoes, and top with the crème fraîche, chopped chives, salt, and black pepper.

HAWK
POWELL PERALTA®
©1983

# "TOE KNEE HOCK" FOR TWO

SERVES 2

I think of this dish in the same way I do skateboarding—the evolution of creativity is taking a trick and building on it. Tony Hawk, a living legend who did as much as anyone to popularize modern skateboarding, gave kids like me an outlet that didn't exist before him. We were pigeonholed as different, but skateboarding gave us a group to be part of, and it also let us be individuals within. This dish may seem like just a play on words, but it's also a play on concepts, recontextualizing and reassembling the parts of leg on a plate . . . well, on a skateboard.

**FOR BRAISING AND FRYING THE TROTTERS AND HOCK:**

**1 gallon Hay Brine (page 284)**
**2 trotters without hocks, about 1 pound each**
**1 large front trotter, hock attached, about 3 pounds (see Note)**
**1 medium yellow onion**
**2 stalks celery**
**1 bulb fennel**
**2 heads garlic, split to expose the cloves**
**2 medium carrots**
**1 bunch thyme**
**¼ cup flat-leaf parsley leaves, stems reserved**
**4 fresh bay leaves**
**Sea salt and freshly ground black pepper**
**Grated zest of 2 lemons**
**1 teaspoon Aleppo chile flakes**
**3 eggs**
**2 cups Seasoned Flour (page 270)**
**2 cups fine bread crumbs**

**FOR THE DISH:**

**6 Chantenay or other small, sweet carrots**
**6 whole small red carrots**
**12 Ruby Crescent or other fingerling potatoes**
**Olive oil, for panfrying**
**1 cup Brusselskraut (page 287)**
**¼ cup flat-leaf parsley leaves, plus 2 teaspoons chopped**
**4 cups reserved trotter braising liquid**
**2 teaspoons unsalted butter**
**¼ cup Hayaioli (page 276), for serving**
**¼ cup whole-grain mustard, for serving**

**NOTE:** Buy the trotter with the hock attached, but ask the butcher to cut the hock off, leaving the leg bone in the hock.

**1.** Combine the brine, all the trotters, and the hock for 2 days, covered, in the refrigerator.

**2.** Preheat the oven to 300°F. Remove the trotters, disposing of the brine, and add the trotters and hock to a braising pan with the onion, celery, fennel, garlic, carrots, and a tightly tied sachet containing the thyme, parsley stems, and bay leaves. Add cold water to cover.

**3.** Place the pan in the oven and cook until the meat is tender, about 3½ hours. Be sure to test the trotters toward the end; you want some give to the meat, but it shouldn't be falling apart. Depending on the size, it could cook a little faster.

**4.** Let the hock and trotters cool in the broth. Once cool, remove the trotters and pick the meat and skin into a bowl. Reserve the hock and the braising liquid, but strain out the vegetables and herbs.

**5.** Season the picked meat to taste with salt and pepper, and add the grated lemon zest, parsley leaves, and Aleppo chile.

*(continued)*

**6.** Lay out a foot-long piece of plastic wrap, still attached to the roll, and place the seasoned meat in the middle. Roll up the meat in several layers of plastic, twisting the ends like a giant Cheech & Chong doobie, making a nice, tight roulade, about 8 × 2 inches. Use a sausage prick or sewing needle to get rid of air bubbles. Letting the meat set in the fridge overnight will make for a much better roulade.

**7.** Cut the roulade into 1½-inch-thick cakes.

**8.** Set up a breading station with the eggs, beaten with a splash of water, in one dish, another dish of seasoned flour, a third of bread crumbs, and a place to put the cakes once breaded. Dip the trotter cakes into the egg, then the flour, and finally the bread crumbs. Double dip them back into the egg and bread crumbs. Set the breaded cakes in the refrigerator until chilled, about an hour.

**9.** Preheat the oven to 300°F. Place the braised hock in a small ovenproof saucepan with ½ cup or so of the strained braising liquid.

**10.** Bake until the hock is hot all the way through, about 10 minutes, basting occasionally so the hock gets a great glaze from the reduced braising liquid.

**11.** While the hock is heating up, place the carrots in a medium saucepan with well-salted cold water and bring to a boil. Reduce the heat to a simmer and cook the carrots until just crisp-tender, about 5 minutes after they come to a boil, then remove them to a tray to cool. They will finish cooking shortly in the braising liquid.

**12.** Boil the potatoes in the salted water until fork-tender, about 15 minutes. Remove from the water and cool on a tray. Peel the skins, keeping the potatoes whole. Keep warm.

**13.** Increase the oven temperature to 375°F. Generously coat a large ovenproof sauté pan with olive oil and set it over medium heat. When it's hot, panfry the trotter cakes on both sides until rich golden, about 3 minutes per side, then place them in the oven to warm through, about 5 minutes.

**14.** In a separate sauté pan, add a slick of olive oil, then toss in the brusselskraut, the parsley leaves, and 2 tablespoons of braising liquid to heat through. Finally, in another pan, cook the carrots in a few splashes of braising liquid until the liquid reduces to a glaze and the carrots are tender. Add the potatoes. Stir in the butter and the chopped parsley.

**15.** To serve, get a big-ass platter, place the glistening hock to one side, followed by a nice spoonful of its glaze as the sauce, then add a pile of glazed carrots and set the potatoes next to them. Add a bed of brusselskraut, then top with the trotter cakes, a dollop of hayaioli on one cake and whole-grain mustard on the other. Take a photo to show your friends on social media, then eat it before it gets cold.

# BRAISED TROTTER, TOMATO & CORONA BEANS

SERVES 4 TO 6

This is a true comfort dish, something you'd remember eating after your Neapolitan great-grandmother slaughtered a hog. It's soft on soft, fat, and flavor; it all melts and marries together as it braises. The hardest part of this recipe is waiting for it to finish cooking.

**2 front pigs' feet, hocks on**
**1 cup red wine**
**Sea salt and freshly ground black pepper**
**2 heads garlic, split to expose the cloves, plus 1 tablespoon sliced**
**2 small yellow onions**
**2 medium carrots**
**2 stalks celery**
**2 bulbs fennel**
**2 fresh bay leaves**
**1 bunch thyme**
**1 branch rosemary**
**6 cups Rich Pork Stock (page 280), plus more as needed**
**4 cups San Marzano tomatoes or heirloom tomatoes (when in season), milled**
**Extra-virgin olive oil**
**1 quart cooked Corona Beans (page 290)**
**Red wine vinegar**
**1 cup mint leaves**
**1 red onion, julienned**
**1 bunch scallions, sliced thin**
**1 cup flat-leaf parsley leaves**

**1.** Rub the trotters with red wine, and season well with salt and pepper. In a large bowl, combine them with the split garlic, onion, carrot, celery, and fennel, and marinate, covered, overnight.

**2.** Place the trotters in a nonreactive braising pan or Dutch oven with the vegetables and a tightly tied cheesecloth sachet containing the bay leaves, thyme, and rosemary. Cover the trotters with pork stock and tomatoes. Preheat the oven to 300°F.

**3.** Place the pan over medium heat and bring the liquid to a simmer. Shake the pan occasionally to make sure the trotters are not sticking. Place the pan in the oven, uncovered, and cook until tender but not falling apart, 2½ to 3 hours. Baste the trotters throughout as the liquid reduces. Remove the trotters and set aside until you're ready to finish the dish.

**4.** Remove all the herbs from the braising liquid, leaving the vegetables, and pour into a blender and puree. Don't put the blender lid on tight; you don't want too much pressure to build up and blow it off, and protect yourself with a kitchen towel. Once smooth, pass the liquid through a strainer, removing any fibers, then pour the sauce back over the trotters.

**5.** Raise the oven to 375°F. In the cleaned braising pan, add a slick of olive oil and heat over medium heat. Sizzle the sliced garlic until fragrant, then add the trotters and sauce. Add the cooked beans, and stir to submerge the beans. Place the pan in the oven to heat through and marry the flavors, about 15 minutes.

**6.** Adjust the sauce with red wine vinegar, glazing the trotters again with the sauce and beans, and then place it all on a large platter.

**7.** Tear the mint leaves. In a mixing bowl, dress the red onion, mint, scallions, and parsley with red wine vinegar, salt, pepper, and extra-virgin olive oil. Serve this salad on top of the trotters.

# CHILE & BONES WITH CAPERS, GARLIC & MINT

SERVES 4

I wanted to do something with bones other than cook them for stock, so I thought of covering them with aromatics, chiles, and herbs, and gnawing on them like chicken wings. Really get in there and gnaw; that way you pick up all the layers of flavor.

**5 pounds meaty pork neck bones (see Note)**
**¼ cup white wine**
**Sea salt**
**1½ tablespoons Spice Rub (page 271)**
**1 medium yellow onion, cut into julienne**
**2 bay leaves**
**½ bunch thyme**
**Lard, for sautéing**
**1½ tablespoons crushed garlic**
**1½ tablespoons salted capers, rinsed**
**½ cup mint leaves**
**½ cup dried chiles, either Calabrian or Sichuan**
**1 long pull of lemon zest off an old-school zester**
**1 long pull of orange zest**

**NOTE:** Using a bone saw, cut the bones into manageable pieces, or ask your butcher to cut the bones into 4-inch lengths.

**1.** Rub the bones with the white wine, an even seasoning of salt, and the spice rub. Place them in a container with the onion, bay leaves, and thyme, and marinate, covered, overnight in the refrigerator.

**2.** The next day, put the bones and aromatics in a lidded, perforated pan set over a pan with 3 inches of water (or use a large steamer) and steam the bones over a simmer until the meat is very tender, about 3 hours. Be sure to check and refill the water level occasionally as it evaporates. Let the bones cool.

**3.** Heat a wok or large sauté pan over high heat with a generous coating of lard. When very hot, sear the bones in batches until well browned on all sides. Add, in the following order with a few seconds in between each to develop their aromas: garlic, capers, mint, chiles, and citrus zest. Be sure not to burn the spices. Repeat this process until all the bones have been browned. Don't worry about dividing the aromatics exactly, because they will be mixed together in the end.

**4.** Pile all the bones on a platter with all the spices, and serve with a pile of napkins.

# FRIED PIG'S TAILS, MARCO POLO–STYLE

SERVES 2

Marco Polo, a Venetian, traveled to Asia and, upon his return, introduced Europeans to spices like black pepper and ginger. This was almost one thousand years ago. Today, we try to make as much as we can with what we have near us. In San Francisco, I forage for wild pink peppercorns and their leaves. This dish is about exploring New World flavors, and referencing the old.

**2 pig's tails (see page 68)**
**Sea salt and freshly ground black pepper**
**1 red Fresno chile, quartered**
**½ cup dried Thai bird chiles or dried Calabrian chiles**
**½ cup crushed garlic**
**¼ cup julienned fresh ginger**
**1 fresh bay leaf**
**Melted lard, to cover (if you are not using sous vide)**
**Rice bran oil or other neutral oil, for frying**
**3 tablespoons duck fat**
**¼ cup fresh black peppercorns**
**¼ cup fresh pink peppercorn leaves, or 1 tablespoon dried pink peppercorns**
**2 tablespoons ground coriander**
**2 tablespoons ground fennel seeds**
**2 tablespoons cacao nibs**

**1.** Season the pig's tails with salt and black pepper. In a Cryovac bag, combine a quarter of the chiles, a quarter of the garlic, a quarter of the ginger, the bay leaf, and a pig tail. Repeat with a second bag. Seal at 100%, then cook in a water bath at 175°F (79.5°C) for 9 hours. Once finished, remove the tails from the bags and let them dry on a sheet tray before frying.

**2.** If you don't have a sous vide setup, you can confit the tails in lard. Preheat the oven to 225°F. Place the tails and the aromatics from the previous step in a Dutch oven and cover with melted lard. Cover and bake for 3 to 4 hours, until tender. Remove the pot from the oven and let the tails cool in the fat before removing them.

**3.** Preheat a deep fryer or a large pot with several inches of oil to 375°F. Carefully lower in and fry the tails, letting them get super crispy, about 8 minutes. (If your fryer is relatively small, fry each tail separately.) Remove and drain the tails on paper towels.

**4.** In a large sauté pan over high heat, add the duck fat. When hot, toss in the peppercorns and leaves, coriander, fennel, cacao nibs, and the remaining chiles, garlic, and ginger. Fry, as in a wok, until very aromatic but not too brown. After about 2 minutes, add the tails and turn to coat, then season with salt. Serve on a platter, leaving the oil in the pan but covering the tails in the cooked spices.

# "TNT" PIG'S TAIL & OCTOPUS TENTACLES

SERVES 4

Ever notice how pigs' tails and octopus tentacles look alike? I thought it would be a fun pairing, grilled crispy. And while I was there, I'd make them spicy, like my favorite Sichuan chicken wings at the San Francisco restaurant Spices. This dish is pure dynamite, mind-numbingly good.

**4 pig's tails (see page 68)**
**Sea salt and coarsely ground black pepper**
**Peel of 1 lemon taken in 5 strips, plus lemon juice to taste**
**4 branches thyme**
**4 fresh bay leaves**
**6 serrano chiles (4 halved, 2 thinly sliced)**
**Melted lard, as needed**
**½ cup plus 1 tablespoon extra-virgin olive oil**
**¼ cup whole garlic cloves, plus 3 large cloves crushed into a paste**
**1 jalapeño, split**
**4 fresh octopus tentacles (2 pounds)**
**1 branch rosemary**
**3 pints mixed cherry tomatoes, halved**
**1 teaspoon red chile flakes**
**¼ cup basil leaves**
**¼ cup flat-leaf parsley leaves**
**¼ cup mint leaves**
**½ small red onion, shaved thinly**
**1 bunch garlic chives, 2-inch batons**
**1 tablespoon fish sauce, preferably Red Boat**

**1.** Season the pig's tails with salt and pepper. Divide them among four Cryovac bags; add to each a strip of lemon peel, a thyme branch, a bay leaf, and a halved serrano chile. Seal the bag at 100% and cook at 175°F (79.5°C) for 9 hours. Chill in an ice-water bath until totally cold throughout.

**2.** Alternatively, if not using sous vide, preheat the oven to 250°F. Place the tails with the seasonings and aromatics from the previous step in a Dutch oven and cover with melted lard. Make sure everything is submerged, then place a circle of parchment, cut to fit the pot, on top and place it in the oven to cook. Confit them until tender, about 3 hours. If the meat easily comes off the bone with the poke of a fork, it's finished. Let the tails cool in the lard, and then remove to the fridge.

**3.** In a large, heavy pot over medium heat, warm the ½ cup of olive oil. Add the garlic and jalapeño and cook for about 2 minutes, until very fragrant. Add the octopus, rosemary, and remaining lemon peel, then cover the pot, lower the heat to medium low, and braise until tender, about 1½ to 2 hours, stirring frequently. Remove from the heat and let cool.

**4.** Fire up a grill to high heat, preferably with live fire. Season the pig's tails and the octopus tentacles with salt and pepper, coat them with some melted lard, and then place them on the grill. Roll them around often to get a nice even crisp all over.

**5.** In a mixing bowl, combine the cherry tomatoes, basil, parsley, mint, chile flakes, and the red onion. Add the garlic chives and the thinly sliced serrano chiles. Toss the ingredients well, then add 1 tablespoon black pepper, 1 tablespoon lemon juice, the fish sauce, and 1 tablespoon extra-virgin olive oil. Adjust to taste with any of the above.

**6.** To serve, place the grilled tails and tentacles in the bowl with the tomato-herb salad; mix well to coat everything in the dressing. Make a pile of grilled tails and tentacles, topped with the salad.

LAMB

BRAIN
TONGUE
STOMACH
SPLEEN
KIDNEYS
RECTUM
LARGE INTESTINE
HEART
LUNGS
SMALL INTESTINE
LIVER

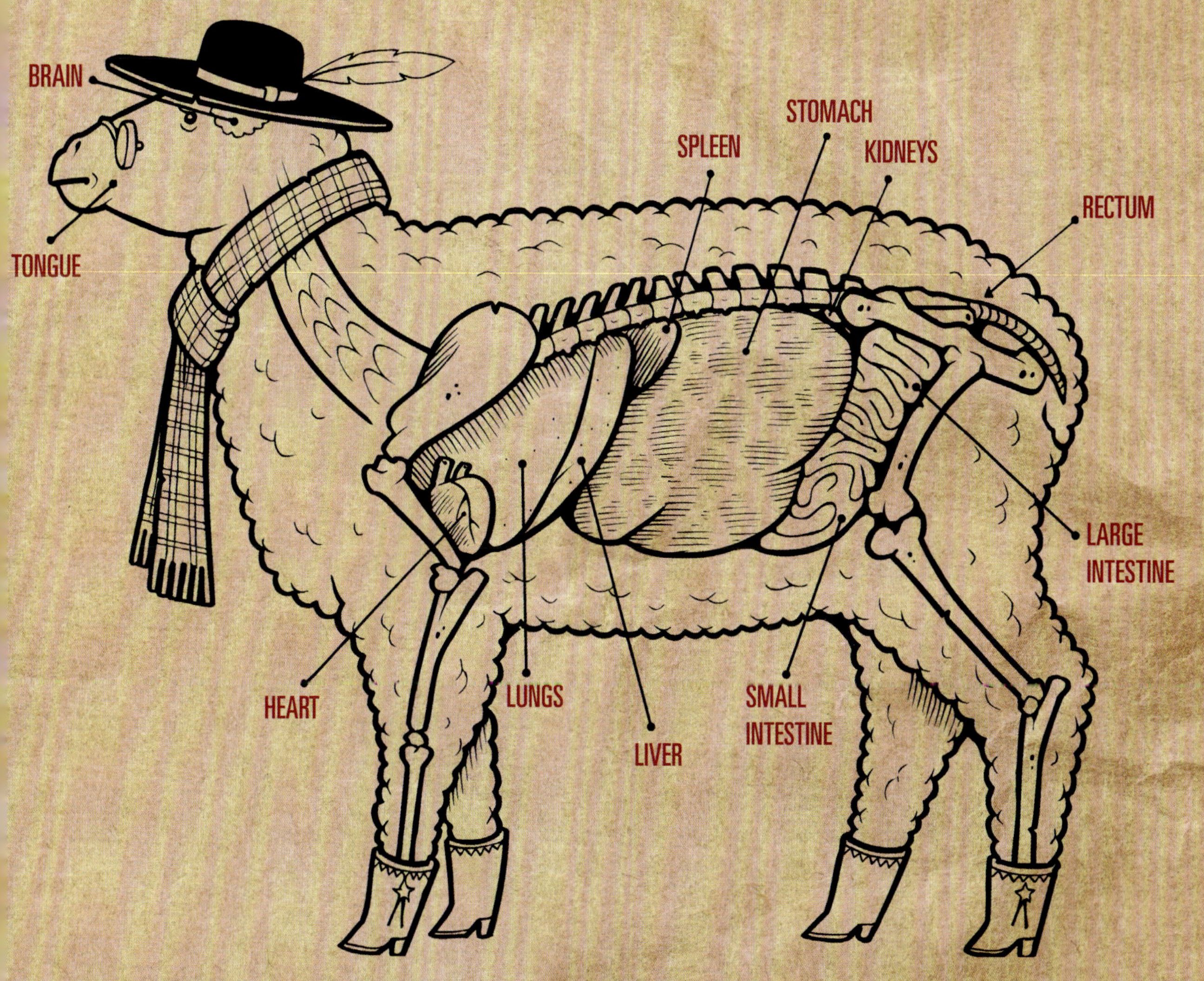

# SHEEP

# SMOTHERED LAMB'S HEAD, ONIONS & LAMB FAT-ROASTED POTATOES

SERVES 2 AS AN ENTRÉE OR 4 AS AN APPETIZER

It feels a little like Dr. Frankenstein, sawing off the back skull cap of a lamb's head to remove and then replace the brain. But this way you can present a beautifully roasted head, with tongue and browned cheek meat, and still serve a custard-like brain.

**1 lamb's head, skinned, with brain, tongue, and eyeballs intact, about 5 pounds**
**Sea salt and black pepper**
**2 cups Court Bouillon (page 280)**
**¼ cup duck fat**
**3 large red onions, julienned**
**3 large yellow onions, julienned**
**8 cloves garlic, thinly sliced**
**2 sprigs rosemary**
**1 cup dry white wine**
**2 cups Lamb Stock (page 282)**
**3 pounds fingerling potatoes**
**2 branches sage, plus 1 leaf**
**2 tablespoons unsalted butter**
**⅓ cup lemon juice, or to taste**
**2 tablespoons chive batons**
**2 tablespoons chive flowers**

**Equipment: Bone saw**

**1.** Using a bone saw, cut a wide square out of the back of the skull, remove the brain, and set it aside. Season the lamb's head all over with salt and pepper and allow it to rest while you prepare the next few steps.

**2.** Bring the court bouillon to a boil in a medium saucepan, season with salt, reduce to a simmer, then add the lamb's brain and let gently simmer until just cooked through, about 5 minutes. Remove the brain and set on a tray to cool in the fridge, covered.

**3.** In a wide heavy-bottomed pot over medium heat, combine duck fat, onions, garlic, and rosemary. Caramelize the onions, stirring constantly, for about 60 minutes, then season with salt. Deglaze the pan with wine, and simmer until reduced by half, about 10 minutes. Add the stock, work up to a simmer, then shut off the heat.

**4.** Preheat the oven to 300°F. Place the lamb's head in a casserole dish or pan with sides as tall as the head. Pour the onion mixture on top and cover tightly with foil. Roast for 3 hours, but after 2 hours, skim some fat off the top—just enough to coat the potatoes. Cover the head with foil and dress the potatoes with the fat, salt, pepper, and the 2 branches of sage. Put them on a sheet tray set on the lowest rack of the oven. Roast the potatoes until cooked through and crispy, about 1 hour. Remove the potatoes from the oven.

**5.** Remove the foil from the head, increase the oven temperature to 375°F, and bake for another 20 minutes, or until well browned. When the head is about to come out of the oven, melt the butter in a small sauté pan over medium heat, then add the brain, presentation-side (the top) down. Baste with the browning butter, then flip it, add a sage leaf, and splash with lemon juice and ⅓ cup of lamb jus from the head braise. Stir together to make a sauce.

**6.** Spoon half the onions onto a platter. Place the lamb's head on the onions, place the brain back into the skull, then cover with remaining onions, chives, and chive blossoms.

# LAMB NECK WITH GREMOLATA & POLENTA

SERVES 6

This dish came to be out of necessity. One year, we couldn't fit the whole lamb in the oven during Easter, so we cut the neck off and cooked it on its own. It ended up being everyone's favorite piece, falling off the bone when prodded with a fork. Plus, it's almost effortless to make.

**2 lemons, diced, seeds removed**
**½ cup peeled garlic cloves**
**2 cups fennel fronds**
**1 cup extra-virgin olive oil, plus more for finishing**
**1 tablespoon coarsely ground black pepper**
**6 lamb necks, about 2 pounds each**
**Sea salt**
**3 cups Lamb Stock (page 282)**
**Sheep's Milk Polenta (page 289)**
**Whole-leaf gremolata (recipe follows)**
**Fresh horseradish, for grating**

**1.** In a meat grinder, grind the lemons, garlic, and fennel fronds, then stir together with the olive oil and black pepper to make a marinade paste.

**2.** Season the necks with salt and pepper and rub them with the marinade paste. Let them marinate, covered, overnight in the fridge.

**3.** Preheat the oven to 200°F. Tray the necks up on a rack set in a sheet pan, and roast until very tender, about 6 hours.

**4.** In a saucepan over medium heat, reduce the lamb stock by half, until it's a rich jus. Taste and season with salt and pepper.

**5.** To serve, spoon a generous portion of polenta on each plate and place one neck on top with a spoonful of lamb jus. Top with the whole-leaf gremolata and a fresh grating of horseradish. Finish with a glug of some good olive oil.

## WHOLE-LEAF GREMOLATA

MAKES ABOUT 4 CUPS

**1 cup parsley leaves**
**1 cup mint leaves**
**1 cup chervil leaves**
**1 cup tarragon leaves**
**Freshly grated horseradish, to taste**
**Grated zest of 2 lemons**
**Sea salt and freshly ground black pepper**
**2 tablespoons extra-virgin olive oil**

**1.** Mix all the herbs with the horseradish and lemon zest, season with salt and pepper, and then add the olive oil. This is not a chopped gremolata; it's more like a whole leaf salad.

# LAMB'S TONGUE, FAVA BEANS, RADISH & ZINFANDEL VINAIGRETTE

SERVES 4

These are the first tastes of spring, straight from the lamb's mouth—simple, crisp flavors served with a zingy dressing that will awaken any palate.

**4 lamb tongues, about 1 pound total, cooked and peeled (see page 29)**
**1 cup shelled fava beans, blanched**
**12 French breakfast radishes, cut lengthwise**
**4 red globe radishes, thinly sliced on a mandoline**
**¼ pound purslane**
**Sea salt and freshly ground black pepper**
**Zinfandel Vinaigrette (page 272), to taste**

**1.** Return the cooked and peeled tongue to room temperature. Cut it into ½-inch slices and place them in a mixing bowl with the favas, radishes, and purslane. Season with salt and black pepper, then dress with the vinaigrette.

**2.** Place on a large platter to share with some lovely friends over a nice bottle of rosé.

# CRISPY LAMB'S TONGUE, POTATOES & PEAS

SERVES 4

During springtime, I like to serve all of the season's flavors together. Here we have freshly dug new potatoes, candy-like peas, and succulent young lamb—such a welcome glut after winter's doldrums.

**4 lamb tongues**
**1 quart Tongue Brine (page 285)**
**1 medium carrot**
**1 medium yellow onion**
**2 stalks celery**
**1 head garlic, split to expose the cloves**
**1 small leek, white and light green parts only**
**1 bulb fennel, top removed**
**2 bay leaves**
**1 bunch thyme**
**1 pound fingerling potatoes**
**Sea salt**
**1 bay leaf**
**1 teaspoon white wine vinegar**
**Extra-virgin olive oil**
**½ cup Roasted Chicken Stock (page 282)**
**1 cup shelled fresh peas**
**10 leaves mint, torn**
**Lemon juice, to taste**
**Freshly ground black pepper, for finishing**
**Flaky sea salt, for finishing**

**1.** Rinse the tongues, then place in the brine, cover, and refrigerate for 24 hours.

**2.** Remove the tongues from the brine and place them in a nonreactive pot with the carrot, onion, celery, garlic, leek, fennel, 1 bay leaf, and thyme; add water to cover. Bring to a boil, then reduce the heat to a low simmer. Skim the scum as it rises. Cook until tender, when the skin will peel off gently, about 60 to 90 minutes. Peel the skin and then let the tongues cool in the liquid.

**3.** Cover the potatoes with cold water in a small saucepan. Salt the water well, add the remaining bay leaf and vinegar, bring to a simmer, and cook until tender, about 20 minutes. Drain the potatoes and let cool. Peel off the skins and cut into ½-inch-thick coins.

**4.** Cut the tongues into ½-inch slices and pat dry. Coat a sauté pan with olive oil over medium heat, then sear the tongue slices on both sides until well browned and crisp, 2 to 3 minutes on each side. Do this in batches as necessary. Deglaze the pan with chicken stock, and add the potatoes and remaining tongue. Once simmering, add the peas and mint. Adjust with lemon juice and oil.

**5.** Divide the mixture among 4 bowls. Finish the dish with black pepper and a little flaky sea salt.

# LAMB TONGUE & FRIES, LAMB'S TONGUE LETTUCE & PICKLED GRAPES

SERVES 8

This is a pressed terrine, with plenty of tongue and balls. More a play on words than an innuendo, it's more delicate than most people's feelings. Here we serve it thinly sliced, but if you'd like, you can cut it thicker and bread and fry it for a hot variation.

**1 lamb neck, about 2 pounds, to make ½ pound picked meat**
**Sea salt and freshly ground black pepper**
**2 medium carrots**
**2 medium yellow onions**
**4 stalks celery**
**2 heads garlic, split to expose the cloves**
**2 small leeks, white and light green parts only**
**2 bulbs fennel, tops removed**
**2 cups white wine**
**1 quart Lamb Stock (page 282)**
**6 lamb tongues, about 1½ pounds total**
**1 quart Court Bouillon (page 280)**
**½ pound lamb fries (testicles)**
**4 sheets gold-leaf gelatin**
**¼ pound mâche or lamb's tongue lettuce, washed**
**Pickled grapes (recipe follows)**
**1 medium red onion, sliced into thin rings**
**Extra-virgin olive oil**

**Equipment: 14 × 4 × 4-inch terrine mold (1½ quarts)**

**1.** Preheat the oven to 275°F. Season the lamb neck with salt and black pepper. In a braising pan or Dutch oven over medium heat, combine 1 carrot, 1 onion, 2 stalks of celery, 1 head of garlic, 1 leek, 1 bulb of fennel, and the white wine. Bring the mixture to a simmer, and reduce by half. Add the seasoned lamb neck, and cover with lamb stock. Top the mixture with a piece of parchment cut to fit the pan, and braise in the oven until the meat is falling off the bone, about 3 hours. Remove the neck from the braising liquid, strain the liquid into a clean pot, then pick the lamb neck meat in large pieces, letting it cool in the strained lamb braising liquid.

**2.** In a large pot, combine the lamb tongues with the remaining carrot, onion, celery, garlic, leek, and fennel, and cover with salted water. Gently simmer over medium heat until the tongues are tender, 60 to 90 minutes. Remove the tongues from the braising liquid, peel them (see page 28), and put them in a bowl, covered with cooking liquid. Let cool.

**3.** In a nonreactive pot, bring the court bouillon to a boil, turn down the heat to just below a simmer, and poach the lamb fries for 4 minutes, being sure not to let them boil. Remove the fries and shock them in a salted ice-water bath. Once the fries are cold, remove the outer membranes and set the fries aside in the fridge until the terrine is being assembled.

**4.** Spray a terrine mold with cooking spray, then line it with plastic wrap and fill the mold with water to settle the plastic. Pour out the water once the air bubbles in the plastic are gone.

**5.** Bloom the gelatin sheets in a small bowl of water, then drain and squeeze them dry. Reduce the lamb braising stock by half, add the bloomed gelatin sheets, and mix until dissolved. Strain through a fine strainer.

**6.** In a large mixing bowl, add the tongues, picked lamb neck meat, and lamb fries. Season with salt and freshly ground black pepper. Gradually add the enriched lamb stock, just enough to bind the meat.

**7.** Press the meat into the terrine mold. Fold the plastic over the top of the mold, press down, and refrigerate overnight.

**8.** To serve, slice the terrine on the meat slicer or with a sharp knife, 6 to 8 thin slices per person. In a mixing bowl, toss the mâche, pickled grapes, and a few onion slices. Dress with olive oil. Gently mix in the terrine and plate.

## PICKLED GRAPES

MAKES 1 POUND

**2 cups apple cider vinegar**
**2 cups champagne vinegar**
**4 cups sugar**
**4 cloves**
**1 red Fresno chile**
**1 teaspoon fennel seeds**
**1 star anise pod**
**1 tablespoon sliced ginger**
**1 pound seedless red table grapes, such as Red Flame, washed**

**1.** Place all ingredients except the grapes in a nonreactive pot, bring to a boil, turn off the heat, and let steep for 1 hour. Cool with the spices in the mixture, then strain.

**2.** Place the grapes in another nonreactive container, and pour the pickling liquid over them. They can be used after 24 hours.

❤ **233 likes**
**offalchris** all sliced and ready to go

# LAMB BRAIN ON TOAST WITH CREAMED NETTLES & MORELS

SERVES 2

This herbaceous and earthy dish melts in your mouth. And it sounds a lot better than "shit on a shingle," a military term for creamed chipped beef on toast, which is kind of where I got this idea in the first place.

**1 quart Court Bouillon (page 280)**
**Sea salt**
**1 fresh lamb brain, about ½ pound**
**3 tablespoons unsalted butter**
**¼ cup finely diced yellow onion**
**½ pound stinging nettles, chopped (see Note)**
**¼ cup heavy cream**
**3 tablespoons crème fraîche**
**Black pepper**
**2 ½-inch-thick slices Pullman loaf or brioche**
**¼ pound fresh morels, trimmed and cleaned**
**4 branches thyme**

**NOTE:** Wear plastic gloves when handling fresh nettles; "stinging" is no misnomer. They are safe to handle and eat once thoroughly cooked.

**1.** In a medium saucepan over medium-low heat, bring the court boullion to just below a simmer and season with salt. Poach the lamb brain in the court bouillon for about 4 minutes, then remove from the court bouillon and set aside to cool.

**2.** In a small sauté pan, melt 1 tablespoon of butter and sweat the onions until translucent, about 3 minutes. Add the stinging nettles, cover the pan, and cook them down until tender, about 5 minutes.

**3.** Add the heavy cream, crème fraîche, and salt and pepper to taste. Remove the pan from the heat.

**4.** Grill or toast the bread.

**5.** In a separate sauté pan over high heat, add the rest of the butter and sear the brain on the presentation side (the top of the brain) until well browned, about 2 minutes. Meanwhile, add the morels and thyme, then flip over the brain and baste with butter until warm all the way through, another minute or two. The mushrooms should be cooked as well at this point.

**6.** Split the brain down the center into 2 lobes. This will allow the brain to cover more of the toast. Spoon a nice amount of hot creamed nettles on the bread, then top each piece with a brain lobe. Cover with sautéed morels.

# LAMB SWEETBREADS, PINE NUTS, CAPERS & RAISINS AGRODOLCE

SERVES 4

Lamb sweetbreads are small, almost thumb size, but they pack an intense punch. This agrodolce is salty, sweet, and sour, and brings out the best qualities of the lambiness, without masking it.

**2 quarts Court Bouillon (page 280)**
**1 pound lamb sweetbreads**
**Sea salt and freshly ground black pepper**
**Extra-virgin olive oil**
**¼ cup sliced shallots**
**2 tablespoons (¼ stick) unsalted butter**
**¼ cup pine nuts**
**1 teaspoon sugar**
**2 tablespoons white wine**
**¼ cup golden raisins**
**2 bay leaves**
**2 tablespoons Lilliput capers**
**3 tablespoons champagne vinegar**
**¼ cup flat-leaf parsley leaves, coarsely chopped**

**1.** Bring the court bouillon to a gentle simmer in a large saucepan. Poach the sweetbreads in the court bouillon until they are half cooked, about 3 minutes. Remove the sweetbreads and place them on a plate with another plate on top. Weigh the plate down with something heavy, like a can of tomatoes, and place in the fridge overnight. This firms them up and removes any excess blood or bitterness.

**2.** The next day, rinse the sweetbreads. Remove any membrane or fat chunks attached to the sweetbreads. Season them with salt and pepper.

**3.** In a sauté pan over medium-high heat, add a slick of olive oil, then the sweetbreads, and sear until golden brown, about 2 minutes, then flip over and cook until browned, another 2 minutes. Remove the sweetbreads and add the shallots to the pan, cooking until golden brown, 3 minutes. Add the butter, then the pine nuts, and cook until the butter has browned, another 2 to 3 minutes. Add the white wine and deglaze. Add the raisins, bay leaf, and capers, and simmer until dry. Add the vinegar, sugar, and olive oil to taste. Adjust the seasoning with salt and pepper.

**4.** Return the sweetbreads to the pan and add the parsley leaves. Serve on a large platter for sharing. This dish is also great served cold.

# LAMB HEART TARTARE PROVENÇAL

SERVES 4

This dish has all the flavors of a southern French braise—tomatoes, olives, capers, and herbs—but lightened by serving the hearts raw instead of stewed. This tartare gets its depth from the fish sauce and briny olives, and its brightness from tomatoes and refreshing herbs.

**1 pound lamb hearts, untrimmed**
**1 tablespoon salted capers, rinsed**
**2 tablespoons pitted and split niçoise olives**
**¼ cup Sweet 100 or cherry tomatoes, blanched, peeled, and halved lengthwise**
**½ teaspoon thyme leaves**
**2 teaspoons chopped fennel fronds**
**2 teaspoons chopped flat-leaf parsley**
**2 tablespoons finely diced red onion**
**2 tablespoons extra-virgin olive oil, plus more to taste**
**1 teaspoon red wine vinegar**
**Sea salt and freshly ground black pepper**
**Fish sauce, to taste (Red Boat brand preferred)**
**Batard slices, grilled, for serving**

**1.** Remove the fat and inner membrane of the heart's chamber, as well as the arteries on top, as instructed on page 38, then grind the meat in a meat grinder for the best texture and place in a mixing bowl. (Otherwise, hand-cut the meat into small dice.)

**2.** Add the capers, olives, tomatoes, thyme, fennel fronds, parsley, onion, and olive oil to the bowl and mix gently.

**3.** Finish with the vinegar, and adjust the seasoning with salt, pepper, oil, vinegar, and fish sauce. Serve the tartare with warm grilled batard slices and a grind of pepper.

# LAMB PLUCK FRA DIAVOLO

SERVES 4

Here, you're playing with the devil's fire. This is super spicy, but it's served with a mint salsa that will soothe the soul. The pluck of the lamb here includes the heart, liver, and kidneys, since we can't get the lungs and trachea traditionally harvested all at once from the throat, a practice known as *coratella* in Italian. This traditionally includes the lungs as well, but since they are difficult to get here, we will have to do without.

**FOR THE MINT SALSA:**

**3 cups mint leaves**
**Kosher salt**
**¼ cup extra-virgin olive oil**

**FOR THE LAMB PLUCK:**

**1 lamb heart, about ½ pound**
**1 lamb liver, about ½ pound**
**2 lamb kidneys, about ½ pound**
**3 tablespoons Salsa Fra Diavolo (page 277)**
**Sea salt and freshly cracked black pepper**
**1 medium red onion, cut into ¾-inch-thick rings**
**3 tablespoons extra-virgin olive oil**
**2 tablespoons torn mint leaves**
**1 tablespoon orange olive oil (see Note), for drizzling**

**NOTE:** There are many good orange-infused olive oils available on the market, but you can make your own by steeping orange peels in oil.

**MAKE THE MINT SALSA:**

**1.** Blanch the mint leaves in 4 cups of boiling water seasoned with 1 teaspoon salt for 20 seconds, then shock in salted ice water. Squeeze dry, then chop, then blend in a blender with extra-virgin olive oil until smooth.

**PREPARE THE LAMB PLUCK:**

**1.** Trim the heart by removing any hard fat, arteries sticking out the side, and tough membranes, then cut it into 1-inch cubes, again trimming out any tough fibrous tissue. Peel any membrane from the liver, then cut the liver into 1-inch cubes. Cut out the valves of the kidneys and peel the external membrane. Cut the kidneys into quarters, and remove as much interior fat as you can. Place all the organs in a mixing bowl and spoon the fra diavolo sauce over them. Let sit for a few hours to marinate, covered, in the refrigerator.

**2.** Salt and pepper the onion rings. Heat a cast-iron pan over high heat with 1 tablespoon of olive oil, and hard-sear the onions. Char on both sides, about 5 minutes, place them in a mixing bowl, and cover with plastic wrap to let them steam; this helps them finish cooking through.

**3.** Using that same cast-iron pan on super-high heat, add 2 tablespoons of olive oil, then add the marinated offal. Season with salt and hard-sear, turning the meat to sear all sides, 6 minutes total. Add the onion rings, separating the rings, and the torn mint. Cook quickly, leaving the meat medium rare.

**4.** To serve, paint a streak of mint salsa on a warm bowl from the base to the rim; this will be the cooling sauce for the searing and spicy heat of the offal. Place the offal in the center of the bowl, and drizzle with orange olive oil and freshly cracked black pepper.

# CORDEDDA, PEAS, MINT & SHEEP'S MILK POLENTA

SERVES 4

This Italian spiedini is from the islands of Sardinia and Sicily, and the southeastern region of Apulia: spleen, liver, and kidneys wrapped in lamb's intestine, like a chunky sausage, and grilled on a stick. As you grill it, all the fat gets crispy. Serve it over soft polenta, and feel your soul warm up.

**1 lamb heart, about ½ pound**
**1 lamb liver, about 1 pound**
**2 lamb kidneys, about ½ pound total**
**2 lamb spleens, about ½ pound total, cooked (see page 51)**
**1 lamb stomach, cooked (see page 49)**
**¼ cup extra-virgin olive oil**
**2 tablespoons oregano leaves**
**2 cups mint leaves, chopped**
**¼ cup garlic cloves, crushed**
**1 tablespoon Aleppo chile flakes**
**1 tablespoon sea salt**
**2 tablespoons freshly ground black pepper**
**¼ cup white wine**
**¼ pound caul fat**
**Salted ice water, for soaking**
**4 lamb intestines, each about 12 inches long**
**4 cups shelled peas**
**1 cup lamb jus**
**Sheep's Milk Polenta (page 289), for serving**

**Equipment: Bamboo skewers, soaked in water**

**1.** Trim and clean the heart (see page 41), liver (see page 46), and kidneys (see page 54), and poach and prep the spleen (see page 51), then cut them all into 1-inch pieces. Cut the stomach into 1-inch pieces.

**2.** Place all the lamb offal in a mixing bowl and season with the olive oil, oregano, chopped mint, garlic, Aleppo chile, salt, black pepper, and white wine. Cover, refrigerate, and marinate overnight.

**3.** Soak the caul fat overnight in salted ice water. Soak and rinse the lamb intestines (see page 57).

**4.** Form the skewers by layering the meat, alternating cuts. (They're more stable on the grill if you use 2 skewers with about ½ inch of space between them.) Braid the lamb casings into it: With all the meat on the skewers, fold a string of lamb intestines, like you would while braiding hair, at the tip of each skewer. Cross the intestines over the meat, then loop them over the skewer and repeat until the intestines reach the bottom of the skewer. Tie the intestines at the bottom before wrapping the skewer in caul fat.

**5.** Let the skewers come to room temperature before you start grilling. Wrap any exposed bamboo in foil so it doesn't burn on the grill. Preheat the grill to medium-high. Season the skewers with salt. When grilling, rotate the skewers often, making sure that the meat is cooking evenly to medium rare and the caul fat and casings are getting crispy, about 10 minutes total.

**6.** Heat the peas up in the lamb jus, just until warm.

**7.** Once finished, season with salt and serve with sheep's milk polenta and peas.

# LAMB BITS, ASPARAGUS, CHILE & PISTACHIO

SERVES 4 TO 6

I love *larb*, the Isaan Thai dish comprised of minced meat mixed with plenty of chiles and herbs. It can be eaten either raw or cooked, but I like mine right in between, served mid rare. I don't chop mine either; instead, it's more of a shaved salad, with nice big, toothsome bites. This dish is larb filtered through my California lens, with asparagus, lemons, and pistachio joining the party.

**12 extra-large spears asparagus**
**½ cup julienned red onion**
**1 serrano chile, sliced thin**
**1 lamb heart, trimmed but left whole (see page 41), about ½ pound**
**½ pound lamb liver, peeled (see page 46)**
**2 lamb kidneys, split and trimmed (see page 54), about ½ pound**
**Sea salt and freshly ground black pepper**
**2 tablespoons extra-virgin olive oil**
**2 tablespoons Lemon Fish Sauce Vinaigrette, page 273, or to taste**
**1 cup mint leaves**
**1 cup Thai basil leaves**
**Fried shallots (recipe follows)**
**¼ cup pistachios, toasted and chopped**

**1.** Using a vegetable peeler and the woody bottom of the asparagus as a handle, shave the rest of the spear into thin ribbons, and put them into a large mixing bowl. What you can't shave, cut into thin pieces, discarding the part you were holding.

**2.** Place the onion in a mixing bowl with ice water for 10 minutes to take out some of the bite. Use a salad spinner to remove the water, then place the onions with the asparagus. Add the serrano chile.

**3.** Season all the trimmed and cleaned meat with salt and pepper. In a sauté pan over medium-high heat, add the extra-virgin olive oil, and when very hot, add the lamb heart, making sure to get color on all sides, cooking it to medium rare, about 8 minutes total. (A quick way to check is to stick your finger into one of the chambers to see if it's warm inside.) In the same pan, cook the liver until medium rare, about 2 minutes per side. Remove liver and set aside, and in the same sauté pan, sear the kidneys over high heat until golden brown, about 2 minutes per side. Let rest.

**4.** Slice the meats thinly against the grain. Cut each piece of meat a slightly different thickness for different mouthfeels. Place them all in a mixing bowl with the asparagus mixture. Season everything with salt and black pepper, then dress with the vinaigrette. Add the mint and basil. Top with fried shallots and lots of chopped pistachios.

## FRIED SHALLOTS

**2 cups rice bran oil or other neutral oil**
**4 large shallots**
**½ cup Seasoned Flour (see page 270)**
**Sea salt**

**1.** Preheat the oil to 375°F in a large saucepan. Slice the shallots on a mandoline into thin rings. Dust with seasoned flour, and fry until crispy and golden brown, about 3 minutes. Fry in small batches as not to crowd the fryer, which would make them soggy. Remove from the oil and drain on paper towels. Season with salt.

# LAMB LIVER CRUDO & BAGNA CAUDA

SERVES 6

A Piedmontese "hot bath," bagna cauda is usually made during the colder months with raw, cooked, and even roasted vegetables presented around a warm dip of anchovies, garlic, olive oil, and butter. Originally a communal dish like fondue, bagna cauda is commonly served in individual terra-cotta pots. Here, we dress the dish as a whole, which makes for far fewer dishes and, I think, is more delicious.

**1 batch bagna cauda (recipe follows)**
**1 pound fresh lamb liver, membrane and veins removed (see page 46)**
**6 radishes, such as red globe or French breakfast, shaved thin on a mandoline**
**1 bulb fennel, shaved thin on a mandoline**
**3 baby carrots, shaved thin on a mandoline**
**1 celery heart, shaved lengthwise on a mandoline**
**12 haricots verts, blanched, shocked in ice water, and split lengthwise**
**¼ cup flat-leaf parsley leaves**
**Sea salt and freshly ground black pepper**

**1.** Place the bagna cauda in a small pot, and gently warm it on the stovetop while preparing the rest of the dish.

**2.** Using a sharp slicing knife, cut thin sashimi slices from the liver. Make sure there are no veins or blemishes. Arrange 4 pieces in a circle on each plate (make sure the plates are cold).

**3.** Toss the vegetables and parsley in a bowl with salt and pepper, then mound them in the center of each plate.

**4.** Remove the bagna cauda from the stovetop, and lightly dress the liver and vegetables with the warm sauce. Don't overdress or the liver will get lost. Serve immediately.

## BAGNA CAUDA

MAKES ABOUT 1¾ CUPS

**¼ cup salt-packed anchovy fillets, rinsed**
**1 cup white anchovy fillets, oil reserved (see below)**
**¼ cup garlic cloves, sliced**
**1½ tablespoons white anchovy oil (reserved from the white anchovies)**
**3 tablespoons unsalted butter**
**¼ cup extra-virgin olive oil**
**3 tablespoons lemon juice**
**Finely rasped zest of 2 lemons**

**1.** Place all ingredients in a small saucepan over medium-low heat and bring to a simmer. Place the hot mixture in a blender and blend to emulsify.

# LAMB'S LIVER, FAVA BEANS & A NICE CHIANTI

SERVES 2

You guessed it: this recipe is an ode to *The Silence of the Lambs*. Hannibal Lecter had very good taste for the finer things in life.

**1 pound lamb liver, peeled, any arteries or veins removed (see page 46)**
**Sea salt and freshly ground black pepper**
**3 tablespoons extra-virgin olive oil**
**1 bunch thyme**
**1 bunch parsley stems**
**¼ cup garlic cloves, crushed**
**3 bay leaves**
**4 tablespoons unsalted butter**
**¼ cup Chianti Classico, or another Tuscan red wine**
**½ cup Roasted Chicken Stock (see page 282)**
**4 cups fava beans, blanched, shelled, and peeled**

**1.** Season the liver with salt and pepper, and dress it with 1 tablespoon olive oil. Cover it with thyme, parsley stems, garlic cloves, and bay leaves, and let it come to room temperature. Reserve the thyme and garlic when you remove the liver; they'll be added to the pan when sautéing.

**2.** Heat a cast-iron skillet over high heat until very hot, reduce the heat to medium, add 2 tablespoons olive oil to the pan, and place the smoother side of the liver down first. Add the reserved thyme and garlic cloves and 2 tablespoons butter, and baste the liver. Caramelize the presentation side of the liver, then flip over and baste continuously with the butter. When the liver is warm through, after about 2 minutes on each side (test it with a cake tester), let the liver rest on a rack near the heat.

**3.** Empty the pan and return to the heat, adding the remaining butter. When the butter has browned, deglaze with red wine, and reduce by half, 1 to 2 minutes. Add the chicken stock and the fava beans. Cook until tender, about 2 minutes. Taste and adjust seasoning as needed. Remove from the heat.

**4.** To serve, slice the liver into 4 pieces, and divide among plates. Top with the Chianti sauce and fava beans. Make a creepy sucking sound and dive in.

# SMOKED LAMB LIVER, SERRANO & MINT BRUSCHETTA

SERVES 12 TO 15 AS A SNACK

This is kind of like having chicken liver and schmaltz, except with cold smoked lamb liver. Smoking is a great way of preserving meat, as we know from things like sausages and jerky, but this dish is made into a spread. A bit more char is added with the grilled chiles and onions. Though this recipe calls it a bruschetta, there have been times when I've made this as a sandwich to go.

**2 pounds lamb liver, membrane and veins removed (see page 46)**
**1 medium yellow onion, cut into 1-inch-thick rings**
**3 serrano chiles**
**Sea salt**
**0.5 gram pink curing salt, such as Instacure #1**
**Freshly ground black pepper**
**Extra-virgin olive oil**
**2 cups mint leaves**
**1 pound butter, cut into cubes, at room temperature**
**Champagne vinegar, to taste**
**¼ pound Padrón chiles**
**6 ½-inch-thick slices batard**

**Equipment: Cold-smoking setup of your choice, or a grill; ¾ cup Pinot Noir barrel shavings or other wood chips; 14 × 4 × 4-inch terrine mold**

**1.** Cut the liver into medium-size pieces.

**2.** Cold smoke the lamb liver for 30 minutes. The best way to cold smoke depends on your kitchen and preference. To make it real easy, you can use a smoking gun, which will produce all the smoke you need. To smoke in a grill, soak your wood chips in water for about 30 minutes. Start a small fire on one end of the grill, and let it burn to embers. Smother the embers with the drained wood chips, and remove any air by shutting all the vents on the lid and closing it. Once the smoke is billowing, put the liver in a pan with ice to keep it cold, and place it all the way on the opposite side of the embers and smoke, so it's away from any heat. Close the lid and check the liver every 10 minutes with a thermometer to make sure the temperature doesn't go over 68°F. Once the liver is smoked, place it in a ziplock bag, then refrigerate it until ready to use in the next step of the recipe.

**3.** Preheat a grill to medium-high heat. Grill the onion slices with the serrano chiles. Once they have a nice char all over, place them in a mixing bowl and cover.

**4.** Season the liver with the sea salt, curing salt, and black pepper. In a sauté pan over high heat, add olive oil to coat the bottom of the pan and then, when it's very hot, add the liver. Sear the liver on both sides, 2 to 3 minutes each, for a nice medium rare. Do this in batches; do not overcrowd the pan.

**5.** Once all the liver is cooked, transfer it, the grilled onions and chiles, and the mint leaves (reserving a few for garnish) to a food processor and blend. Slowly add the butter and adjust the seasoning with vinegar and salt. Once all the butter is incorporated, pass the whole mixture through a tamis or fine-mesh strainer for a smooth consistency.

**6.** Spray a terrine mold with cooking spray and line it with plastic wrap. Pour in the liver mixture, then cover with the plastic wrap to seal tight. Let it rest in the refrigerator overnight before serving.

**7.** Blister the Padrón chiles in a sauté pan over high heat until they have nicely charred spots, about 4 minutes. Grill the bread. Spread a thick amount of liver spread onto the bread and top with the warm blistered chiles, reserved torn mint, sea salt, black pepper, and a nice drizzle of olive oil; serve.

# LAMB LIVER BOTTARGA, MÂCHE, RADISH & SHEEP'S MILK BUTTER ON TOAST

SERVES 4

Bottarga is a salt-cured fish roe, used mostly as a dish finisher to add tons of depth and flavor. Taking that idea, I've made "bottargas" from livers and blood. The liver is prepared using the same process as traditional bottarga and becomes an umami bomb as it ages, like grated Parmesan cheese over pasta.

**4 1-inch-thick slices country bread**
**Peel and juice of 1 lemon**
**2 tablespoons unsalted butter (sheep's milk, if available)**
**6 red globe radishes, shaved thin**
**6 French breakfast radishes, quartered**
**4 cups mâche (a.k.a. lamb's tongue lettuce)**
**Sea salt, to taste**
**Extra-virgin olive oil, to taste**
**3-inch piece Lamb Liver Bottarga (page 288) (or enough for 40 thin slices)**

**1.** Grill or toast the bread on both sides. Rub the crisped bread with lemon peel on both sides. Then spread a nice layer of butter on the bread.

**2.** In separate mixing bowls, dress the radishes and mâche with lemon juice, salt, and olive oil.

**3.** Divide the radishes among the bruschetta, then top with the mâche. Shave the lamb liver bottarga over the bruschetta using a mandolin or a bonito shaver for beautiful curls.

# LAMB TRIPE & PORCINI

SERVES 6 TO 8

Jean-Louis Palladin was a kind, brilliant, and sharing person. He changed the way people ate in this country; in the 1980s, when many restaurants were still relying on canned or frozen vegetables, he was one of the first Michelin-starred French chefs to come here and insist on using only the freshest and best ingredients. He encouraged chefs to go directly to the farm and use every scrap of food, whether meat or vegetable. This dish does exactly that. Lamb tripe has a very intense flavor, but I cook it with mint "bones"—just the stems—to temper it. Palladin would pair offal with extravagant ingredients, like caviar, truffles, and porcini mushrooms, to prove these lesser cuts could commingle with haute produce. This is an homage to him.

**2 pounds lamb tripe, rinsed and trimmed of excess fat and blemishes**
**Sea salt and freshly ground black pepper**
**2½ cups white wine**
**1 medium carrot**
**1 whole medium onion, plus 1 large onion, medium-diced**
**2 stalks celery**
**1 head garlic, split to expose the cloves, plus 2 tablespoons sliced**
**1 small leek, white and light green parts, plus 1 sliced into rings, white part only**
**1 bulb fennel, top removed**
**1 bunch mint stems**
**2 bay leaves**
**1 bunch thyme**
**¼ cup extra-virgin olive oil**
**2 cups Lamb Stock (page 282)**
**2 pounds porcini mushrooms, cleaned and cut into ¼-inch slices**
**Sherry vinegar, to taste**
**2 tablespoons chopped nepitella**
**A dozen slices of grilled baguette**

**1.** In a bowl, season the lamb tripe with salt and pepper. Add 2 cups of white wine and the carrot, whole onion, celery, split garlic, 1 leek, and fennel, and let sit overnight, covered, in the refrigerator.

**2.** Transfer the tripe mixture to a pot. Add a tightly tied cheesecloth sachet containing the mint stems, bay leaves, and thyme. Cover with cold water and bring to a boil. Skim any fat or scum and reduce the heat to a simmer. Cook until tender, about 2 hours; let the tripe cool in the braising liquid. Once cool, remove the tripe from the liquid and cut into 1-inch squares.

**3.** In a braising pan over medium heat, add 2 tablespoons olive oil and sweat the diced onions, leek rings, and sliced garlic, about 10 minutes. Once the vegetables are tender, deglaze with the remaining ½ cup white wine, and cook until dry. Add the tripe and lamb stock, and bring to a simmer.

**4.** In a separate sauté pan over high heat, add 2 tablespoons olive oil and the porcini, sear for 2 minutes or until golden brown, and then season with salt and pepper. Do this in batches to avoid crowding the pan. Add the porcinis to the tripe pot and let simmer to heat through, a couple minutes. The goal is to marry all the flavors and reduce the tripe liquid to a nice saucy consistency, while not overcooking the mushrooms. Adjust the seasoning with sherry vinegar, salt, and black pepper. To serve, add the chopped nepitella and serve with grilled bread.

# LAMB INTESTINE, SHEEP'S MILK RICOTTA, MINT, PENNE & BLACK PEPPER

SERVES 4

This pasta dish, found in old trattorias of Rome, is called *pajata* and traditionally uses the intestines of a calf, which has only fed on its mother's milk. The *chyme* (milk) is left in the intestines, and when heat is applied, it reacts with the natural rennet to make a creamy sauce. The tubular penne is used to reinforce the shape of the intestine itself. This version is a little more accessible, using cleaned tripe and ricotta instead.

**Sea salt**
**2 tablespoons extra-virgin olive oil, plus more for drizzling**
**1 cup finely diced yellow onion**
**2 tablespoons sliced garlic**
**¼ cup white wine**
**1 pound lamb tripe, cooked (see page 47) and cut about the size of penne**
**2 cups Roasted Chicken Stock (page 282), plus more as needed**
**1 pound dried penne pasta**
**2 tablespoons unsalted butter**
**1 cup sheep's milk ricotta**
**Freshly cracked black pepper**
**½ cup torn mint leaves**
**Pecorino, for grating**

**1.** Bring a pot of salted water to boil for the pasta. While the pasta water is coming to a boil, start the sauce.

**2.** In a large sauté pan over medium heat, add the olive oil and onions. Sweat until the onions are tender, stirring, about 6 minutes, then add the garlic and cook until tender but not browned, about 3 minutes. Deglaze with the white wine and cook until the vegetables are dry, about 3 minutes. Add the tripe and chicken stock, and simmer until the liquid is reduced by half, about 10 minutes. Season with salt to taste.

**3.** When the salted water boils, cook the pasta to al dente; drain, then return the pasta to the pot. Add the tripe sauce, butter, and ricotta, and mix well. Season with salt and pepper, and add the mint. If the sauce is too thick, add some more chicken stock.

**4.** Transfer the pasta to a large serving platter, grate some fresh pecorino on top, drizzle with olive oil, and add more freshly cracked black pepper.

# SICILIAN LAMB SPLEEN BRUSCHETTA, CACIOCAVALLO CHEESE & SALSA PICANTE

SERVES 6

*Pani ca meusa*—slices of tender, minerally spleen covered in shredded cheese and wrapped in paper—is the O.G. Sicilian grab-and-go sandwich that will make a mess of your shirt, like a badge of offal honor.

Here we make this as an open-face sandwich, so you don't have to stuff a *vastedda* (the soft roll traditionally used in Palermo) until it's about to bust.

**2 quarts Court Bouillon (page 280)**
**12 lamb spleens, about 1¼ pounds total**
**Sea salt**
**4 tablespoons unsalted butter**
**⅓ cup slivered garlic**
**Freshly ground black pepper**
**6 ½-inch-thick slices country bread**
**¼ pound arugula**
**Caciocavallo cheese, for grating**
**Salsa Picante (page 279)**

**1.** Bring the court bouillon to a bare simmer in a large saucepan. Add the spleens and poach them for 10 minutes, then remove them from the heat and let cool. Remove any veins or loose membranes, then split each spleen in half lengthwise. Pat them dry and season them with salt.

**2.** Heat a large sauté pan over medium heat and add the butter, letting it brown. Add the spleens and sear them, getting nice color on both sides, about 6 minutes total, adding the garlic halfway through and seasoning them with salt and pepper.

**3.** Grill or toast the bread. Place one slice on each plate, and top each with arugula and 4 spleen halves. Drizzle the garlic butter from cooking the spleens on each bruschetta. Top with grated caciocavallo. Finish with a nice amount of salsa picante. Serve immediately.

# LAMB KIDNEYS, LENTILS, CHILE & MINT

SERVES 2

This dish is no more than whole kidneys cooked in butter, served over a pile of nutty Umbrian lentils. It's so easy and satisfying that you'll find yourself craving a warm bowl on brisk nights.

**4 lamb kidneys, 1 pound total**
**1 cup Umbrian lentils**
**1 head garlic, split to expose the cloves, plus ¼ cup slivered and 2 whole cloves, smashed**
**1 bunch thyme, 1 branch reserved**
**1 bay leaf**
**1 bunch parsley stems**
**4 cups Roasted Chicken Stock (page 282)**
**Sea salt**
**½ cup all-purpose flour**
**Freshly ground black pepper**
**2 tablespoons extra-virgin olive oil, plus more for drizzling**
**1 small onion, finely diced**
**1 medium carrot, finely diced**
**½ Fresno chile, thinly sliced**
**3 tablespoons lemon juice**
**1 cup mint leaves**
**2 tablespoons (¼ stick) unsalted butter**

**1.** If the kidneys are super fresh, simply cut out the valves and fat. If they are a little funkier, soak them in salted ice water as described on page 53.

**2.** Rinse the lentils in cold water, then place them in a medium saucepan and cover with water. Bring to a boil over high heat. Drain and rinse again with cold water. Return the lentils to the pot with the split garlic head, the herbs tied in a bundle, and the chicken stock. Simmer the lentils gently until they are tender, 20 to 25 minutes. Once tender, salt to taste and allow the lentils to cool in their cooking liquid, removing the split garlic and bundle of herbs. Strain and discard liquid, or reserve it for another use.

**3.** Season the flour with salt and pepper. Dry the kidneys well, season with salt and pepper, and lightly dust with the flour mixture.

**4.** In a medium sauté pan, heat olive oil over medium heat. Sweat the fine dice of carrot and onion, then sizzle the slivered garlic and fresno chile until the garlic is light golden brown, about 5 minutes. Add the lentils and toss gently to coat. Deglaze the pan with the lemon juice, season with salt and pepper to taste, and toss in the torn mint.

**5.** Heat the butter in a large sauté pan over medium-high heat. Add the smashed garlic cloves and the reserved thyme branch, sizzle for a minute, and then add the kidneys. Sear until golden brown, about 3 minutes, then flip over and cook until medium rare, about another 3 minutes.

**6.** Divide the lentils among warmed plates, top with the kidneys, drizzle with olive oil, and serve immediately.

# FRITTULA

SERVES 4

Here's another Sicilian street food from Palermo. All the scratchings and trim from the lamb slaughter are boiled, pressed to remove the water, and then fried in lard. Guys with covered baskets, called *panaru,* take a handful and place it on waxed paper or stuff it in a sesame bun. I've added some shaved fried artichokes and lemon to liven up the dish.

**4 lamb's feet, cleaned (see page 63)**
**2 lamb's ears, cleaned (see page 31)**
**2 lamb's stomachs, cleaned (see page 49)**
**Sea salt and freshly ground black pepper**
**1 cup white wine**
**1 medium carrot**
**1 medium yellow onion**
**2 stalks celery**
**1 head garlic, split to expose the cloves**
**1 small leek, white and light green parts only**
**1 bulb fennel, top removed**
**6 baby artichokes**
**4 lemon wedges, plus more for acidulating the water**
**2 cups Seasoned Flour (page 270)**
**Rice bran oil or other neutral oil, for frying**
**½ cup mint leaves**

**1.** Marinate the lamb parts with salt, pepper, white wine, carrot, onion, celery, garlic, leek, and fennel overnight, covered, in the fridge.

**2.** In a large nonreactive stockpot, place a diffuser or wire rack in the bottom. Add the marinated vegetables, with the meats on top. Cover with salted water, bring to a gentle simmer, and cook until the meats are tender, 3½ to 4 hours.

**3.** Cool the meats in the braising liquid. Separate the meat and skin from the feet, and pat the feet dry. Remove the stomachs from the liquid, dry them off, and cut into 1-inch squares. Cut the ears into strips, ½ inch thick and no more than 3 inches long, and pat dry. Using a mandoline, shave the artichokes ¼ inch thick into acidulated water.

**4.** Preheat a deep fryer or a pot with several inches of oil to 350°F. Dredge the meats in a light coating of seasoned flour. Fry the meats in batches until crispy, about 5 minutes, then drain on paper towels and season with salt and pepper. Drain and pat dry the artichokes, then dredge and fry them until crisp, about 3 minutes. Drain them on paper towels and season with salt. Place everything on a large piece of butcher paper. Quickly fry the mint leaves and place them on top. Serve with a few wedges of lemon.

# LAMB FRIES, SWEETBREADS, BACON & CAPERS

SERVES 1 OR 2

Let's put this "anything's better with bacon" rule to a test. Serving lamb testicles with sweetbreads and thick rashers of bacon will leave you asking for more! I came up with this recipe after butchering a lamb and thinking about what to do with the two sweetbreads and the pair of fries. Of course, you can scale it up to serve more.

**2 lamb sweetbreads**
**Sea salt and freshly ground black pepper**
**1 bunch thyme**
**1 bay leaf**
**1 head garlic, split to expose the cloves**
**1 strip lemon peel**
**2 quarts Roasted Chicken Stock (page 282)**
**1 pair of lamb fries (testicles)**
**2 slices bacon**
**1 teaspoon capers, drained**
**2 tablespoons unsalted butter**

**1.** Season the sweetbreads with salt and pepper. Put the thyme, bay leaf, garlic, and lemon peel in a stockpot and cover with chicken stock. Bring the stock to a simmer over medium heat and cook for 20 minutes, then add the sweetbreads. Poach for 4 minutes, until medium rare, then remove and plunge the sweetbreads into salted ice water, reserving the chicken stock and refrigerating it overnight.

**2.** Remove the sweetbreads from the ice water and press out the liquid by weighting them with some cans on a plate. Chill, covered, overnight. This will remove the extra blood and bitterness.

**3.** The next day, peel off the membranes, devein the sweetbreads, and set aside.

**4.** In a large saucepan, bring the reserved chilled stock to a boil. Blanch the fries for 2 minutes, then drop them in an ice-water bath to cool. Holding the fries in one hand, cut each one across the membrane with a knife, slicing the three membranes but not the meat. Remove the meat from inside the membrane.

**5.** Preheat a sauté pan over medium heat. Add the bacon. Let the bacon release some of its fat, then add the sweetbreads. Season and sauté the sweetbreads until they are golden brown on one side, about 3 minutes, then flip them. Once they start to brown on the second side, after about 3 minutes, add fries, capers, and butter. Once there's color on all the meats, after a few more minutes, deglaze the pan with about ⅓ cup of the stock. Stir the mixture to emulsify. Season with salt and pepper, then serve.

CHICKEN

TURKEY

DUCK

SQUAB

RABBIT*

*because the USDA's classification system is weird and rabbit is considered poultry

# FOWL

# CRISP SKINS

Ashkenazi Jews use chicken-skin scraps to make schmaltz, but it's the by-product, crispy skin bits called gribenes, that are eaten as a snack. I think of it as the potato chip of Judaism. I like mine baked thin, and I even use them as croutons for a salad. This is a method more than a recipe, as it works for pretty much any poultry skin you can think of, but you'll have to watch the time—thinner skins will crisp much faster.

**Skin of 1 bird, or many**
**Sea salt**
**Freshly ground black pepper**

**1.** Preheat the oven to 325°F. Put on a pot of water and bring it to a boil. Blanch each piece of skin for a few seconds, just enough to firm up the skin and make it somewhat translucent. Drain and pat the skin pieces very dry with paper towels. Spread the skins out nice and flat in a single layer on a Silpat- or parchment-lined sheet tray, and season with salt and pepper. Cover the skins with another Silpat or parchment paper, then place another sheet tray on top. Bake until crispy. Each skin crisps differently, and the ones at the edges of the pan may finish first, so watch the pan, rotate it, and expect anywhere from 5 minutes up until they're done, sometimes as much as 50 minutes. Let them cool, break them into shards if you want, and store in an airtight container for a couple days, but they're better the sooner you use them.

# ROASTED SQUAB HEADS WITH SQUAB LIVER AIOLI

SERVES 4

Every serious food lover knows about eating ortolans in France, where diners famously put napkins over their heads when they chomp down to get at the birds' brains. (And they know that eating ortolans is illegal now.) Well, what I like to do with squab heads won't require you to get a lawyer or cover yourself in linens, but you might end up covering yourself in their spicy umami coating. The beak is a great built-in handle. Dip it in the Liver Aioli, then enjoy some brains!

**24 very fresh squab heads, necks removed**
**Sea salt and freshly ground black pepper**
**3 tablespoons duck fat**
**6 cloves garlic, unpeeled**
**½ bunch thyme**
**1 serrano chile, sliced paper thin**
**1 teaspoon Aleppo chile flakes**
**½ cup thinly sliced scallions**
**2 teaspoons fish sauce, preferably Red Boat**
**Liver Aioli (page 274, preferably made with squab livers), for serving**

**1.** Preheat the oven to 375°F. Season the heads with salt and pepper. Preheat a large ovenproof sauté pan over medium heat, add some duck fat, and cook the heads in batches. Roll them around in the pan for a good all-around sear. Add the garlic and thyme, then transfer the pan to the oven and bake for 5 minutes. They're done when the eyes have liquid coming out of them.

**2.** Toss the heads in a large mixing bowl with the serrano, Aleppo chile, scallions, fish sauce, and 2 teaspoons black pepper. Split the heads by taking the tip of a knife, stabbing the skull, and slicing down through the beak.

**3.** Serve with squab liver aioli as a dipping sauce.

# CRISPY DUCK TONGUES & BIRDSEED

SERVES 4

You'll pop these in your mouth as if they were Chex Mix or your favorite bar snacks. Fried and puffed quinoa, farro, and rice—giving true meaning to "eating like a bird"—well, it only seemed fitting to crisp up some duck tongues to go with them.

**2 ounces sunflower seeds**
**Extra-virgin olive oil**
**Sea salt**
**2 ounces pumpkin seeds, hulled**
**2 ounces barley**
**2 ounces quinoa**
**2 ounces freekeh**
**Neutral oil, for frying**
**Freshly ground black pepper**
**1 cup rosemary needles**
**1 pound duck tongues, prepped and braised (see page 29)**
**1 cup fried shallots (see Note)**

**NOTE:** Fried shallots are available in Asian markets, and they are delicious. To make them yourself, slice 1 pound of shallots ⅛ inch thick on a mandoline, and place them in a pot with neutral oil to generously cover, about 4 cups. Place this over medium-low heat and cook, stirring more often as the shallots go from sizzling, to sticky, to "fluffy," 35 to 45 minutes total. Strain (the oil is delicious for drizzling and dressings) and drain the shallots in one layer on paper towels. Season with salt, let cool, and then store them in an airtight container in the refrigerator for up to a few weeks.

**1.** Preheat the oven to 300°F. Toss the sunflower seeds with a little bit of olive oil and salt. Roast until golden brown, about 4 minutes. Repeat with the pumpkin seeds. Once the two seeds are cool, mix together.

**2.** Simmer the barley, quinoa, and freekeh in separate pots, covered with water, until they bloom and become tender. The time differs from grain to grain, so make sure they are cooked by taking a taste; they should be toothsome but not hard. Once all the grains are cooked, drained, and cooled, keep them separate and dry them in a dehydrator overnight, or place them on sheet trays in an oven with the fan on cool and the oven off. This will dry the grains and let them puff.

**3.** Preheat a fryer or a large pot with several inches of oil to 375°F. Fry each grain separately until crispy, drain on paper towels, and season a bit with salt and black pepper. Fry the rosemary needles until just crisp, then season with salt and set aside to drain on a paper towel. Once all the grains are done, fry the duck tongues in batches until they puff, which should be real quick, about 1 minute. Mix tongues, grains, and fried shallots together, and serve with a great crisp beer.

# FRIED RABBIT EARS & CARROT AIOLI

SERVES 6 TO 8

While pig ears usually fry up crisp and chewy, thin rabbit ears fry up more like chips. Keeping with the theme, carrot juice is folded into an aioli for serving alongside, and a little *pluche* of chervil sits atop like a carrot top.

**Sea salt**
**2 pounds rabbit ears**
**Freshly ground black pepper**
**Neutral oil, for frying**
**1 cup Seasoned Flour (page 270)**
**½ cup chervil pluches**
**1 cup Carrot Aioli (page 274)**

**1.** In a large nonreactive pot, bring a gallon of water to a boil. Add 2 tablespoons of salt and blanch the rabbit ears for a minute, just to loosen the skin. Dump the water and start over again. Bring the water up to a boil, then add the ears, reduce the heat to a simmer, and cook until the hair and skin start to slide off, about 15 minutes.

**2.** Drain the ears and quickly remove the hair and outer skin layer. Do this while they're hot—it will be much easier. Lay them on a sheet tray, pat dry, and season with salt and pepper while they are still warm, then let them cool.

**3.** Preheat a deep fryer or a large pot with several inches of oil to 350°F. Toss the rabbit ears in the seasoned flour and fry in small batches until crispy, about 4 minutes. Place the fried ears in a bowl lined with paper towels and season lightly with salt and pepper. To serve, place them in a paper cone or on a piece of paper with the chervil pluches and a ramekin of carrot aioli.

❤ **368 likes**
**offalchris** a perfect snack of rabbit and carrot

# TURKEY LUNGS ON TOAST WITH SAGE BROWN BUTTER

SERVES 6

Every year I go up to Sonoma to visit Jim Reichardt, who owns Sonoma County Poultry. We harvest heritage breed turkeys with the 4-H kids so they can sell birds for the Thanksgiving holiday to raise money for the schools, and I get all the weird bits. I serve these as an appetizer, as the lungs are small. You have to soak them in salted water for 30 minutes to get the blood out, but then you press them so that, when cooked, they have a texture similar to crispy tofu that's still creamy on the inside.

**1 pound turkey lungs**
**Salt**
**2 quarts Court Bouillon (page 280)**
**Freshly ground black pepper**
**4 tablespoons unsalted butter**
**12 large sage leaves**
**2 tablespoons sherry vinegar**
**2 cups Roasted Chicken Stock (page 282)**
**4 1-inch-thick slices sourdough batard, toasted or grilled**

**1.** Trim the lungs of any tubes, then soak them in salted ice water for 24 hours to remove any blood. Remove the lungs from the water, place them in a large pot with the court bouillon, and simmer until tender, about 35 minutes, skimming continuously to remove all of the scum and impurities. Once cooked through, strain them from the liquid, place in a perforated pan set over another one to catch the liquid, weight them down to press them, and refrigerate overnight.

**2.** The next day, remove the lungs from the fridge and pat dry.

**3.** Season the lungs with salt and black pepper. In a large sauté pan over high heat, melt 2 tablespoons butter, and, when the butter is foaming, add the lungs. Sear until crispy, about 4 minutes on high heat, then flip the lungs, add the sage, and deglaze with sherry vinegar. Once the vinegar has nearly cooked dry, add the chicken stock and mount in the remaining butter, knob by knob, until the mixture is emulsified.

**4.** Place the toasted bread on plates, top with the lungs and sauce, and serve.

# CONFIT GIBLETS, POACHED DUCK EGG & DANDELION

SERVES 4

A great side for Thanksgiving, the giblets are marinated in an herbaceous salt to add a lot of flavor, then confited in duck fat to impart a richness. You'll want to ensure there are leftovers, just so you can have it again for breakfast with a soft poached egg on top.

**1 pound duck hearts, cleaned (see page 41)**
**1 pound duck gizzards, cleaned (see page 72)**
**Sea salt and freshly ground black pepper**
**0.1 gram pink curing salt (just enough to fit on just the tip of a paring knife), such as Instacure #1**
**1 bunch thyme**
**2 bay leaves**
**1 bunch parsley stems**
**1 head garlic, split to expose the cloves**
**½ gallon duck fat, or to cover**
**2 cups ½-inch-diced stale bread**
**3 cups red wine**
**4 duck eggs**
**1 pound duck liver, cleaned (see page 46)**
**½ pound baby dandelion greens**
**¼ cup sliced shallots**
**Sherry Vinaigrette (page 272)**

**1.** In a nonreactive heatproof container, combine the hearts and gizzards and season with salt, black pepper, and the curing salt. Toss with the thyme, bay leaves, parsley stems, and garlic, and let sit, covered, in the refrigerator overnight.

**2.** Remove the giblets (gizzards and hearts) from the refrigerator and let them come to room temp. Preheat the oven to 250°F. Warm the duck fat on the stove until hot but not very hot, and reserve a little for crisping croutons and sautéing livers. Pour the rest of the fat over the hearts and gizzards with all the herbs and garlic.

**3.** Place the giblets and duck fat in the oven. Cook until tender, about 2 hours. When they are done, remove the giblets from the fat and keep warm.

**4.** In a sauté pan over medium heat, add some of the reserved duck fat and sauté the croutons until golden brown and crispy, about 3 to 4 minutes. Season with salt. Set aside.

**5.** In a separate pot, combine the red wine, 1 cup of water, and a teaspoon of salt, and bring to a boil. Crack in the duck eggs, one at a time, and turn the heat to the lowest setting, making sure to poach them soft, about 4 minutes.

**6.** Pat the liver dry with paper towels and season with salt and pepper. Heat a large sauté pan over high heat, add the remaining reserved duck fat, and when the fat is very hot, sauté the liver, flipping once, until medium rare, about 3 minutes total.

**7.** In a large mixing bowl, toss together the dandelion greens, shallots, and crispy croutons. Add the giblets and liver to the salad at the last minute. Dress with the sherry vinaigrette, and adjust the seasoning with salt and black pepper.

**8.** Divide the salad among 4 plates, then top each with a warm poached egg, season with salt and black pepper, and serve.

KETTLE
67 & 69. West
NEWPORT

# GRILLED DUCK HEARTS, HAZELNUT OIL & BLACK PEPPER

SERVES 4

Izakaya restaurants in Japan often serve a little bowl of sesame oil with their grilled chicken hearts. You dip the warm, tender hearts into the nutty oil, then dab them into another bowl of spicy black pepper, and you keep going back for more and more. Here we use meaty duck hearts and sweet hazelnut oil as a riff. Kanpai!

**1 pound fresh duck hearts**
**Sea salt**
**Olive oil, for the grill**
**¼ cup hazelnut oil**
**4 lemon wedges**
**Coarsely ground black pepper**

**Equipment: Bamboo skewers**

**1.** Soak the skewers in water so they won't burn when you are grilling.

**2.** Trim the hearts, making sure to remove any hard bits and squeezing to remove any excess clotted blood from the chambers. Preheat a grill to medium heat.

**3.** Distribute the hearts evenly among the skewers, making sure there is a little space between the hearts. Season with salt, oil the grill grates, and then grill the hearts, rotating evenly so they get nice color all over. Once they are medium rare, about 4 minutes total, place the skewers on a plate with the lemon wedges. Serve with a side of hazelnut oil and salt and pepper to season as you wish.

# BEST PARTS OF THE CHICKEN RISOTTO

SERVES 4

This risotto is inspired by a classic Torino dish called *finanziera*, which translates to "the financiers." Using all the best parts of the bird, it was made for the money guys who came to market. It's a true testament to how many flavors and textures can come from one bird. This serves several people, but of course if you want to be like the finanziera, you can be greedy and hog it all yourself.

**1 bunch thyme**
**4 chicken thighs, skin removed and crisped (see page 234)**
**Sea salt and freshly ground black pepper**
**One good pull of peel from a lemon, plus grated lemon zest, for garnish**
**2 cloves garlic**
**2 bay leaves**
**2 quarts Roasted Chicken Stock (page 282), hot**
**¼ cup extra-virgin olive oil, plus more for searing the livers**
**1 medium onion, small dice**
**2 cups Vialone Nano Fino or other risotto rice**
**½ cup white wine**
**12 confit chicken hearts (prepared as on page 239)**
**12 confit chicken gizzards (prepared as on page 239)**
**4 cockscombs, cleaned and cooked (see page 72)**
**12 chicken livers**
**2 large egg yolks**
**Crisp Skin (page 234), to garnish**

**1.** Preheat the oven to 300°F. Pick 2 tablespoons of leaves from the thyme and reserve them for finishing the dish. Season the thighs with salt and black pepper. Place them in an ovenproof pan with the lemon peel, garlic cloves, the remaining thyme stems, and 1 bay leaf, and cover with hot chicken stock. Place in the oven until just cooked through, about 30 minutes. Let the thighs cool in the liquid, then remove them and pull the meat into bite-size pieces. (Save the liquid to braise the cockscombs.) This liquid will be then used to make the risotto.

**2.** Warm the reserved chicken stock in a saucepan on the stove and keep hot. In a 12- to 14-inch skillet, heat the olive oil over medium heat. Add the onion and cook until softened and translucent but not browned, 8 to 10 minutes. Add the rice, and stir with a wooden spoon until toasted and opaque, 3 to 4 minutes. Add the wine and remaining bay leaf to the rice, and cook until nearly dry. Add a 4- to 6-ounce ladle of stock, and cook, stirring, until it is absorbed. Continue adding the stock a ladleful at a time, waiting until the liquid is absorbed before adding more, until the rice is tender and creamy yet a little al dente, using about 6 cups of liquid and cooking for 15 to 20 minutes. Just before adding the last addition of stock, add the confit chicken bits, cockscombs, and pulled thigh meat.

**3.** At the same time, heat a medium sauté pan until very hot, pat the chicken livers dry, and season them with salt and pepper. Film the pan with olive oil, and sear the livers until browned and medium rare, about 1½ minutes per side.

**4.** Take the risotto off the heat, and stir in the egg yolks until well mixed and thickened. Adjust the seasoning with salt, pepper, and lemon zest. Top with the reserved thyme and crispy chicken skin.

# DUCK BLOOD SOUP, GRILLED HEARTS & SEED QUACKERS

SERVES 6 TO 8

Blood soup is a classic in many cuisines, known in Poland as *czernina,* in Sweden as *svartsoppa,* and in the Philippines as *dinuguan.* This is the poultry version of the pork-based, vinegar-laced dinuguan. All the seeds of a duck's feed season the thin, crunchy "quacker."

**¼ cup duck fat, plus more for finishing**
**1 medium yellow onion, medium dice**
**1 medium carrot, medium dice**
**1 head fennel, top removed, medium dice**
**3 ribs celery, medium dice**
**6 cloves garlic, chopped**
**1 teaspoon thyme leaves**
**2 cups red wine**
**6 cups duck stock (see page 282, using duck bones instead of chicken)**
**2 teaspoons balsamic vinegar**
**Sea salt and freshly ground black pepper**
**6 cups duck blood**
**24 fresh duck hearts**
**2 tablespoons extra-virgin olive oil, plus more for drizzling**
**2 bunches chives, cut into 1-inch lengths**
**1 cup chervil leaves**
**¼ cup celery leaves**
**¼ cup flat-leaf parsley leaves**
**Red wine vinegar, to taste**
**Seed quackers (recipe follows)**

**1.** Heat the duck fat in a large, nonreactive pot over medium heat, add the onion, carrot, fennel, celery, garlic, and thyme, and cook until the vegetables are lightly caramelized, about 15 minutes, constantly stirring so they cook evenly. Deglaze the pot with the red wine and cook until nearly dry, then add the duck stock and bring it to a simmer. Cook for 20 minutes over low heat.

**2.** Place this soup base in a blender in batches, and blend until smooth, being careful to protect your hand with a towel while blending hot liquids. Pass the soup through a fine strainer, and put it back on the stove over medium low heat. Add balsamic vinegar and salt and pepper to taste.

**3.** When the soup comes back up to a simmer, using a stick blender, slowly mix in the blood at a medium pace, blending to emulsify. Bring the soup back to a simmer, then turn it down to the lowest heat just to keep the soup warm, and readjust the seasoning with salt and pepper.

**4.** Preheat a grill to high heat.

**5.** Season the duck hearts with salt and pepper, coat them with olive oil, and then grill until medium rare, about 2 minutes a side.

**6.** In a mixing bowl, add all the herbs and season with salt and pepper, a drizzle of extra-virgin olive oil, and a spritz of red wine vinegar. Gently warm a little duck fat in a pot for finishing the soup.

**7.** Ladle the soup into individual bowls. Evenly distribute the duck hearts among the bowls, then top the soup with some herb salad. Drizzle a little duck fat on the soup, and lay a seed quacker along the edge of the bowl.

*(continued)*

## SEED QUACKERS

MAKES ABOUT 15 CRACKERS, WHICH GIVES YOU A FEW EXTRA FOR SNACKS

**½ teaspoon active dry yeast**
**1½ cups all-purpose flour**
**½ teaspoon sea salt**
**1 tablespoon honey**
**Extra-virgin olive oil, as needed**
**⅓ to ½ cup room-temperature water**
**1 egg, beaten**
**Flaky sea salt, to taste**
**1 teaspoon poppy seeds**
**1 teaspoon sesame seeds**
**1 teaspoon fennel seeds**
**1 teaspoon black sesame seeds**
**1 teaspoon caraway seeds**

**1.** Mix the yeast, flour, salt, and honey in a bowl until it makes a smooth dough consistency, then place it in a bowl lightly coated with olive oil. Cover with plastic wrap and let it sit at room temperature until it doubles in size, about 30 minutes. Punch the dough down, wrap it in plastic wrap, and place it in the fridge to cool before rolling it out.

**2.** Preheat the oven to 350°F. On a lightly floured surface, with a rolling pin, roll the dough out to ¼-inch thickness, about 12 x 12 inches, then cut it into 6 × 1½-inch pieces, and place them on a sheet tray lined with parchment paper. Brush the tops with the beaten egg, and top with flaky salt and the mixed seeds. Bake until golden brown, about 5 minutes, rotating the sheet tray halfway through to cook evenly. Let cool on a wire rack. Quackers may be stored in an airtight container for a few days, but they're best when fresh.

# DUCK BLOOD SAUSAGE À L'ORANGE

SERVES 4

Italians claim *canard à l'orange* originated in Italy, then migrated to France. The English bastardized it by swapping in squash gravy for the orange sauce. I just took the whole thing and made it into a self-lacquering sausage.

**2 tablespoons unsalted butter**
**4 duck blood sausages (recipe follows)**
**¼ cup orange juice**
**1 cup duck stock (see page 282, using duck bones instead of chicken)**
**1 tablespoon duck fat**
**¼ cup sliced shallots**
**¼ pound Bloomsdale spinach**
**Sea salt and freshly ground black pepper**
**2 oranges, supremed or segmented**

**1.** Preheat the oven to 375°F. In a cold ovenproof pan, melt the butter over medium heat. Add the blood sausages and cook them on one side until the sausages turn very dark black, about 4 minutes, then flip them over and place the pan in the oven until the sausages are hot all the way through, about 10 minutes more.

**2.** While the sausages heat through, in a saucepan over medium heat, reduce the orange juice by three-fourths until very thick, about 5 minutes. Add the duck stock and simmer until the mixture has a rich but not gloppy consistency, about 5 minutes.

**3.** In a separate pan, heat the duck fat and sweat the shallots over medium heat until tender, about 4 minutes. Add the spinach, let it wilt, and season with salt and pepper. Remove the sausage pan from the oven, and add the orange sauce and the orange supremes.

**4.** To serve, plate a small bed of wilted spinach, top with a duck blood sausage, and some orange sauce and orange supremes.

## DUCK BLOOD SAUSAGE

MAKES ABOUT 5.5 KILOS / 12 POUNDS OF SAUSAGE

As with many of my curing and baking recipes, precision is vitally important, and so you'll need to use a scale and work in grams for this recipe. These sausages keep in the refrigerator for up to 4 days, or for 1 month in the freezer.

**Bundle of large natural hog casings**
**100 grams fine white bread crumbs**
**100 grams whole milk**
**80 grams fine sea salt**
**4 grams dark brown sugar**
**500 grams heavy cream**
**1 kilogram duck skin, with fat attached**
**1 kilogram onions, finely chopped**
**2.3 grams freshly ground black pepper**
**1.2 grams ground fennel**
**6 grams Aleppo chile flakes**
**16 grams lemon thyme leaves**
**10 grams grated orange zest**
**150 grams orange juice**
**2 kilograms duck blood**
**1 kilogram duck hearts, ground fine**

**1.** Flush and rinse the casings of salt with fresh water.

**2.** In a small bowl, soak the bread crumbs in milk, making a panade.

**3.** Mix the salt and brown sugar with the cream in another bowl.

**4.** In a large, nonreactive pot over medium-low heat, melt the fat from the duck skin and cook slowly until the fat is all rendered. Add the onions, pepper, fennel, Aleppo chile, lemon thyme, and orange zest, and cook until the onions are translucent, about 8 minutes. Deglaze the onion mixture with the orange juice and cook until dry, about 3 minutes, stirring constantly.

**5.** Add the blood, the panade, and the cream mixture. Fold in the ground heart meat. Mix together using a wooden spoon, quickly breaking up the panade mixture, being sure the meat is evenly distributed.

**6.** Immediately remove the blood sausage mixture from the heat and get ready to stuff your casing. Fit the casing over a funnel, then ladle some of the blood sausage mixture into the funnel and start to fill the casing, leaving the other end open to allow the air to escape as you fill it, so be conscious of not letting the filling come out the other end. Once the filling is almost at the end, tie off the end of the casing itself with a traditional knot. Once the casing is fully stuffed, twist the sausages off into 3 sections and tie off the remaining open end.

**7.** Using a sausage prick or needle, remove any air pockets and air bubbles while twisting the sausage into 6-inch links. This will prevent air pockets from forming in the finished sausage, which might cause it to burst while cooking.

**8.** Poach the blood sausage in 165°F (barely simmering) salted water, keeping the sausage submerged in the water with a kitchen towel. Never boil the water, and make sure to keep the temperature constant. Cook the sausage until firm, about 45 minutes. To test, prick the sausage; when it doesn't leak blood, it's finished.

**9.** Once cooked, remove the sausage from the water and let cool in a salted ice-water bath until cold. Then set in the refrigerator to cool overnight before using.

# DUCK LIVER TERRINE & PICKLED CHERRIES

SERVES ABOUT 10

Liver terrines are often the gateway offal. Originally a peasant food, they're now very haute, but this can be justified by the fact that it does take some skill to make them particularly well. Which means you should be careful here—terrines can overblend and separate. Having all your mise en place ready and blending this quickly is the best way to get a great final product. Serve this just a bit cooler than room temperature, so it keeps its shape.

As with many of my curing recipes, I prefer using metric measurements for precision here.

**760 grams duck livers, cleaned (see page 46)**
**85 grams shallots, thinly sliced**
**60 grams Vin Santo wine**
**12 grams sea salt, plus more to taste**
**2 grams freshly ground black pepper**
**0.8 gram aniseed, ground**
**2 teaspoons thyme leaves**
**1 bay leaf**
**.1 gram pink curing salt (just enough to fit on just the tip of a paring knife), such as Instacure #1**
**Grated zest of 1 orange**
**65 grams duck fat**
**55 grams unsalted butter, cubed, at room temperature**
**Pickled cherries, for serving (recipe follows)**
**Grilled baguette, for serving**

**Equipment: 14 × 4 × 4-inch terrine mold (1½ quarts)**

**1.** Combine the livers and all other ingredients, excluding the duck fat, butter, cherries, and bread. Marinate, covered, for 3 hours in the refrigerator.

**2.** Remove the bay leaf, pat the livers very dry, and season them with salt. In a large sauté pan over high heat, add some duck fat to coat the pan. When the fat is very hot, add the livers in small batches. Cook for about 2 minutes per side, getting good color on them, and then transfer them to a food processor. Blend while the livers are still warm, adding the butter bit by bit so it emulsifies. Taste and adjust with salt if necessary. Pass the liver mixture through a tamis or fine-mesh strainer to make it super smooth.

**3.** Spray a terrine mold with cooking spray and line it with enough plastic wrap to double over the top. Melt the remaining duck fat, but don't let it get too hot. Pack the liver mixture into the terrine mold while still warm, then top with the duck fat to seal it. Wrap the plastic over it and chill until set, about 12 hours.

**4.** Served with pickled cherries, grilled baguette, and a spoon.

## PICKLED CHERRIES

MAKES 2 POUNDS

**1 teaspoon black peppercorns**
**1 tablespoon coriander seeds**
**1 teaspoon fennel seeds**
**3 cups red wine vinegar**
**1½ cups sugar**
**2 tablespoons kosher salt**
**2 strips of orange zest, about 1 x 3 inches each**
**1 bay leaf**
**2 pounds Bing cherries, pitted and cut in half**

**1.** Toast the peppercorns, coriander, and fennel in a medium saucepan over medium heat until fragrant, about 1 minute. Add the vinegar, sugar, salt, orange zest, and bay leaf, and bring to a boil. Reduce the heat to a simmer and cook for 10 minutes. Remove from the heat and let cool until just warm. If the liquid is too hot, the cherries will get mealy.

**2.** Place the cherries in a bowl and pour the liquid over them. They should be completely submerged. Seal or cover the cherries, and refrigerate for up to 1 month.

❤ **974 likes**
**offalchris** Cooking in the backyard with @meatmaven for our friends

# FOIE GRAS CRUDO, CORN & VANILLA SALT

SERVES 8 TO 10

Raw foie gras has a velvety and rich texture as the fat melts away in your mouth. With corn and tarragon, this dish tastes a little like butter dripping off a fresh cob. I like returning the animal back to its feed, and this is a pairing of flavors that always works.

**1 lobe grade A foie gras, 1½ to 2 pounds**
**2 large ears corn**
**3 tablespoons lemon juice**
**2 teaspoons extra-virgin olive oil**
**Sea salt and freshly ground black pepper**
**Vanilla salt or flaky sea salt (see Note)**
**1 tablespoon tarragon leaves**

**NOTE:** Vanilla salt is available from specialty salt dealers; I love the one by Jacobsen Salt Company. If you'd like to make it yourself, keep any vanilla beans you've scraped for another recipe and put them in a jar with good-quality salt. Screw on the lid and let the pod infuse the salt.

**1.** To clean the foie gras, remove any veins or external clumps of fat. Set aside.

**2.** With a sharp knife, shave the corn kernels from the cobs, making sure there are no corn silks, and don't cut so deep into the cob that the corn will be tough.

**3.** Fill a bowl with hot water. Dip a thin, sharp knife into the water, making sure the knife is hot before cutting the foie gras into thin, wide sashimi-like pieces.

**4.** Lay 3 slices of foie on the center of each plate. Be sure to save all the scraps for terrines or another dish.

**5.** In a small mixing bowl, dress the corn kernels with the lemon juice and olive oil and season with salt and pepper. Dress the foie gras slices with the corn mixture, then season with vanilla salt and black pepper. Finish with some tarragon and serve.

# HOT MESS: FOIE GRAS, PIG'S FEET, STRAWBERRY JAM, BRIOCHE

SERVES 4

When you call someone a "hot mess," I believe it refers to a beautiful person who's a mess in life, maybe even childish in their behavior. For them, this is my version of a grown-up peanut butter and jelly.

**1 pound grade A foie gras, cut into 4-ounce portions**
**Sea salt and freshly ground black pepper**
**1 tablespoon pork fat**
**1 pound Braised Trotter meat (recipe follows), picked**
**1 quart Trotter Jus (recipe follows)**
**1 pint strawberries, cut in half and hulled**
**16 Pickled Green Strawberries (recipe follows), cut in half**
**Zinfandel vinegar, or any other red wine vinegar, to taste**
**4 ½-inch-thick slices brioche, crusts removed**
**Strawberry Jam (recipe follows), as needed**
**1 bunch chives, cut into ¾-inch lengths**

**1.** Preheat the oven to 350°F. Score the foie gras to make cross-hatch marks with a sharp knife, then season well with salt and black pepper. Heat the pork fat in a sauté pan over high heat. When the fat is very hot, add the foie gras, scored-side down, gently holding it down and searing it to a nice golden brown, about 2 minutes. Flip the foie gras and baste, searing until it's golden brown on the second side, warm, and jiggly through the center, about 2 minutes more.

**2.** In a separate pan over medium-low heat, combine the picked trotter meat and the trotter jus. Once the mixture reaches a simmer, add the strawberries, both fresh and pickled. Adjust the seasoning with zinfandel vinegar and salt to taste.

**3.** Toast the brioche dry, then top it with the jam and foie gras. Add the rendered foie fat to the trotter-strawberry sauce, and smother the foie gras and toast with it. Top with chives and serve.

## BRAISED TROTTERS

MAKES 1 TO 1½ POUNDS MEAT

**2 trotters, with the hock on, 2 to 3 pounds total**
**Sea salt and freshly ground black pepper**
**1 medium onion**
**1 bulb fennel**
**1 medium carrot**
**1 head garlic, split to expose the cloves**
**1 bay leaf**
**1 bunch thyme**
**1 jalapeño, split**
**Peel of 1 lemon**
**½ cup white wine**
**2 gallons Roasted Chicken Stock (page 282)**

(continued)

**1.** Season the trotters liberally with the salt and pepper. Transfer to a nonreactive container with the onion, fennel, carrot, garlic, bay leaf, thyme, jalapeño, lemon peel, and white wine. Let marinate, covered, overnight in the refrigerator.

**2.** In a nonreactive pot, place the marinated vegetables and a splash of their liquid in the bottom to help prevent the trotters from sticking. Place the trotters on top, and cover with stock. Bring to a simmer over medium heat. Let the trotters cook until they're tender and you can easily pull the meat and skin from the bones, about 4 hours. Pick the meat and set it in a pan, covered with a bit of braising liquid. Reserve the rest of the braising liquid and the bones for the trotter jus.

## TROTTER JUS

MAKES 1 QUARTS

**2 tablespoons pork fat**
**3 reserved trotter bones**
**1 medium onion, medium dice**
**1 medium carrot, medium dice**
**1 bulb fennel, medium dice**
**2 ribs celery, medium dice**
**1 cup white wine**
**2 quarts trotter braising liquid**
**1 bay leaf**
**1 bunch thyme**

**1.** In a heavy-bottomed pot over medium heat, combine the pork fat and the bones and cook, stirring frequently, until golden brown, about 10 minutes. Remove the bones from the pot, set them aside, and add the vegetables. Caramelize the vegetables, stirring occasionally, for about 10 minutes (you're browning the vegetables on the outside, but not cooking them through). Return the bones to the pan and deglaze with the white wine. Cook until dry, add the trotter braising liquid, bay leaf, and thyme. Let the liquid reduce by half, about 30 minutes, skimming as you go.

**2.** Pass the sauce through a fine strainer.

## PICKLED GREEN STRAWBERRIES

MAKES 1 POUND PLUS PICKLING LIQUID

**1 teaspoon yellow mustard seeds**
**1 teaspoon coriander seeds**
**1 teaspoon fennel seeds**
**1 teaspoon black peppercorns**
**1 teaspoon red peppercorns**
**1 cup champagne vinegar**
**1 cup sugar**
**⅛ teaspoon sea salt**
**1 fresh bay leaf**
**1 pound green strawberries**

**1.** In a small nonreactive saucepan, toast the spices over medium heat until aromatic, a minute or so. Add the vinegar, sugar, salt, and bay leaf. Heat until the salt and sugar dissolve. Take the pot off the heat and chill it down in an ice-water bath.

**2.** While the liquid is cooling, wash the strawberries, then stem and cut them in half. Put them in another nonreactive container. When the liquid is completely cold, pour it over the berries, and let them pickle in the refrigerator overnight, covered, before use. Remove them from the pickling liquid before adding them to the trotter sauce.

## STRAWBERRY JAM

MAKES 2 CUPS

**1⅓ pounds strawberries, trimmed and cut in ¼-inch pieces**
**¾ pound sugar**
**Pinch of salt**
**2 teaspoons fruit pectin**
**1 teaspoon molasses**
**1⅔ tablespoons lemon juice**

**1.** Chill a plate in the freezer. Toss the strawberries in a mixing bowl with the sugar, salt, and pectin. Place the mixture in a nonreactive pot with the molasses and lemon juice.

**2.** Cook the fruit over medium-high heat until the mixture looks jammy. Drop a small spoonful on the cold plate; if the jam sets, it's done. If not, continue cooking. Cool the jam down by adding it to a bowl and then placing the bowl in an ice-water bath to help keep the vibrant red natural color. Store in the refrigerator, where it will last a month or more.

❤ **132 likes**
**offalchris** a quick pickle of Green strawberries

# CHICKEN LIVERS SALTIMBOCCA

SERVES 4 TO 6 AS FINGER FOOD

I remember eating so many of these bites as a kid. A neo-traditional Italian American dish, these are inspired by saltimbocca, literally meaning "jump in your mouth." While the original is usually a veal or chicken cutlet wrapped in prosciutto and sautéed, my parents made these as little passed items. These morsels will always be around at your dinner parties after you try them, and I'm sure you'll sneak a few before you put out a fresh tray for guests.

**1 pound chicken livers, cleaned (see page 46)**
**Sea salt and freshly ground black pepper**
**¼ pound country ham, sliced very thinly (use Benton's Smoky Mountain Country Ham, if you can find it)**
**Sage leaves, 1 per piece of liver, plus a few more to fry for garnish**
**4 tablespoons unsalted butter, plus a bit more to finish**
**2 bay leaves**
**2 tablespoons white wine**
**½ cup Roasted Chicken Stock (page 282)**

**1.** Pat the livers dry and season them with salt and black pepper. Lay a slice of country ham on a cutting board, and place a sage leaf in the middle with a piece of liver. Use just enough ham to wrap each liver into a nice little package in one layer; using too much will cause the liver to undercook. If you need toothpicks to hold them together, that's fine; just be creative while searing and be sure to remove the toothpicks before serving.

**2.** In a sauté pan over medium heat, add the butter, fry the reserved sage leaves until just darkened and crisped, 1 minute or less. Remove the sage and drain on paper towels. Fry the ham-wrapped chicken livers, and cook until golden brown on one side, 2 minutes. Flip them over, add the bay leaves to the butter, and get a little color on the other side of the livers, another minute or two. Remove the livers, then deglaze the pan with the white wine and reduce the liquid until almost evaporated. Add the chicken stock, and swirl in a small spoonful of butter to make a smooth sauce. To serve, put the livers on a plate and top with sauce, a grind of fresh black pepper, and crisped sage leaves.

# SAUTÉED CHICKEN LIVERS, FIGS & PICKLED ONIONS BRUSCHETTA

SERVES 4

The richness of liver with a lovely, sweet, ripe fig just can't be beat. In this dish, they're like doppelgängers, mimicking each other in form, and the pickled onions tie them all together. The mix of sweetness, minerality, and acidity is a perfect balance on the palate. The flavors complement each other so well, this will be a regular on your recipe list.

**4 1-inch-thick slices country bread**
**2 tablespoons duck fat, melted**
**12 fresh figs, quartered**
**Sea salt and freshly ground black pepper**
**2 tablespoons torn mint leaves**
**2 pounds chicken livers, cleaned (see page 46)**
**2 tablespoons unsalted butter**
**3 tablespoons Pickled Red Onions (page 286)**

**1.** Brush the bread with a little melted duck fat, then grill or toast until crisp.

**2.** Put a piece of bread on each serving plate. Place 3 whole figs on each piece of bread, then crush them. Season with salt and black pepper and sprinkle with mint. Leave at room temp while you prepare the livers.

**3.** Pat the livers dry with paper towels and season with salt and pepper. Heat the remaining duck fat and butter in a large sauté pan over medium-high heat, until the butter is melted and foaming. Before the butter begins to color, lay the livers in the pan without crowding them. (Cook in batches if necessary.) Cook the livers for 1½ minutes, or a bit more until they're browned on the underside, then turn them over. Cook for about 1½ minutes on the second side, until they are nicely browned all over and slightly pink inside.

**4.** Place the livers on the bread, top with a few rings of pickled onions, and serve.

# THYME-ROASTED CARROTS & RABBIT BITS À LA MOUTARDE

SERVES 4

Dijonaise cuisine boasts the famous *lapin à la moutarde* (rabbit in mustard sauce), but here we flip the scale. Instead, we make the rabbit's feed—carrots—the focus of this dish, and top them with a mustardy rabbit offal ragù.

**1 pound baby heirloom carrots, preferably a mix of colors**
**Salt and freshly ground black pepper**
**Extra-virgin olive oil**
**1 bunch thyme, separated into branches, plus 1 tablespoon of leaves**
**½ pound rabbit livers, cleaned (see page 46)**
**½ pound rabbit kidneys, cleaned (see page 52)**
**2 tablespoons unsalted butter**
**6 cloves garlic**
**¼ cup white wine**
**1 cup Roasted Chicken Stock (page 282)**
**1 bay leaf**
**1 tablespoon whole-grain mustard**
**1 tablespoon Dijon mustard**
**2 tablespoons crème fraîche**
**Chives, cut into ½-inch batons, for garnish**

**1.** Preheat the oven to 350°F. On a sheet pan, season the carrots with salt and pepper, sprinkle with some olive oil and 1 tablespoon thyme leaves, then roast until tender, about 20 minutes.

**2.** While the carrots are cooking, heat a sauté pan over medium-high heat. Pat the livers and kidneys dry and season with salt. Add the butter, garlic, and remaining thyme branches to the pan, and, when the butter is foaming, cook the livers and kidneys on each side until golden but still rare, about 3 minutes total. Deglaze with white wine and reduce the liquid by half. Add the chicken stock, bay leaf, whole-grain mustard, Dijon, and crème fraîche, and bring just to a simmer. Adjust the seasoning with salt and black pepper.

**3.** When ready to serve, remove the thyme branches and add the chives to the sauté pan. Spoon over the roasted carrots and serve immediately.

# GOOSE NOODLE SOUP

SERVES 4

You don't have to be sick to enjoy this brothy noodle soup. Goose intestines are cooked until tender, then cut to look like anellini pasta. You won't be able to tell the "noodles" apart!

**2 pounds goose intestines, cleaned of fat (see page 57)**
**1 medium carrot**
**1 medium yellow onion**
**2 stalks celery**
**1 head garlic, split to expose the cloves**
**1 small leek, white and light green parts only**
**1 bulb fennel, top removed**
**Sea salt**
**¼ pound dried anellini pasta**
**½ gallon Roasted Chicken Stock (page 282)**
**2 cups shelled and peeled fava beans**
**1 cup leeks, cut into thin rings, cleaned of grit**
**½ pound fava leaves**
**Lemon juice, to taste**
**3 tablespoons goose fat, melted**
**Cracked black pepper**

**1.** Rinse the goose intestines inside and out very well, then place them in a pot with the carrot, onion, celery, garlic, leek, and fennel; cover with well-salted water. Bring to a boil, then skim, and reduce to a simmer. Cook until tender, about 2 hours. Once done, cool in the cooking liquid.

**2.** Cook the pasta to al dente in a pot of well-salted boiling water, then drain and spread it out on a sheet tray to cool. Don't shock the pasta in cold water or oil it; this will ruin the flavor or make the soup oily. Spreading out the pasta prevents it from sticking together.

**3.** Cut the intestines into strips 3 inches long, then split them open lengthwise.

**4.** Heat the chicken stock until boiling in a pot, season it with salt to taste, and cook the fava beans in it until just tender. Add the cooked goose intestines and leek rings and let them simmer together for 3 minutes. Add the fava leaves and pasta to warm them through. Adjust the seasoning with salt and lemon juice.

**5.** Divide the soup among 4 bowls. Drizzle the goose fat over the top, and sprinkle with a crack of black pepper. Serve immediately.

# GOOSE SCHMALTZ SPREAD

SERVES 10

Smother and spread this on bread, fold it into mashed potatoes, or even drizzle it on top of a soup. It's a versatile fat that will render you speechless (aside from the "mmms").

**2 cups (1 pound) goose fat, melted**
**2 pounds yellow onions, cut into thin julienne**
**1 bay leaf**
**Sea salt**
**12 sage leaves**
**Whole-grain seeded bread, sliced 1 inch thick, for grilling**
**12 chestnuts, peeled**
**Flaky salt, to finish**
**Freshly ground black pepper, to garnish**

**Equipment: 14 × 4 × 4-inch terrine mold (1½ quarts)**

**1.** Add ¾ cup of the goose fat to a braising pot or Dutch oven over medium heat. Reserve a small handful of the onions and add the rest and the bay leaf to the pot. Salt the onions in the pot and cook them slowly, stirring regularly, until golden brown and tender, about 45 minutes. Remove the bay leaf from the onions, place the onion mixture in a blender, add 1 cup of fat, and blend until smooth. Place the mixture in a terrine mold lined with plastic wrap and top with 6 sage leaves, then let cool.

**2.** To serve, grill the bread slices and let them cool.

**3.** Slice the chestnuts into thin rings. Heat the remaining ¼ cup of goose fat in a sauté pan over medium heat, and fry the remaining sage leaves until crisp, about a minute if not less. Remove and crumble. Fry the chestnut slices until browned and crispy, about a minute. Set aside on a paper towel and season with salt.

**4.** To assemble the dish, smear a nice heaping amount of fat on the grilled bread. Top with thin slices of raw onions, the crispy chestnuts, and a few fried sage pieces. Finish with flaky salt and pepper.

# CONFIT DUCK FEET WITH SAGE & BLACK PEPPER GRAVY

SERVES 4

This dish is reminiscent of Thanksgiving flavors and nods to the braised chicken feet popular in Chinese dim sum. Confiting the feet leaves them sticky and messy in a good way, like chicken wings. As an alternative to serving them in a sauce, as we do here, the confited feet are also delicious deep-fried until crisp.

**12 duck feet, washed**
**2 teaspoons kosher salt**
**1 teaspoon freshly ground black pepper**
**1 branch rosemary**
**1 branch sage**
**1 branch thyme**
**1 bay leaf**
**1 jalapeño, split**
**1 head garlic, split to expose the cloves**
**Peel of 1 lemon**
**4 cups duck fat, or to cover, melted**

**1.** Preheat the oven to 250°F. While the oven preheats, cut the talons off the feet with scissors, and place the feet in a nonreactive ovenproof pan. Season with salt and pepper, and then add all the herbs, jalapeño, garlic, and lemon peel. Cover the feet with duck fat, making sure each foot is completely submerged in the fat. Place in the oven, covered, and cook until the feet are tender and you can easily separate the skin from the bone, about 2 hours. Make sure the fat doesn't boil; if it does, turn down the oven temperature and add a little more duck fat. Once the feet are tender, let the feet cool in the fat. To remove them from the cold fat, gently heat the pan in the oven until the feet can be removed (they are best the next day).

**2.** Confited duck feet can be enjoyed in a sauce as follows, or deep-fried until crisp.

## SAGE AND BLACK PEPPER GRAVY

**2 tablespoons unsalted butter**
**6 sage leaves**
**1 cup Roasted Chicken Stock (page 282)**
**Confit Duck Feet (see above)**
**1 tablespoon freshly ground black pepper**
**1 bunch scallions, sliced in thin rings**
**Lemon juice, to taste**

**1.** In a large sauté pan over medium-high heat, brown the butter and add the sage leaves. Fry until they are crisp, about 1 minute. Add the chicken stock and bring it to a boil. Add the duck feet and let them simmer until the sauce is sticky and has glazed the feet. Add the black pepper and scallions. Adjust with plenty of lemon juice.

**2.** Serve on a platter with a pile of moist towelettes, and gnaw on the feet.

# DUCK BRODO, UNFORMED EGGS, DUCK FRIES & MATSUTAKE

SERVES 4

This is sex soup: Man, woman, and child, all in one dish. The broth gets a rich umami boost and an incredible pinewood-like aroma from the mushrooms and is balanced by the tender bite of the fries and egg.

**2 quarts duck stock (see page 282, using duck bones instead of chicken)**
**Sea salt**
**¼ pound duck fries, rinsed**
**¼ pound unformed duck eggs**
**¼ pound duck tongues, braised (see page 29)**
**1 pound matsutake mushrooms, cleaned**
**Lemon juice, to taste**
**2 tablespoons minced chives**
**2 tablespoons duck fat, melted**
**4 duck eggs, poached**

**1.** In a medium pot over medium heat, bring the duck stock to a simmer and season with salt. Add the duck fries and unformed eggs. Gently simmer until they are firm and the color changes, about 4 minutes. Add the duck tongues, to warm through.

**2.** Slice the matsutakes very thin on a mandoline and add them to the broth. Adjust the seasoning with salt and lemon juice to taste.

**3.** Serve in 4 warm bowls. Top with minced chives and a drizzle of duck fat on the top. Finish with a poached duck egg.

# CANDIED COCKSCOMBS, RICE PUDDING & POMEGRANATE

SERVES 4

Cockscomb has a rubbery texture; braising softens them to a chew similar to that of gummy bears. By infusing them with pomegranate juice, they look like gummy bears, too. Playing on this, I love making a dessert of rice pudding garnished with chewy "candies" of cockscomb. Prepare the cockscombs a few hours before serving, or the night before.

**FOR THE COCKSCOMBS:**

**12 cockscombs, cleaned (see page 72), but not cooked**
**2 vanilla beans, split and scraped**
**8 cups sugar**
**3 cups pomegranate juice**
**3 tablespoons pomegranate molasses**
**¼ cup lemon juice**

**FOR THE RICE PUDDING:**

**1 cup short-grain Italian rice, like Arborio or Carnaroli**
**5¾ cups whole milk**
**1 bay leaf**
**1 vanilla bean, split and scraped**
**¼ cup sugar**
**1 cup heavy cream, or as needed**

**1 cup pomegranate seeds**

**PREPARE THE COCKSCOMBS:**

**1.** In a heavy-bottomed pot, place the cockscombs in 2 quarts cold water and bring to a boil. Remove the cockscombs and rinse with cold water. Re-cover the cockscombs with fresh water, add 2 cups of sugar and 1 vanilla bean pod (use seeds in the pudding), and stir. Cook the cockscombs at a moderate simmer, skimming any scum off the surface of the water, until they are soft, about 1½ hours.

**2.** Meanwhile, prepare the syrup by combining the remaining sugar, the remaining vanilla bean and seeds, and pomegranate juice in a heavy stockpot over medium heat. Whisk the pomegranate molasses into the syrup and adjust the flavor with lemon juice. Remove from heat and set aside until the cockscombs finish cooking.

**3.** Drain the cockscombs. Heat the pomegranate syrup to just below a simmer and add the cockscombs. Stir well, and cook over a very gentle heat, stirring occasionally, until the cockscombs look like gummy bears melting in your pocket, 30 to 45 minutes. Cool, and refrigerate the cockscombs in the syrup.

**MAKE THE RICE PUDDING:**

**1.** Place the rice, milk, bay leaf, and vanilla bean in a heavy-bottomed pot. Bring to a boil over medium heat, stirring occasionally. Turn the heat to low, stirring every few minutes to ensure the rice does not stick to the bottom. Cook until the rice is tender and creamy, 20 to 30 minutes, then remove from heat.

**2.** Remove the bay leaf and vanilla bean, and stir in the sugar. Pour the pudding into a container and press plastic wrap directly on the surface. Refrigerate until chilled.

**3.** When ready to serve, slowly stir in the cream until the pudding is loose but will still hold some shape on a plate or in a bowl.

**4.** To serve, place a few heaping spoonfuls of rice pudding in the center of each plate. Take 3 warm cockscombs and arrange them atop the pudding. Garnish with pomegranate seeds and some pomegranate syrup.

# BASICS

# BASICS

# SPICE MIXTURES

## SEASONED FLOUR

MAKES 2 CUPS

**2 cups all-purpose flour**
**2 teaspoons sea salt**
**2 teaspoons finely ground black pepper**

Mix all the ingredients together. Store in an airtight jar at room temperature; the seasoned flour will keep well for over a month.

## SPICY DREDGE

MAKES ABOUT 1¼ CUPS

**½ cup all-purpose flour**
**½ cup fine cornmeal**
**1 tablespoon celery salt**
**1 teaspoon sea salt**
**1½ teaspoons pimentón de la Vera (smoked paprika)**
**1½ teaspoons freshly ground black pepper**
**1½ teaspoons ground fennel seed**
**1½ teaspoons Aleppo chile flakes**
**1½ teaspoons onion powder**

Mix all the ingredients together. Store in an airtight jar at room temperature; the dredge will keep well for over a month.

# SPICE RUB

MAKES ABOUT ¼ CUP

**2 tablespoons fennel seeds**
**2 tablespoons black peppercorns**
**2 tablespoons coriander seeds**
**2 tablespoons red chile flakes**

Toast all the seeds in a moderately hot pan until very aromatic, add the chile flakes, then grind them together until fine in a spice grinder. When cool, store the rub in an airtight container; it will keep for over a month at room temperature, but is best used fresh.

# PASTRAMI SPICE

MAKES ABOUT ¾ CUP

**2 cinnamon sticks**
**2 tablespoons red peppercorns**
**2 tablespoons black peppercorns**
**2 tablespoons yellow mustard seeds**
**2 tablespoons brown mustard seeds**
**2 tablespoons coriander seeds**
**2 tablespoons fennel seeds**
**2 tablespoons red chile flakes**
**2 tablespoons allspice berries**
**1 whole nutmeg, crushed**
**2 tablespoons whole cloves**
**24 dried bay leaves, crumbled**

Burn the cinnamon sticks on an open flame to char them, bringing out their natural oils. Crush all the spices in a mortar and pestle until coarse, then mix them together. Alternatively, you can use a spice grinder, but pound the cinnamon in a mortar and pestle; that should be a more medium-coarse grind. Store in an airtight container at room temperature for up to two weeks.

# VINAIGRETTES

## MUSTARD VINAIGRETTE

MAKES ¾ CUP

**1 tablespoon whole-grain mustard**
**1 teaspoon Dijon mustard**
**¼ cup champagne vinegar**
**½ cup extra-virgin olive oil**
**Sea salt, to taste**
**1 teaspoon freshly ground black pepper, or to taste**

In a mixing bowl, combine the mustards and the champagne vinegar. Whisk in the olive oil, and season with salt and pepper. Store in the refrigerator until ready to use. It can keep for a month.

## ZINFANDEL VINAIGRETTE

MAKES 1 CUP

**¼ cup Zinfandel or good red-wine vinegar**
**¾ cup extra-virgin olive oil**
**Sea salt and freshly ground black pepper, to taste**
**1 teaspoon lemon juice**

Pour the vinegar into a mixing bowl, then whisk in the olive oil. Season with salt and pepper, and adjust with lemon juice. It keeps its flavor for a week or longer in the fridge.

## SHERRY VINAIGRETTE

MAKES ABOUT 1 CUP

**1 teaspoon Dijon mustard**
**¼ cup minced shallots**
**¼ cup sherry vinegar**
**½ cup extra-virgin olive oil**
**Sea salt and freshly ground black pepper, to taste**

Combine the mustard, shallots, and vinegar in a mixing bowl. Whisk in the olive oil until combined, and season with salt and pepper. The vinaigrette keeps for a week in the fridge.

# LEMON ANCHOVY VINAIGRETTE

MAKES ABOUT 1½ CUPS

**3 salted anchovies**
**3 white anchovies**
**1 clove garlic**
**½ cup lemon juice**
**1 teaspoon champagne vinegar**
**1 cup extra-virgin olive oil**
**Sea salt and freshly ground black pepper, to taste**
**Sugar, to taste**

Pound all the anchovies in a mortar and pestle with the garlic to make a paste, and place it in a mixing bowl. Add the lemon juice and champagne vinegar. Slowly whisk in the olive oil. Adjust with salt, black pepper, and sugar. The vinaigrette keeps for a week in the fridge.

# LEMON FISH SAUCE VINAIGRETTE

MAKES 1 CUP

**4 cloves garlic**
**½ cup olive oil**
**1 teaspoon black peppercorns, crushed**
**¼ cup lemon juice, plus more as needed**
**2 tablespoons fish sauce, preferably Red Boat, plus more as needed**

Crush the garlic in a mortar and pestle until it's a paste, then place it in a mixing bowl, add the remaining ingredients, and mix, but don't emulsify it completely. Taste and adjust the seasoning with more acid or fish sauce. The vinaigrette keeps for up to a month, refrigerated.

# AIOLIS, SAUCES & CONDIMENTS

## BASIC AIOLI

MAKES ABOUT 1¾ CUPS

**1 clove garlic**
**Sea salt**
**2 large egg yolks**
**1 teaspoon Dijon mustard**
**1½ cups pure olive oil**
**Extra-virgin olive oil, for finishing**
**1 tablespoon freshly squeezed lemon juice, plus more as needed**
**Freshly ground black pepper**

In a mortar and pestle, pound the garlic with a pinch of salt until it forms a paste. Add egg yolks and mustard and stir with pestle until combined. Slowly drizzle in 2 tablespoons pure olive oil while stirring vigorously with the pestle. Once the aioli begins to emulsify, transfer it to a larger mixing bowl and slowly whisk in the remaining oil in a slow and steady stream, whisking constantly. After all the oil has been incorporated, finish with extra-virgin olive oil to taste, season with salt and pepper, and adjust the acidity with lemon juice. If you don't have a mortar and pestle, you can use a food processor to achieve the same result.

## CARROT AIOLI

MAKES 1½ CUPS

**2 cups carrot juice**
**1 cup Basic Aioli (left)**

In a nonreactive pot over medium heat, reduce the carrot juice by three-fourths. Once cool, fold it into the aioli. The aioli will keep, covered, in the refrigerator for a week or two.

## LIVER AIOLI

MAKES 1½ CUPS

**¼ pound chicken livers**
**Extra-virgin olive oil, as needed**
**1 clove garlic**
**Kosher salt**
**1 large egg yolk**
**½ teaspoon Dijon mustard**
**½ cup pure olive oil**
**Freshly ground black pepper**
**¼ teaspoon lemon juice**

In a sauté pan over high heat, sear the chicken livers in extra-virgin olive oil until golden brown and medium, about 1½ minutes per side. Let cool.

In a mortar and pestle, combine the cooled chicken livers, garlic, and a pinch of salt, and pound with a pestle until a paste forms. Add the egg yolk and mustard, and stir with the pestle until combined. Slowly drizzle in 2 tablespoons of pure olive oil while stirring vigorously with the pestle. Once the mixture begins to emulsify, transfer it to a bowl and slowly add the remaining pure olive oil in a slow, steady stream, whisking constantly. Finish by whisking in a drizzle of extra-virgin olive oil to taste. Season to taste with salt, pepper, and lemon juice.

Alternatively, to use a food processor, finely mince or mash the garlic and add it to the pure olive oil in a bowl. Combine the egg yolk and mustard in the food processor and process until well blended. Then add the seared livers. With the motor running, very slowly add the olive oil–garlic mixture in a fine stream until the mixture begins to emulsify. When all of the olive oil–garlic mixture has been added, finish with some extra-virgin olive oil. Season to taste with salt, pepper, and lemon juice.

Use right away, or cover and refrigerate for up to 2 days.

## BRAINAISE

MAKES 1½ CUPS

**1 clove garlic**
**Kosher salt**
**1 large egg yolk**
**½ teaspoon Dijon mustard**
**½ cup pure olive oil**
**3 ounces pig brain, poached (see page 34)**
**¼ cup extra-virgin olive oil, for drizzling**
**Freshly ground black pepper**
**¼ teaspoon lemon juice**

In a mortar, combine the garlic and a pinch of salt, and pound with a pestle until a paste forms. Add the egg yolk and mustard and stir with the pestle until combined. Slowly drizzle in 2 tablespoons of the pure olive oil while stirring vigorously with the pestle. At this point, start adding the brains. Once the mixture begins to emulsify, transfer it to a bowl and slowly add the remaining pure olive oil in a slow, steady stream, whisking constantly. After the pure olive oil has been incorporated, finish by whisking in a drizzle of extra-virgin olive oil. Season to taste with salt, pepper, and lemon juice.

Alternatively, to use a food processor, finely mince or mash the garlic and add it to the pure olive oil in a bowl. Combine the egg yolk and mustard in the food processor and process until well blended, then add the brain. With the motor running, very slowly add the olive oil–garlic mixture in a fine stream until the mixture begins to emulsify. When all of the olive oil–garlic has been added, finish with the extra-virgin olive oil. Season to taste with salt, pepper, and the lemon juice.

Use right away, or cover and refrigerate for up to 2 days.

# HAYAIOLI

MAKES 1½ CUPS

**1 clove garlic**
**Kosher salt**
**1 large egg yolk**
**½ teaspoon Dijon mustard**
**½ cup Hay Oil (recipe follows)**
**¼ cup extra-virgin olive oil, for drizzling**
**Freshly ground black pepper**
**¼ teaspoon lemon juice**

In a mortar, combine the garlic and a pinch of salt, and pound with a pestle until a paste forms. Add the egg yolk and mustard and stir with the pestle until combined. Slowly drizzle in 2 tablespoons of the hay oil while stirring vigorously with the pestle. Once the mixture begins to emulsify, transfer it to a bowl and slowly add the remaining hay oil in a slow, steady stream, whisking constantly. After the hay oil has been incorporated, finish by whisking in a drizzle of extra-virgin olive oil. Season to taste with salt, pepper, and the lemon juice.

Alternatively, to use a food processor, finely mince or mash the garlic and add it to the hay oil. Combine the egg yolk and mustard in the food processor and process until well blended. With the motor running, very slowly add the oil-garlic mixture in a fine stream until the mixture begins to emulsify. When all of the oil-garlic mixture has been added, finish with the extra-virgin olive oil. Season to taste with salt, pepper, and the lemon juice.

Use right away, or cover and refrigerate for up to 2 days.

## HAY OIL

MAKES 1 CUP

**1 cup neutral oil**
**1 cup hay**

In a small saucepan, combine the oil and hay. Warm this over very low heat for 1 hour. Strain through a fine mesh strainer.

# SAUCE GRIBICHE

MAKES ABOUT 1½ CUPS

**3 eggs**
**½ cup very finely diced red onion**
**Kosher salt**
**½ teaspoon red wine vinegar**
**1 tablespoon salted capers, rinsed**
**¼ cup chopped flat-leaf parsley**
**½ cup chopped chervil leaves**
**½ cup chopped tarragon leaves**
**2 tablespoons minced chives**
**1 small clove garlic, minced**
**½ teaspoon lemon zest**
**Freshly ground black pepper**
**4 to 6 tablespoons extra-virgin olive oil**
**Splash of lemon juice (optional)**

Hard-boil the eggs, let cool, and remove the shells.

Put the onion in a bowl, sprinkle with a pinch of salt, and let stand for 5 minutes. Add the vinegar and let stand for an additional 10 minutes.

In a small bowl, combine the capers with water to cover, and let stand for 10 minutes.

In another bowl, combine the parsley, chervil, tarragon, chives, garlic, and lemon zest. Squeeze out the vinegar from the onions, like you're ringing out a wet T-shirt. Add the onion to the bowl with the herbs.

Drain the capers, pat dry, coarsely chop, and add to the bowl.

Sprinkle the mixture with a little salt and pepper and then whisk in the olive oil to achieve your preferred consistency. Sieve the whites and yolks into the sauce by pushing them through a baking rack with ½-inch squares or coarsely chopping them. Taste and adjust the seasonings with salt, pepper, and lemon juice. Let the sauce stand for 1 hour before serving to allow the flavors to develop. Any leftover sauce may be covered and refrigerated for up to 2 days.

## REMOULADE

MAKES ABOUT 1½ CUPS

**1 cup Basic Aioli (page 274)**
**3 tablespoons Dijon mustard**
**1 teaspoon fish sauce, preferably Red Boat**
**2 tablespoons minced shallots**
**1 tablespoon chopped flat-leaf parsley**
**2 tablespoons grated fresh horseradish**
**1 tablespoon chopped chives**
**1 tablespoon chopped tarragon**
**1 tablespoon Aleppo chile flakes**
**1 teaspoon grated lemon zest**
**1 teaspoon lemon juice**
**1 tablespoon salted capers, rinsed and chopped**
**Sea salt, to taste**

Combine all the ingredients except the salt in a bowl and mix well. Add salt to taste, then refrigerate in an airtight container. Use within a week or two, but it tastes best fresh.

## SALSA FRA DIAVOLO

MAKES 1½ CUPS

**3 serrano chiles**
**3 red Fresno chiles**
**2 jalapeños**
**4 cloves garlic**
**1 bunch thyme, leaves picked**
**3 bay leaves**
**1 tablespoon red chile flakes**
**1 tablespoon smoked pimentón de la Vera picante**
**½ cup extra-virgin olive oil**
**Zest and juice of 1 orange**

Remove the stems from the chiles, chop the bay leaves and thyme, and place all the ingredients in a blender. Blend until smooth. The sauce will keep, covered in the fridge, for two weeks. After that, it begins to age and the flavor changes but is still delicious.

# LOBSTER MARINARA

MAKES ABOUT 2½ QUARTS

**Salt**
**2 2-pound lobsters**
**3 tablespoons extra-virgin olive oil**
**1 medium yellow onion, medium dice**
**2 medium carrots, medium dice**
**1 head fennel, medium dice**
**2 stalks celery, medium dice**
**6 cloves garlic, coarsely chopped**
**1 cup red wine**
**1 bunch thyme**
**1 fresh bay leaf**
**2 28-ounce cans San Marzano tomatoes, milled**

Bring a large pot of well-salted water to a boil. Add the lobsters and boil for 5 minutes per pound, so 10 minutes in total. This will undercook them a little; we will cook them further in the sauce. Remove and shock in salted ice water until cool. Once cool, remove the meat and roe from the shells, reserving the shells for the sauce and saving all the meat and roe for the finished sauce

Heat a braising pan or Dutch oven over medium heat with the olive oil. Add the broken lobster shells to the oil and caramelize over medium heat, stirring, for 15 minutes; they should be bright red and smell amazing. Add the vegetables and cook until they caramelize a bit, about 10 minutes, stirring constantly for even cooking.

Deglaze the pan with the red wine and cook until it's dry, then add the thyme, bay leaf, and tomatoes.

Bring the mixture to a boil, then turn the heat down to a simmer. Simmer until deep red, about 30 minutes. Blend the sauce in a blender in batches, to break up the shells, but not too finely. Strain the sauce through a strainer to remove the bits of shell. When reheating the sauce with the final dish, add the lobster per the recipe instructions, or just add the lobster and heat through to make an amazing pasta sauce.

# LOBSTER BOTTARGA

MAKES 6 OUNCES (OR VARIES)

**6 ounces lobster roe (or as much as you have)**

Place the lobster roe in a Cryovac or heavy zip-top plastic bag and push it all down to the bottom of the bag. Roll up the bag, forcing the roe into a tube shape, and use a few layers of plastic wrap to roll it up tight. Bring a pot of water to boil over high heat and boil the bag for 15 minutes or until the lobster roe is cooked firm. Place the roe in an ice bath and cool until cold. To use, grate the roe over a dish.

Wrapped tightly in plastic, the bottarga will keep in the fridge for up to two weeks, or in the freezer for up to two months.

## SALSA VERDE

MAKES ABOUT 3 CUPS

**1 medium red onion, finely diced**
**Kosher salt**
**1 tablespoon red wine vinegar**
**2 tablespoons salted capers, rinsed**
**1 cup parsley leaves**
**1 cup chervil leaves**
**½ cup tarragon leaves**
**½ cup mint leaves**
**¼ cup minced chives**
**1 teaspoon grated lemon zest**
**3 garlic cloves, finely grated**
**Freshly ground black pepper**
**½ to ¾ cup extra-virgin olive oil**
**Lemon juice (optional)**

Place the onion in a bowl and add a pinch of salt and the red wine vinegar; macerate for 15 minutes.

Soak the capers in cold water for 10 minutes to remove the extra salt. Drain the capers, chop, and set aside. Note, the salt will sink to the bottom of the bowl, so be sure to lift the capers out of the water rather than pour the water over the capers in a sieve.

Wash and thoroughly dry the herbs, then chop them coarsely. Place them in a mixing bowl and add the lemon zest, garlic, and chopped capers. Squeeze any excess vinegar from the onion, and then add the onion to the herb mixture, discarding the vinegar (or saving it for vinaigrettes). Mix well. Season with salt and pepper. Add the olive oil to cover, about ½ cup, but if you want it looser, add more. Finish seasoning to taste, adding some lemon juice if more acid is needed. Allow to rest for 1 hour before serving so the flavor develops. Cover and refrigerate if not using immediately; it's best within the first few days.

## SALSA PICANTE

MAKES 1 PINT

**8 dried sweet New Mexico red chiles, stemmed**
**3 dried cayenne chiles, stemmed**
**4 dried cascabel chiles, stemmed**
**2 serrano chiles, stemmed**
**6 red Fresno chiles, ribs and seeds set aside, finely diced**
**1 cup extra-virgin olive oil**
**1 medium red onion, finely diced**
**2 tablespoons grated lemon zest**
**2 tablespoons lemon juice**
**2 cups flat-leaf parsley leaves, chopped**
**Kosher salt**
**Freshly ground black pepper**

In a blender, combine all the dried chiles with seeds, the serranos, and the ribs and seeds of the red Fresnos with ½ cup extra-virgin olive oil. Blend on high until the oil is red, about 4 minutes. Pour the chile puree into a mixing bowl. Add the diced Fresnos and red onions, and mix well. Add the lemon zest and juice.

To finish, add the parsley, and season with salt and black pepper to taste. Let it sit for 2 hours at room temperature, so it can develop its flavor. The flavor is best the first few days after it's made, but it can keep in the fridge for a week.

# STOCKS

## COURT BOUILLON

MAKES 1 GALLON

**1 cup roughly chopped onion**
**½ cup roughly chopped whole leek**
**½ cup roughly chopped celery**
**1 head garlic, split to expose the cloves**
**½ bunch thyme**
**1 bay leaf**
**½ tablespoon sea salt**
**½ tablespoon fennel seed**
**½ tablespoon black peppercorns**
**Peel and juice of ½ lemon**
**¼ cup white wine**

Combine all ingredients with 1 gallon water in a large nonreactive stockpot and bring to a boil. Turn down the heat, and let simmer for 10 minutes, then strain before use.

## RICH PORK STOCK

MAKES ABOUT 2½ GALLONS

**10 pounds pork neck bones**
**¼ pound onion, roughly cut**
**¼ pound carrot, roughly cut**
**¼ pound celery, roughly cut**
**¼ pound fennel, roughly cut**
**1 head garlic, split lengthwise**
**1 teaspoon black peppercorns**
**1 teaspoon coriander seeds**
**2 bay leaves**
**½ bunch parsley stems**
**½ bunch thyme**
**15 quarts chicken stock**

Preheat the oven to 350°F. Place the pork bones on a sheet tray and roast until golden brown, about 45 minutes. Place the hot bones in a large nonreactive pot and add the vegetables and aromatics. Cover with the chicken stock. Bring to a simmer over high heat, then lower the heat to maintain a simmer. Skim the surface of scum. Simmer, partially covered, for 6 hours. Add water as necessary if the level drops too low. Let cool, strain, and chill. The stock will keep in the fridge for up to a week, but it can keep in the freezer for months.

# RICH TROTTER STOCK

MAKES ABOUT 1½ GALLONS

This is a souped-up stock, extremely silky and deep flavored. Make it after you've cooked pig trotters and have the cooking liquid on hand.

**3 pounds pork bones**
**1 white onion, halved**
**1 head garlic, split to expose the cloves**
**2 gallons pork trotter cooking liquid (see page 62)**
**1 gallon chicken stock**

Preheat the oven to 375°F. Place the pork bones on a sheet tray and roast until golden brown but not burnt, about 45 minutes. Heat a heavy pan or skillet over high heat until very hot. Place both onion halves in the pan, cut-side down, and sear until blackened, about 5 minutes.

Add the roasted pork bones, blackened onion, and garlic to a large nonreactive stockpot, and cover with the trotter braising liquid and chicken stock. Bring to a boil, and then reduce to a simmer. Let simmer until reduced by half, about 3 hours. Let cool. Strain, and chill. The stock will keep in the fridge for a week, or a month or longer in the freezer.

# VEAL STOCK

MAKES ABOUT 2 GALLONS

**12 pounds veal bones, knuckles preferred**
**¼ pound onion, roughly cut**
**¼ pound carrot, roughly cut**
**¼ pound celery, roughly cut**
**¼ pound fennel, roughly cut**
**1 head garlic, split lengthwise**
**¼ cup tomato paste**
**2 bay leaves**
**1 teaspoon black peppercorns**
**1 teaspoon coriander seeds**
**½ bunch parsley stems**
**½ bunch thyme**

Preheat the oven to 350°F. Place the veal bones on a sheet tray and roast until golden brown, about 45 minutes. Place the bones in a large nonreactive stockpot. Mix the vegetables and tomato paste together, set on the sheet tray, and roast until the vegetables are golden brown, about 30 minutes. Combine all ingredients in the stockpot, then cover with 15 quarts of water. Bring to a simmer, skimming the surface of scum, and simmer for 8 hours, partially covered; add more water as necessary if the level drops too low. Let cool, strain, and chill.

## LAMB STOCK

MAKES 2½ GALLONS

**10 pounds lamb bones**
**15 quarts chicken stock**
**¼ pound onion, roughly cut**
**¼ pound carrot, roughly cut**
**¼ pound celery, roughly cut**
**¼ pound fennel, roughly cut**
**1 head garlic, split lengthwise**
**2 bay leaves**
**1 teaspoon black peppercorns**
**1 teaspoon coriander seeds**
**½ bunch parsley stems**
**½ bunch thyme**

Preheat the oven to 350°F. Place the lamb bones on a sheet tray and roast until golden brown, about 35 minutes. Place the bones, vegetables, and aromatics in a large nonreactive stockpot and cover with the chicken stock. Bring to a simmer, skimming the surface of scum, and simmer, partially covered, for 6 hours. Add water as necessary if the level drops too low. Let cool, strain, and chill.

## ROASTED CHICKEN STOCK

MAKES 2½ GALLONS

**10 pounds chicken bones**
**2 pounds chicken feet**
**¼ pound onion, roughly cut**
**¼ pound carrot, roughly cut**
**¼ pound celery, roughly cut**
**1 head garlic, split lengthwise**
**½ pound leek, roughly chopped**
**1 bay leaf**
**1 sprig thyme**
**Handful of parsley stems**
**1 teaspoon black peppercorns**
**1 teaspoon coriander seeds**

Preheat the oven to 350°F. Place the chicken bones and feet on a sheet tray and roast until golden brown, about 40 minutes. Remove from the oven and place in a nonreactive pot. Roast the vegetables on the same pan as the bones; when golden, after about 15 minutes, add them to the pot. Cover with 15 quarts of water and add the aromatics. Bring to a boil, skim the scum, and simmer for 6 hours, partially covered. Add water as necessary if the level drops too low. Let cool, strain, and chill.

# BRINES

## SMOKED MEAT BRINE

MAKES ABOUT 2½ GALLONS

**3 cups kosher salt (see Note)**
**2 cups sugar**
**2 tablespoons Pastrami Spice (page 271)**
**½ cup maple sugar**
**2 heads garlic, split to expose the cloves**
**3 large yellow onions, julienned**
**1 bunch thyme**
**1 bunch parsley stems**
**6 bay leaves**
**½ cup julienned fresh ginger**
**85 grams pink curing salt, such as Instacure #1**

**NOTE:** I prefer Morton brand kosher salt; if you're using Diamond Crystal, increase the quantity to 5 cups.

Mix all ingredients except the curing salt in a large pot. Add 2 gallons water and bring to a boil. Remove the pot from heat, let it cool, then add the curing salt. Chill the brine in the refrigerator until cold before adding the meat.

## CORNING BRINE

MAKES 1½ GALLONS

**1 teaspoon yellow mustard seeds**
**1 teaspoon brown mustard seeds**
**12 juniper berries**
**1 cinnamon stick, charred, then crushed**
**8 allspice berries**
**12 black peppercorns**
**12 whole cloves**
**2 cups dark brown sugar, packed**
**2⅓ cups sea salt**
**3 fresh bay leaves**
**1 teaspoon red chile flakes**
**1 teaspoon ground ginger**
**1 bunch thyme**
**1 head garlic, split to expose the cloves**
**1 red Fresno chile, split**
**1 onion, sliced**
**1 carrot, sliced**
**1 stalk celery, sliced**
**1 bulb fennel, top removed**
**⅔ ounce pink curing salt, such as Instacure #1**

Toast all the spices, then crush them in a mortar and pestle. Place them in a large nonreactive pot with the remaining ingredients and 6 quarts of water. Bring to a boil, then cool immediately. Once cool, submerge your meat.

## HAM BRINE

MAKES 3 GALLONS

**5 teaspoons allspice berries**
**3 tablespoons plus 1 teaspoon black peppercorns**
**2½ teaspoons whole cloves**
**5 teaspoons juniper berries**
**1 pound onions, julienned**
**1 bunch thyme**
**1 bunch parsley stems**
**8 fresh bay leaves**
**2 cups sea salt**
**2 cups sugar**
**2 ounces pink curing salt, such as Instacure #1**

Toast all the spices, then crush them in a mortar and pestle. Once crushed, place them in a large nonreactive pot with the remaining ingredients and 3 gallons of water. Bring to a boil, then cool immediately. Once cool, submerge your meat.

## HAY BRINE

MAKES 3 GALLONS

**¼ cup peppercorns**
**2 tablepoons juniper berries**
**2 heads garlic, split to expose the cloves**
**3 pounds yellow onions, julienned**
**2 bunches fresh thyme**
**2 bunches parsley stems**
**5 bay leaves**
**1 pound alfalfa hay**
**2¼ cups sea salt**
**2 cups sugar**
**1 ounce pink curing salt, such as Instacure #1**

In a dry skillet, toast the peppercorns and juniper, then crush in a mortar and pestle. Once crushed, place them in a large nonreactive pot with all the other ingredients and 3 gallons of water. Bring to a boil, then cool immediately. Once cool, submerge your meat of choice.

# TONGUE BRINE

MAKES 1 GALLON

**2 cups sugar**
**2⅔ cups sea salt**
**12 juniper berries, toasted**
**12 cloves, toasted**
**12 peppercorns, toasted**
**1 head garlic, split to expose the cloves**
**1 jalapeño, split**
**1 large yellow onion, julienned**
**3 bay leaves**
**1 bunch thyme**
**⅔ ounce pink curing salt, such as Instacure #1**

Combine all the ingredients except the curing salt with 1 gallon of water. Bring to a boil, then chill until cold; add the curing salt and mix until dissolved. Refrigerate until ready to use.

# PRESERVED ITEMS

## PRESERVED SUDACHI

MAKES ABOUT 2½ POUNDS

**2½ pounds fresh sudachi (Japanese sour oranges)**
**¼ cup sea salt**
**2 bay leaves**
**1 tablespoon coriander seeds, toasted**

**Equipment: Quart-size wide-mouthed mason jars, crocks, or a fermentation device**

Trim both ends off the sudachi, taking care not to cut into the flesh. Slice the sudachi top to bottom as if to quarter them, but keep the base intact. Sprinkle the interior of the sudachi with sea salt, then layer them in your mason jars. Sprinkle with some more sea salt, then mash with a wooden spoon or dowel until the rinds of the fruit begin to soften and they release their juices. This combines with the salt to create a brine, which will break down the sudachi. Continue mashing, salting, and mashing until your oranges fill the jar and rest below the level of the brine. Add the bay leaves and coriander.

Ferment at room temperature for 3 to 4 weeks. Sudachi can be kept under the brine for up to 2 years.

## PICKLED RED ONIONS

MAKES ABOUT 1 PINT

**1 cup red wine vinegar**
**1 cup sugar**
**1 fresh bay leaf**
**2 allspice berries, toasted**
**2 tablespoons black peppercorns, toasted**
**1 clove**
**¼ bunch thyme**
**1 large red onion, sliced into ¼-inch rings**

Place all the ingredients except the onion in a medium nonreactive saucepan. Bring the mixture to a boil, then turn off the heat and let it infuse for 30 minutes. Place the sliced onions in a heat-proof bowl. Strain and pour the hot liquid over the onions. Let the onions sit covered in the fridge overnight before use.

# BRUSSELSKRAUT

MAKES A LITTLE MORE THAN 2 QUARTS

**4½ pounds Brussels sprouts**
**3 tablespoons fine sea salt**

Cut the bottoms off the Brussels sprouts, then slice them very thin using a food processor with the slicer attached, or sit there like an idiot, like I did for the first time, and use a mandoline.

Layer the Brussels sprouts in a nonreactive container, sprinkling salt in between each layer, then top with a piece of parchment paper and press the mixture down with a heavy stack of plates. If the liquid that seeps out doesn't cover the Brussels sprouts, make a brine by mixing 2 cups of water with 1 tablespoon sea salt and add enough of it to keep the Brussels sprouts fully submerged.

Cover the container with cheesecloth to keep the outside world's crap out.

Let the batch sit at room temperature for 3 weeks before transferring to the refrigerator to stop the fermentation process.

# BLOODTARGA

MAKES 2 LOGS, ABOUT 8 OUNCES EACH

**1,360 grams pig's blood**
**90 grams meat glue (transglutaminase)**
**34 grams sea salt**
**34 grams Aleppo chile flakes**
**.01 gram pink curing salt, such as Instacure #1**
**Salt, for packing**

Mix all ingredients together very well, then place them into Cryovac bags in the shape of otter pop bags—you know, those frozen popsicles. Seal the bags, then tie them with string so they're round and very tight.

Cook in a water bath with a circulator at 189°F (87.2°C) for 35 minutes. Remove the bloodtarga to an ice-water bath and chill hard. Remove the bloodtarga from the Cryovac bag, then wrap it in cheesecloth. Pack the logs fully in salt for 12 hours.

Remove the logs from the salt and either dry in a dehydrator or hang for 7 days at room temp. They are best kept in an airtight container to preserve their flavor, and will keep for a week to a month, depending on if they're exposed to any moisture.

## LAMB LIVER BOTTARGA

MAKES 800 GRAMS

**500 grams sea salt**
**500 grams sugar**
**3 bay leaves**
**1 cup mint leaves**
**2 grams pink curing salt, such as Instacure #1**
**2,270 grams lamb liver**
**100 grams coarsely ground black pepper, enough to cover**

Combine the salt, sugar, bay leaves, and mint with the curing salt in a large bowl.

Place the lamb liver in a nonreactive container, then rub and cover the liver with the salt mixture. Let sit for 2 weeks, covered, in the refrigerator. Make sure it's cured through; it will have lost a lot of liquid and should feel pretty solid.

Once the liver has released most of its liquid, it will become very tough. Rinse off the salt mixture, pat dry, and rub with black pepper, then either dry in a dehydrator, or hang wrapped in cheesecloth for 2 months, until it is dry and can be shaved like Parmesan cheese.

**VARIATIONS:** Use the same method to make Pork Liver or Beef Heart Bottarga.

## PORK LIVER BOTTARGA

MAKES 800 GRAMS

**500 grams sea salt**
**500 grams sugar**
**2 grams pink curing salt, such as Instacure #1**
**3 bay leaves**
**14 grams thyme leaves**
**2,270 grams pork liver**
**100 grams black peppercorns, toasted and cracked, enough to cover**

## BEEF HEART BOTTARGA

MAKES 800 GRAMS

**500 grams salt**
**500 grams sugar**
**3 grams pink curing salt, such as Instacure #1**
**4 bay leaves**
**19 grams rosemary needles**
**14 grams picked thyme**
**2,270 grams beef heart, 1.35 kilograms**
**100 grams black peppercorns, toasted and cracked**

# SIDES, ETC.

## CREAMY POLENTA

SERVES 6

**1 cup coarse-ground polenta**
**2 cups whole milk, plus more as needed**
**½ cup unsalted butter**
**½ cup mascarpone cheese**
**1 cup grated Parmesan cheese**
**Kosher salt and freshly ground black pepper, to taste**

In a heavy-bottomed pot, combine the polenta and 5 cups cold water. Bring this to a simmer, slowly, over medium heat, constantly whisking the polenta so it doesn't stick to the bottom of the pot. Once the water has been absorbed, feed the milk into the polenta ½ cup at a time, and let it absorb completely before adding more. Cook at a gentle simmer for about 45 minutes, until the polenta gains a creamy consistency.

Add the butter, in pieces, and mascarpone and cook for 15 minutes more, whisking often, then add the Parmesan. Remove from the heat.

Taste and adjust the seasoning to your liking with salt and pepper. If the polenta gets too thick, add more milk to adjust the consistency.

**VARIATION:** Sheep's Milk Polenta
Replace 1 cup of water with sheep's milk whey, and replace the Parmesan with pecorino. Proceed as for Creamy Polenta.

# SUET CRUST

MAKES 1 CRUST

**250 grams all-purpose flour**
**125 grams fresh beef suet, ground ($\frac{3}{16}$ die)**
**Pinch of salt**
**Pinch of freshly ground black pepper**
**125 to 150 milliliters ice-cold water**

Place the flour and suet in the bowl of a mixer with the salt and pepper. Using a paddle attachment, mix slowly, breaking up the fat. Slowly add the water, just enough to bring it all together. Once a paste is formed, wrap it in plastic wrap and chill it hard before rolling.

When rolling out or lining a terrine mold, you don't have to work as quickly as you would with butter, because the suet won't melt as fast. Your pies and en croutes will be flakier than ever before.

# CORONA BEANS

MAKES 1½ QUARTS

**1 pound dried corona beans**
**1 medium carrot, roughly chopped**
**1 bulb fennel, roughly chopped**
**1 medium onion, roughly chopped**
**1 head garlic, split to expose the cloves**
**1 peeled russet potato (see Note)**
**1 branch rosemary**
**1 bay leaf**
**Sea salt and freshly ground black pepper to taste**
**2 tablespoons extra-virgin olive oil**

**NOTE:** An enzyme in the potato stops the beans from bursting by softening their casings.

Cover the beans with water and let them soak overnight, covered, at room temperature. Be sure to add a little extra water, as the beans will soak up more than you think.

In the morning, strain off the water, rinse the beans, and place them in a large nonreactive pot. Cover with fresh water and add the vegetables, potato, rosemary, and bay leaf. Bring to a simmer, covering with a piece of parchment paper cut to fit the pot, until creamy and tender, about 2 hours. Test by eating a few to see if they're done; if they're still firm in the middle, let them go a little longer. Season with salt, black pepper, and olive oil. Cool and refrigerate the beans in their liquid until you're ready to use them.

# ACKNOWLEDGMENTS

Tatiana, we met when I was a young, overly eager cook with outsized dreams. You introduced me to sushi, the absolute decadent pleasure of eating a ripe, raw heirloom tomato, and cultured me with museums, nurturing a deep connection I didn't even know I had to classic and contemporary art. But the most important thing was how you taught me to understand how to fit things into a larger context, revealing my own place in the world. After coming into my own as a chef, I realized I really wanted to write a book on offal, but I had no idea where to begin. For years, people and publishers denied the idea, but you, ever supportive, worked with me to shape a proposal, even while bickering over my grammar and poorly written recipes. You helped me find my voice and follow the original vision we'd begun discussing nearly a decade ago, setting the course for what this book has become. Thank you, Tatiana. Without your help I would still be struggling to tell my story. Your love and support makes me feel lucky every day, challenging me to be the best husband I can be for you.

To Easton, my awesome, kind, and cool son, I love making "ham" burgers with you and I'm so proud of the young man you're becoming. Being your father is the most important job I've ever had.

To my mother, Susan, thanks for your love and support, even though I know you would sooner kiss a Yeti than to eat offal. I love you, Mom.

Michael, you have been with me on this journey for ten years shooting photos, and then, somehow, I roped you into writing this with me. Thank you for your boundless optimism, loyalty, and belief in this project from day one. You are a great friend and I couldn't have done this without you.

To Sammy Jo, thank you for being my second set of eyes. You're a strong and confident cook, and so naturally translated my style for the page.

To Alexa, you made the dishes look great on camera while still looking like real food. Thank you.

Jeremy Fish, thank you for your friendship and amazing artwork, you are keepin' SF real!

Francis Lam, my editor, you got this book by default, but with composure and class, you saw it through, and I thank you for putting together something I'm so proud of.

Mark Pastore, thank you for letting me cook all these cuts of meat at Incanto without the fear of people being scared. We truly changed the world one "head to tail" at a time.

Mark Miller, I owe you a debt of gratitude for the many history lessons on food. You are a great teacher and an amazing friend. To the greats: Jean Louis Paladin, I constantly go back to when you said, "cook for your guest, not the reviewer, and everything will work." Rosalie Cosentino, my great-grandmother who inspired it all, I would not be the chef I am today without those days standing on a chair making pasta. Pierre Kaufmann, for teaching me to debone trotters at La Tante Claire. Marco Pierre White, for inspiring me to be myself and slamming a door in my face when I tried to stage at Harveys. Harold McGee, for always answering my crazy questions about food and helping me when I was stuck—without you, the food world would never have evolved as quickly.

I would like to thank all the past staff of Incanto for their hard work and dedication, you all know who you are. Thanks to the team at Boccalone, past and present, for making such delicious cured meats. And to my team at Cockscomb, for sticking with me in pursuit of not only great food, but also believing in what we cook. I am proud of each and every one of you. Stand strong and remember nothing is impossible. Jeremy Emmerson, my secret weapon, thanks for always being there, you really are the best!

Thanks, in no particular order, to this group of industry standouts: Fergus Henderson, Derek Dammann, Jamie Bissonette, Staffan Terje, Matt Jennings, Traci Des Jardins (my chef mom), Martin Picard, April Bloomfield, David Chang, Francis Derby, Ed Lee, Alex Stupak, Sean Brock, Fred Morin and Dave McMillan, Daniel Boulud, Anthony Bourdain, José Andrés, Paul Cunningham, Mario Batali, Andrew Zimmern, Rene Redzepi, and Chris Ying. You all play a significant role in my life; your friendship, candor, and care means everything to me. To all the chefs past and present for the constant inspiration and friendships, there are too many of you to call out, but thanks for having my back or stabbing it.

To all my great farmers and ranchers without whom I would have nothing: Andy Griffin of Marquita Farms for your friendship and your exemplary produce, Jim Reichart of Liberty Ducks, Cream Co. Meats for your amazing heritage beef, Hamada Farms for your delicious fruits, Poli Yerena of Yerena Farms for the best of berries, and Don Watson of Napa Valley Lamb.

My business partner, Oliver Wharton, thanks for always pushing me to do more. We're an odd couple, but it works. To Zach Field, my agent, thanks for being a thoughtful navigator. Phillip Baltz and the Baltz team, thank you for the constant encouragement and direction. And, finally, to Dr. Heung, I'm so grateful to you for getting my guts back on track, so I could have the guts to write this book about guts.

JACOBSEN

# SOURCES

### Boccalone
**boccalone.com**
For all of your cured-meat needs. Yes, I know it's my company, but I think we do a good job.

### Butcher & Packer
**butcher-packer.com**
Sausage casings of all sizes, curing salts, and specialty equipment

### The Butchers Guild
**thebutchersguild.org**
A great source to help you find good butchers in your area who can provide quality meat and offal cuts

### Casa de Case
**casadecase.com**
Amazing olive oils, vinegars, dried beans, and a lot of specialty Italian ingredients

### Cayson Designs
**caysondesigns.com**
They make the best chef coats and aprons around.

### Cockscomb
**cockscombsf.com**
And yes, this is my restaurant too. But if you see an organ you like and you don't feel like cooking it, be sure to stop by. I might be serving it tonight.

### Cream Co.
**eatcream.co**
Lots of specialty beef and pork, as well as offal cuts: udder, liver, heart, oh my!!

### D'Artagnan
**dartagnan.com**
A great source for game birds, head and feet on birds, foie gras, and a lot of unique parts

### Don Watson and Napa Valley Lamb

**woolyweeders.com**

Don is my go-to for all things lamb. Not only is the product delicious, he is an amazing human.

### Fresca Italia

**frescaitalia.com**

Italian cheeses, cured tuna heart, and so much more

### Jacobsen Sea Salt

**jacobsensalt.com**

Highest quality American-made sea salts, including smoked, vanilla, and regular flake salt; they also sell top-notch kosher salt

### Liberty Farm Ducks

**libertyducks.com**

Jim Reichart is the best of the best; his ducks are amazing and delicious.

### National Pork Board

**porkfoodservice.org**

Their website has a lot of great information for professionals and interested home cooks.

### Offalgood

**offalgood.com**

My website is a source for all things fun about offal and what I have going on.

### Williams Sonoma

**williams-sonoma.com**

For serving utensils, and some harder-to-find kitchenware, this is your place.

# INDEX